Naked, Short and Greedy

Wall Street's Failure to Deliver

Dr. Susanne Trimbath

First published January 2020

by Spiramus Press Ltd

102 Blandford Street

London W1U 8AG

Telephone +44 20 7224 0080

www.spiramus.com

© Spiramus Press Ltd

ISBN

9781910151341 Paperback

9781910151839 Digital

All rights reserved. No part of this publication may be reproduced in any material form (including photocopying or storing it in any medium by electronic means and whether or not transiently or incidental to some other use of this publication) without the prior written permission of the copyright owner except in accordance with the provisions of the Copyright, Designs and Patents Act 1988 or under the terms of a licence issued by the Copyright Licensing Agency Ltd, 90 Tottenham Court Road, London W1P 4LP.

British Library Cataloguing-in-Publication Data.

A catalogue record for this book is available from the British Library.

The right of Susanne Trimbath to be identified as the author of this work has been asserted by her in accordance with the Copyright, Designs and Patents Act, 1988.

Printed and bound in Great Britain by Grosvenor Group (Print Services) Ltd

About the author

Susanne Trimbath, Ph.D. is business instructor for Cochise College in southeastern Arizona. Dr. Trimbath started her training in finance and economics at the Federal Reserve Bank of San Francisco. She worked in operations at depository trust and clearing corporations in San Francisco and New York, including Depository Trust Company, a subsidiary of DTCC, a privately-run central clearing agency in the US. Dr. Trimbath served as Senior Advisor on a US Agency for International Development project to develop capital market infrastructure in Russia after the fall of communism. She was a consultant on similar projects in several other countries including Romania and Poland at a time when few people understood the details of post-trade processing in a centralized clearing environment. She was Senior Research Economist in capital markets at the Milken Institute (where Michael Milken serves as Chairman) before forming STP Advisory Services, LLC. Her Ph.D. in economics is from New York University's Graduate School of Arts and Sciences. She taught economics and finance at New York University and University of Southern California (Marshall School of Business).

Acknowledgements

The impact of trade settlement failures in equity markets was first brought to my attention by Tom Montrone, Ray Riley, Carl Hagberg and members of the Securities Transfer Association, Inc. in 1993. Ten years later, I was made aware of the worsening impact on small businesses by Wes Christian, Carl Koerner and Bud Burrell. Finally, the impact on the investors who believe in and want to encourage those small businesses was driven home for me by Sandra Mohr. I am grateful to each of them for their encouragement in my endeavor to describe it here. The impact of trade settlement failures in bond markets was first brought to my attention by members of the Open Market Operations department at the Federal Reserve Bank of New York. I am grateful to the participants in the Credit Risk & Credit Derivatives session at the International Economics and Finance Association's 6th NTU International Conference on Economics, Finance and Accounting, Financial Engineering and Financial Intermediation (Taipei May 2008). They not only provided encouragement and useful comments on my draft paper on trade settlement failures in US bond markets, but they also made me aware of the impact of fails and other issues in the market for credit default swaps that would play an important part in understanding the financial crisis that devastated global credit markets in 2008.

Contents

About the author iii
Acknowledgements... iii
Contents v
Abbreviations.. ix

PART I. OPENING..1
Shareholder democracy in shambles 1

Chapter 1. A Primer..7
Terminology 8
The triumvirate of trouble: shorts, loans and fails..................... 11
Economics of phantom shares 16

Chapter 2. Start at the Beginning.. 19

PART II. BACK TO WHERE I LEFT OFF 31
Chapter 3. A Sidewalk Café in New York 31
Chapter 4. Blind Men Describe an Elephant............................ 39

PART III. COMMITTING TO A CAUSE 45
Chapter 5. Real Experts Meet 45
Chapter 6. STA White Paper... 51
Chapter 7. Tax Consequences... 56
Bond trades... 56
Stock trades 59

PART IV. SUCCESS SEEMS POSSIBLE 61
Chapter 8. Regulation SHO 61
Chapter 9. Criminal Cases Reveal Evidence.......................... 124
Chapter 10. The Battle Goes Public.. 131
A public forum in Washington DC... 133

PART V. ESCALATING COMMITMENTS 139
Chapter 11. Byrne's War 139
Online interview for The Sanity Check 143

Chapter 12. Publicity Ramps Up..**162**
    Media, mainstream and otherwise..166
    The FBI calls 170

Chapter 13. Naked Short and Greedy – the Event.......................**174**
    Press release 175

PART VI. ALL SEEMS LOST...**179**

Chapter 14. Resistance from Wall Street......................................**179**
    Everyone knew by 2003..180
    CFA-LA press release 186

Chapter 15.   Corporate Governance Fails at Overstock........**191**

Chapter 16. Senate Inaction **197**

PART VII. WHEN THE MUSIC STOPS **202**

Chapter 17. Media Interest after the Financial Crisis **204**

Chapter 18. CMKM and the UnShareholders **208**
    In the end… 208
    Examples of Messages from CMKM UnShareholders..............224
    Military...224
    Canada 225
    Switzerland..225
    USA..225

Chapter 19. Two Documentary Films **228**
    Transcript of November 7, 2008 interview by producers and directors of The Wall Street Conspiracy (2012)..........................230
    Credit default swaps and mortgage bonds................................233
    Beyond the US...236
    Phantom shareholders 236
    Ferreting out the data..240
    Economics = Accounting + Finance...241
    An explosion in FTDs..242
    How does that make you feel? 244
    Phantom votes..247

CDS: phantom or real?.. 249
Where is my perp-walk? 252
America sneezed.. 254
Why small companies are targeted... 255
Can it be fixed? 258

PART VIII. THE TRAGEDY OF A DOWNER ENDING 261

Chapter 20.   GAO faults SEC and Other Revelations 263

Chapter 21. Barker Minerals' Unique Approach 274

PART IX. UNRESOLVED REGULATORY CRISIS..................... 278

The latest numbers 280
How do you solve a problem 282
Epilogue 283

References 287

Appendix 1: Report for Barker Minerals, Review of Data and Documents, October 14, 2010... 290

Clarification of terminology.. 290
Prior research on settlement failures 291
Background 293
Purpose of study.. 294
Settlement process... 294
Why settlement fails... 295
Analysis 297
Identifying settlement failures.. 298
Conclusions 300
Suggestions for further analysis... 301
Appendix: Trading range as percentage of opening price 305
Appendix: Excerpt of Broker Trading Activity Chart............... 306
Appendix: Excerpt 2 of Broker Trading Activity Chart............ 307
Appendix: One Clear Example – documentation suggestion .. 308
Appendix: Glossary – presentation suggestions....................... 309
Appendix: Limitations and Disclaimers 309

Appendix 2: Report for Barker Minerals – Updated Review of Data and Documents (July 16, 2012)..311
  Executive summary..311
  Background and the 2010 report.................................312
  Introduction to 2012 report...315
  Update on recommendations.......................................316
  Updated statistical analysis..324

Barker minerals' strategy 327
  Summary..328
  References...332

APPENDIX 3: Manipulative Market Practices Derived from TMPG (2007) 334

APPENDIX 4: Barker's Event Analysis 336

Index..342

Endnotes..347

Abbreviations

Abbreviation	Meaning
401(k)	Tax-deferred retirement savings account, named for a section of the IRS code
AIG	Stock symbol and common name for American International group
AMEX	American Stock Exchange, now known as NYSE American
BD	Broker-dealer
BIS	Bank for International Settlements
BoD	Board of Directors
BoNY	Bank of New York
CCS	Centralized Clearing and Settlement
CDS	Credit Default Swap; also the initials of the Canadian Depository for Securities
Cede & CO	(or CEDE & Co) is a nominee name for DTC. It originated with the acronym "CD" which stood for "central deposits," a department at the NYSE
CEO	Chief Executive Officer
CFA	Chartered Financial Analyst; CFA-LA is the Chartered Financial Analyst Society of Los Angeles
CFRN	Christian Financial Radio Network
CMKM	Stock Symbol and short name for CMKM Diamonds, Inc.
CNS	Continuous Net Settlement
CSJ	Christian Smith and Jewell
CUSIP	Unique numbering system for securities, developed by the Committee on Uniform Securities Identification Procedures
DFA	Dodd-Frank Wall Street Reform and Consumer Protection Act of 2010, commonly known as the

Abbreviation	Meaning
	Dodd-Frank Act
DJIA	Dow Jones Industrial Average
DTC	Depository Trust Company, a subsidiary of DTCC
DTCC	Depository Trust and Clearing Corporation
ECSDA	European Central Securities Depositories Association
ETF	Exchange Traded Fund
FAST	Fast Automated Securities Transfer program under contract between DTC and a TA
FBI	United States Federal Bureau of Investigation
FCIC	Financial Crisis Inquiry Commission
FINRA	Financial Industry Regulatory Authority, formed in 2007 by the merger of the National Association of Securities Dealers with some SRO functions of the NYSE
FOIA	Freedom of Information Act
FRB	Federal Reserve Bank or Federal Reserve System
FRB-NY	Federal Reserve Bank of New York
FTD	Fail to deliver (or failure to deliver)
GAO	United States Government Accountability Office
GDP	Gross Domestic Product
IIROC	Investment Industry Regulatory Organization of Canada
IPO	Initial Public Offering
IRA	Individual Retirement Account
IRS	United States Internal Revenue Service (tax authority)
JGTRRA	Jobs and Growth Tax Relief Reconciliation Act of 2003 (United States)
MBS	Mortgage-backed securities (bonds)
MIS	Management Information System

Abbreviation	Meaning
NASAA	North American Securities Administrators Association
NASDAQ	Electronic stock exchange in the US. Originated as an acronym for "National Association of Securities Dealers Automated Quotations."
NHHI	New Horizons Holdings, Inc., successor to CMKM Diamonds, Inc.
NSCC	National Securities Clearing Corporation, a subsidiary of DTCC
NSS	Naked Short Sales or Naked Short Selling
NYSE	New York Stock Exchange
NYU	New York University
OLP	O'Quinn Laminack and Pirtle
OSTK	Stock Symbol for Overstock.com
OTC	Over-The-Counter, stock trading not on an organized exchange
OW	DTCC's Obligation Warehouse Service
R&T	Registrar & Transfer Company
RECAPS	DTCC's Reconfirmation and Pricing Service
Reg SHO	Regulation SHO, SEC rules defining ownership of securities, aggregation of long and short positions, and requiring broker-dealers to mark non-exempt sales in all equity securities "long" or "short"
S&P	Standard and Poor's Financial Services, LLC
SBP	Stock Borrow Program (at NSCC)
SEC	United States Securities and Exchange Commission
SIA	Securities Industry Association
SLP	Stock Lending Program (at DTC)
SPDRs	Exchanged-traded fund that tracks the S&P 500 Index

Abbreviation	Meaning
SRO	Self-Regulatory Organization
STA	Securities Transfer Association International
STAMP	Signature Guarantee Medallion Program
T+3	Trade date plus three business days; variations include T+5 and T+2
TA	Transfer Agent
TMPG	Treasury Market Practices Group (at the Federal Reserve Bank of New York)
UCC	Uniform Commercial Code
US-AID	United States Agency for International Development
UST	United States Treasury securities (bills, notes and bonds issued by the federal government)
WSC	The Wall Street Conspiracy (2012 documentary film)

PART I. OPENING

Shareholder democracy in shambles

Investors and the entrepreneurs they support are being harmed by fails-to-deliver (FTDs) and stock lending/borrowing under rules approved by the Securities and Exchange Commission (SEC). Neither the government regulators nor the financial industry self-regulatory organizations are capable of correcting themselves. This is the definition of a Regulatory Crisis.[1]

If you are not already aware of the problem, this book will show that there are failures to deliver securities to settle trades throughout the global financial system. Although the data and examples in this book are primarily (though not exclusively) from the United States (US), it happens everywhere that the financial industry includes self-regulatory organizations.

- Some of the fails to deliver last for years in the US because the centralized clearing and settlement organization provides that fails to settle on a given day will be resubmitted with a new settlement date the next day, *ad infinitum*.
- The New York Stock Exchange (NYSE) admitted in a public forum in Washington, D.C. on November 30, 2005 that using the central clearing organization's stock borrow program to cover up these failures to settle has resulted in the violation of the "one share, one vote" rule. Some shares of stock have no votes in corporate governance issues, or sometimes just a fraction of a vote. The broker-dealer firm makes choices about which votes to count in a completely opaque process. They have made a sham of shareholder democracy.
- No regulation in the US requires the borrower of shares to close out long-term outstanding stock loans and settlement failures, the combination of which can be blamed for universal over-voting in matters of corporate governance. All rights of

ownership go with the stock share to the borrower, including the right to lend the share to another borrow.
- Finally, numerous companies have been the subject of aggressive trading attacks that are enabled by the lack of action by regulators. Aggressive trading tactics such as naked short selling can, at a minimum, impair access to capital and at the worst have driven small companies to ruin.[2]

The US central clearing and settlement organization, Depository Trust and Clearing Corporation (DTCC) and its subsidiaries, claim that they have no power or legal authority to regulate or stop the practice of lending stock without a close-out requirement (i.e. no due date for the loans) and no power to force their member firms to close out or resolve fails to deliver. This is not technically true. Since the DTCC's subsidiary, the National Securities Clearing Corporation (NSCC), makes itself the counterparty to both sides of every transaction involving a failure to deliver, DTCC has the same power and authority to compel a resolution or close out as would an original customer who does not receive the shares he pays for. It is more correct to say that DTCC *chooses* not to resolve or buy-in trades where the seller fails to deliver the shares they sold. DTCC and its subsidiaries can and do change their own rules and procedures after notice to the public and approval by the SEC. Their rules allow them to credit their members with an entitlement for undelivered shares, which allows their members to credit the account representing the buying investor in a failed trade. This process creates extra shares of the stock of public companies – all within the rules.

The problem became so serious in late 2003 that some companies, mostly entrepreneurial companies who accessed what they believed to be fairly operating capital markets, approached the DTCC's subsidiary Depository Trust Company (DTC) in hopes of either finding a resolution to the problem or moving their stock out harm's way, out of the system. DTC turned to the SEC and got approval for a rule to prohibit the companies from taking action to protect themselves. If you asked the DTC about this particular instance, they will only tell you that they cannot honor requests from issuers to exit the system because it "has not been permitted by the SEC" without mentioning the fact that the DTC *initiated* the SEC rule that stops companies from protecting themselves, their assets, and their investors.[3]

Similarly, DTCC approached the SEC for rulemaking to protect its members from having to close out failed trades by forcing an open market purchase in a process known as "a buy-in" where the buyer can purchase the shares from another party and then charge back the cost to the seller who failed to deliver.[4] This situation is getting worse instead of better. The more rules that are put in place to support this flawed infrastructure, the more the risk created by a build-up of unsettled trades in the system will look like the asbestos of the 21st century: just because fire-safety regulations required the use of asbestos in schools and public buildings in the 1970s did not make it any less dangerous in the 1990s. Likewise, just because financial regulations allow fails to deliver in the 2000s will not make it any less dangerous to the economy in the 2020s.

This problem was created by and is sustained by the very rules the regulators put in place with the intention of protecting investors and providing orderly capital markets. When the DTC got the rulemaking from the SEC to prevent companies from refusing to allow their shares to be held in the flawed system, they submitted comment letters insisting that the NSCC's stock borrow program satisfies the need for shares when trades fail so they can make sure that trades don't fail. If that sounds like double-speak, that is because it is. They say that they prevent trades from failing by enabling trades to fail. The DTC further stated that the lender cannot loan shares multiple times. Unfortunately, the buyer whose trade was "settled" with borrowed shares can and does lend the shares. It is not just a matter of semantics. Although one owner cannot loan the same share twice, nothing in the rules, regulations or accounting systems prevents lending by the owner who got a borrowed share at settlement. Each time a share is loaned, it leaves behind another phantom share.

Simply put, how do we explain year-long failures to settle? How do we explain that some companies are on the SEC's list restricting short selling in their shares for repeated periods? How do we explain that at least half of the trades that fail to settle are more than two months old? There is only one explanation: lax management at the self-regulatory organizations on Wall Street, a complete failure in oversight by the SEC and a willingness to look the other way when broker members, who hold positions on the Board of Directors at the self-regulatory organizations and who may have ambitions to political appointments at the SEC, violate their duty to perform in the best interest of investors.

This is not a glitch or bookkeeping problem; this is a problem of very large dimensions created by a gaping hole in the capital market infrastructure supported by the regulators and overseen by the SEC. This hurts businesses seeking access to the brightest capital markets in the world by allowing unsettled trades to be covered with borrowed shares that are then re-sold and re-loaned until the number of phantom shares in circulation surpasses the number allowed by the articles of incorporation filed with the Departments of Corporations in all 50 states. It takes away the rights of shareholders to exercise control over companies by voting their shares. The failure to enforce the close out of stock lending and to enforce final settlement is generating phantom shares which, through the most basic laws of supply and demand, depress the prices of stocks by increasing the supply of shares.

The circumstances present in the securities industry where the self-regulatory organizations on Wall Street all adhere to the rules that they wrote and got approved by the regulators in Washington is no less a Regulatory Crisis. In the context of the constitution, Levinson and Balkin (2009) describe a "Type Two" crisis that occurs "when all relevant actors comply with their widely accepted constitutional duties and roles, but following the accepted understandings of the Constitution fails to resolve an existing political crisis or leads to disaster. (Thus, one might say that type two crises arise in situations where the Constitution really is a suicide pact.) Type two crises involve failures of constitutional structures that the relevant actors do not dispute or attempt to escape. If type one crises feature actors who publicly depart from fidelity to the Constitution, type two crises arise from excess fidelity, where political actors adhere to what they perceive to be their constitutional duties even though the heavens fall" (p. 729). Wall Street and Washington follow and write rules that they can follow with "excess fidelity" even in the face of protests from investors, entrepreneurs and the general public; even in the face of the collapse of global financial markets in 2008.

When I set out on this journey in 2003, I firmly believed that the only possible solution was for Congress to act to force the settlement of all outstanding trades. I believed that until I talked to Congress (Chapter 7). Then I believed that the only possible solution was in the courts. I believed that until I was brought in as a fact- and expert-witness in several lawsuits either filed or considered by a multitude of public companies (Chapter 9). Most of those fell under opposition from Wall Street's rules. Then I believed that the only possible solution was through the criminal justice system. I believed that until I talked to the Department of Justice and the Federal Bureau of Investigation (Chapter 12). Now I believe that we face a true regulatory crisis. The current system may not survive.

The complete lack of transparency on Wall Street raises questions that may never be answered. Earning income from covering fails with stock loans provides an economic incentive for maintaining the status quo to the detriment of shareholders and entrepreneurs. There are unanswered questions about the total income received in payments from stock lending. We know from industry reports that borrowed shares are not restricted in any way so that they cannot be lent again; once the borrowed share is delivered to the purchaser they are able to vote, receive dividends – and lend the share without restriction. Stock lending resolves only 18% of total fails, the remaining 82% of outstanding fails may remain open for years.

Who will protect the interests of shareholders and entrepreneurs being damaged by the system of self-regulation in global financial markets? This is the story of a handful of investors and entrepreneurs who made a valiant attempt to change that system. I will warn you in advance that there is no happing ending to this story.

Chapter 1. A Primer

"And, probably, a lot of what you know is lies-to-children. Just as 'survival of the fittest' captured the imaginations of the Victorians, so 'DNA' has captured the imaginations of today's public. However, imaginations thrive best if they are left free to roam: they grow tired and feeble in captivity. Captive imaginations do breed quite effectively, because they are protected from the terrible predator known as Thought."

The Science of Discworld, Terry Pratchett, Ian Stewart & Jack Cohen, Ebury Press, Random House, London 2002

If you are new to the world of finance and economics, there are some concepts that will appear in this book that you may not be familiar with. If you are already knowledgeable about financial markets, you may still want to read this Primer to understand the economic implications of the events described in *Naked, Short and Greedy*. Otherwise, the informed reader may skip this chapter without loss of continuity.

The purpose of this Primer is to give the reader enough background to understand the problems caused by the events covered in *Naked, Short and Greedy*. It is not intended to be a complete college course in finance or economics. To keep the narrative flowing, we also do not cover all of the existing regulations and past episodes of financial crises. For a more complete discussion of the role of regulatory issues in the 2008 and prior financial crises, including a review of the changes implemented in the Dodd–Frank Wall Street Reform and Consumer Protection Act of 2010, please look for *Lessons Not Learned* (Spiramus, 2015) available directly from the publisher or on Amazon. Chapter 7 of *Lessons Not Learned* includes a brief explanation of short selling and settlement failures and their connection to the 2008 financial crisis. Chapter 4 covers the issue as it specifically relates to the behavior of financial firms (banks).

Terminology

This list has the especially important terms for understanding the events described in this book. If you come across some term or concept you are not familiar with while reading, Internet websites like Investopedia offer simple explanations, as do most of the bank, broker and investment advisor websites.

Shares or Securities: To simplify the terminology in this book discussion, we will use "shares" to refer to stocks and bonds. "Security" is a more general term that can refer to a share of stock, a bond, and other more exotic financial products like warrants, debentures, derivatives, etc.

Outstanding shares: When a company decides to go public, they identify a fixed number of shares to be sold (initial public offering or IPO). Companies in the US are required to register shares in two places. They identify the total number of shares "authorized" with the state where they are incorporated. Companies do this even if they are going to remain private. Then, before a company can sell shares to the public, the shares must be "registered" with the Securities and Exchange Commission (SEC). Shares that are issued may be held by the company as Treasury shares, in which case they are not "outstanding." We clarify these categories further below.

> **Authorized shares**: A company is authorized by its Board of Directors to issue shares. The number of authorized shares is included in the articles of incorporation and by-laws. After shares are issued, any material change in the number of authorized shares must be approved by the shareholders (existing owners who will experience an economic impact). Authorized shares include all the shares that are identified to

the state, which may exceed outstanding shares which are only those that have been issued.

Registered shares:
(1) Before a public offering, a number of authorized shares (not always 100%) are registered for sale with the SEC. Registration assures that shares are only issued once.
(2) Valid ownership is recorded when shares are registered on the issuer's books and records.
(3) Registered is also used to differentiate shares that are directly registered for the beneficial owner in the issuer's records from shares that are held in "street name" (see definition below).

Issued and Outstanding shares: When registered shares are sold, they are issued in exchange for money. At this point, the shares are outstanding (in the market). Shares can be authorized, issued and outstanding, but not registered if, for example, they are given to insiders, used to pay consultants, etc. These shares are restricted from the public markets because they are not registered for sale with the SEC ("registered" definition (1)).

Float: Finally, another term used to count the number of shares that should be available for trading in financial markets is "float." Float excludes authorized shares that are not outstanding; any authorized shares held by the company (for any reason); and usually shares held by insiders (executive officers or anyone who has restrictions on selling shares). Simply put, float is the number of shares that can be bought and sold without restrictions in the stock market.

Street name: Shares registered in a nominee name can be held either directly for the nominee (proprietary shares) or on behalf of beneficial owners (customer shares). A nominee name is used to register securities that are being held in trust for another party. For example, all the shares held by DTC are registered in their nominee name, Cede & Co. and held on behalf of the Participant (member) who deposited the shares.

Proxy voting: a ballot cast by one person on behalf of a shareholder of a corporation. When stock shares are left in "street name" the beneficial owner is not a registered shareholder with the corporation. In that case, the investor receives a statement describing the issues to be voted on, along with a form to return to the broker indicating how they want their shares voted and designating the broker as their "proxy" for voting purposes. The proxy voting process in the US is regulated by the SEC.

Settlement: the exchange of cash and shares after the trade. In the US, most trades are scheduled to settle three business days after the trade date, known as T+3 ("Trade date plus three business days"). Settlement is the final step in completing a securities transaction and includes the transfer of ownership in a security and the associated transfer of payment for the transaction.[5]

Institutional investor: An institution can be any party (person or company) that trades share quantities (or dollar amounts) that are large enough to qualify for special treatment and lower commissions. For example, where individual (retail) investors usually trade in lots of 100 shares, an institution would trade in lots of 10,000 shares or more. Institutional investors are usually investing money for someone else, like a pension plan or a school district.

Self-Regulatory Organization (SRO): An SRO exercises some regulatory authority in the securities industry in place of government regulation (or in addition to it). The New York Stock Exchange (NYSE) and the Financial Industry Regulatory Authority (FINRA), for example, are SROs that create and enforce certain requirements related to stock trading and broker activities. The Depository Trust Company (DTC) is the SRO responsible for holding the stocks and bonds that its members ("Participants") use to settle trades based on instructions from the National Securities Clearing Corporation (NSCC), the SRO that clears trades.

Clearing and settlement: The easiest way to understand what happens in the post-trade processing is with an analogy to air traffic control. Much like an airport control tower makes sure other planes are out of the way before a flight is allowed to land, the central clearing organization "clears" trades in each stock for each broker to make one end-of-day figure for settlement. When a trade is "cleared," both the buyer and the seller have agreed to all the details (price, number of shares, etc.). In this analogy, settlement is like touchdown: shares and money change hands like passengers disembarking the plane at the end of their flight to reach their final destination.

Buy-in: After a seller fails to deliver shares for settlement, the buyer (or the clearing organization, under certain rules) may purchase the shares on the open market and charge any difference in cost back to the failing seller.

Regulation SHO: SEC rules initially approved in 2004 (with compliance beginning in January 2005) to update short sale regulations first adopted in 1938, "and to address concerns regarding persistent failures to deliver and potentially abusive 'naked' short selling."
(See https://www.sec.gov/investor/pubs/regsho.htm.) Important amendments are discussed in Chapter 8.

The triumvirate of trouble: shorts, loans and fails

There are three financial market activities that produce problems for investors and issuers. Each will result in the circulation of more shares than the company has outstanding. These are 1) short sales,

2) stock lending and 3) settlement failures. "Naked short selling" is a special type of short sale, which will be discussed in the next section. The term "naked short selling" was often used to marginalize complaints in the years leading up to the 2008 financial crisis about the extra shares in circulation.

Short sales

In an ordinary trade (buy/sell) of stocks or bonds, the buyer believes that the value of the shares will increase in the future, or that the value of the accumulated dividends will provide an income flow sufficient to warrant the investment. In a short sale, the seller believes the value of the shares will *decrease* in the future. The seller sells shares without owning them. In an ordinary short sale, the seller will borrow the shares from someone else to deliver them to the buyer at settlement.

"Naked short sales" are market trades where the seller does not borrow the shares for delivery at settlement. In addition to being a short sale, this activity always results in a settlement failure (see below). Naked short sales are legal in the US in only very limited conditions.

Whether an ordinary short sale or a naked short sale, the theory behind this investment strategy requires the seller to monitor the market price of the shares for two reasons. First, if the price rises instead of falls, the seller will be required to put additional funds aside for the eventual purchase of shares to either repay the stock loan or to close out the settlement failure. Second, the seller must eventually close out the short sale (i.e. repay the loan or buy shares to close settlement). A short sale that remains open indefinitely is not an investment strategy – it is basically a fraudulent sale because the seller never intended to deliver shares to the buyer.

Any time a share is sold short, there will ultimately be more shares in circulation than there are outstanding shares. In an ordinary short sale, the borrowed shares leave the lender with the "extra" shares (see below). In the naked short sale, the buyer believes they own shares that, in fact, do not exist. (For the technical aspects of owning a real share versus owning an entitlement, which is what is created for the party who "buys" shares from a short seller, see *Lessons Not Learned*, especially reference to Article 8 of the Uniform Commercial Code in Chapter 7.)

Stock lending

Ordinary short sales will be "covered" with borrowed shares (i.e. not "naked"). The seller contacts a broker who either owns or has a client who owns the shares. That broker then lends the shares to the short seller; the borrowed shares are delivered to the buyer at settlement. At this point, the original owner may or may not be aware that their shares have been loaned. The standard brokerage customer agreement includes a section on "Loan or Pledge of Securities" (see box) that most investors do not notice. It gives the broker the right to lend shares from their account without notifying them. While the shares are out on loan, they will receive instructions to vote in corporate elections but the broker cannot turn in the vote to the company. The broker is under no obligation to tell you that your vote will not be counted. The voting rights go to the buyer who received the borrowed shares at settlement. This clause in the standard brokerage customer agreement is also the place where the broker advises investors that they will not receive tax-qualified dividends; the "payment in lieu" of dividends that they receive is not qualified for favorable tax treatment from the IRS. Again, the actual dividend will go to the buyer who received the borrowed shares at settlement, shares that the broker loaned from a retail investor's account.

> **Loan or Pledge of Securities**
>
> I authorize [broker name] to lend either to itself or to others any Securities and/or Other Property held by [broker name] in my Margin Account to the extent permitted by law. I understand that within the limitations imposed by applicable laws, rules and regulations all of my securities and other property may be pledged and repledged and hypothecated and rehypothecated by [broker name]. This can occur from time to time without notifying me, either separately or together with other Securities and/or Other Property of other customers of [broker name], for any amount due [broker name] in any Account in which I have an interest. In certain circumstances, such loans may limit, in whole or in part, my ability to exercise voting rights of the securities that are lent by me. In addition, if any Securities in my Margin Account are lent out on the dividend record date for such securities, I understand that I may receive a payment in lieu of dividend (also known as a substitute payment) from [broker name], instead of the actual dividend from the issuer or its transfer agent. Payments in lieu of dividends are treated differently than qualified dividend income under U.S. tax laws. I understand that [broker name] does not offer tax advice and that I will consult with my tax advisor as necessary.
>
> Source: Broker name redacted from brokerage customer agreement, [Online, Accessed June 30, 2019]

One other thing that the broker does not tell retail investors is that the broker will receive a fee for lending the shares – and they will not share that fee with a retail investor. The longer the loan remains outstanding, the more fees the broker will collect for lending shares that belong to retail account holders. Therefore, the broker has no incentive to get the shares back from the borrower – the longer the short sale position stays open, the longer the loan is outstanding, the more money the lending broker makes on the shares retail investors entrust to them for safekeeping.

Settlement failures

As hard as it may be to believe, the US centralized clearing and settlement (CCS) system offers the option to fail. There are CCS systems in other countries that either reverse unsettled trades or fine participants who fail to deliver securities in time for settlement. In the US, most financial market participants are only penalized if they failed to deliver money for settlement.[6] That seems odd if you keep in mind that one dollar bill is the same as the next and that even foreign currency can easily be exchanged for US currency to use at settlement. However, if the brokers sell more shares of, say Microsoft than that company has issued, they cannot get more shares of Microsoft by exchanging shares of, for example, Apple, Inc. Furthermore, Microsoft cannot simply print more shares of stock the way the US government can create more dollars. Recall from the terminology above that the number of shares authorized by the company is part of the state registration; and the number of shares they are permitted to sell in the financial markets has to be registered with the SEC. As bizarre as it sounds, settlement failures are tolerated in US capital markets and, before about 2004, the CCS organization was not required to disclose this information to the public. Even after 2004, they are only required to list the number of shares of each company that was not received in time for settlement (see www.sec.gov/fails). They are not required to disclose which brokers are the failing parties.

Settlement failures will always happen after a naked short sale, since no shares were borrowed to make delivery (fail-to-deliver). When the broker executes the trade, they are required to indicate if the sale is short or not – but that does not always happen. Some trades that are not "marked short" end up failing at settlement anyway. No one seems to keep track of whether or not the trade was short when it was executed, so settlement failures have come to be used as a way to measure naked short sales, although, again, not all trades that fail to settle were marked "short" at execution. The lack of transparency (and often accountability) for the records of individual trades is an important reason for focusing on fails to deliver and not just naked short sales. It also puts the emphasis squarely on the need for regulatory reform and not on simply chasing down one wrongdoer after another.

Economics of phantom shares

We refer to the extra shares put into circulation by shorts, loans and fails as "phantom shares." So far, we have explained the problems of shorts, loans and fails from the perspective of the investor. The economics of phantom shares also impact the company who issued the shares plus governments that use debt to finance deficits, which is the federal government and most states, counties, cities, school districts, etc. The economic impact on the government, in turn, affects all citizens whether or not they are investors. I call the combination of shorts, loans and fails the "Triumvirate of Trouble."

Because the difference in price from short sale to buy-to-replace is taken as profit, an unscrupulous short seller has an economic incentive to sell as much as possible – to attempt to drive the price down – in order to increase profits. A simple concept from economics is at work here: prices fall when supply increases. It is as true for cars as it is for shares. For stocks, we call this decrease in price a "dilution of share value" because the price of the shares is falling not because the company performed badly but because there are simply more shares in circulation (an increase in supply). The same price decrease could be seen if the company issued extra shares. Of course, the difference there would be that the company would get the money from the sale of the shares to use for capital investments. In a short sale, the money for the extra shares goes to the seller and their broker to do with as they please.

In a covered short sale, the seller pays to borrow the shares. The cost and fees associated with that loan put pressure on the seller to close out their position.[7] In a naked short sale the shares are not borrowed: there is no additional expense or incentive to close out the short sale. With legitimate short selling (naked or otherwise), the dilution of share value and shareholder rights will be corrected when the short positions are closed: the market price of the shares will move toward the real value of the firm as shares are borrowed to cover the short sale and ultimately as shares are purchased to repay the loan.

When settlement failures are added to the picture, none of the short sellers have an incentive to cover. The trade may be allowed to remain unsettled indefinitely. When a trade is executed, regardless of whether the trade is marked "long" or "short," if the shares are not presented at settlement, the customer pays for those shares and they are led to believe that they have those shares in their account when they do not.

To be perfectly clear, the source of the problem is three-fold – short selling, stock lending and settlement failures. The short sellers can harm a company's reputation and damage the share price, both of which limit the firm's ability to access capital. Investors are damaged by settlement failures because they are not getting real ownership of shares after making payments. Institutional investors, including pension funds like California's teachers and public employees' retirement funds, try to stand on both sides of the problem: as investors, they see the value of their portfolio shares eroded by the short sellers. But, unlike individual investors, big institutional investors can get a share of the money earned by the broker for lending shares from their portfolio. They still relinquish their voting rights, but they are able to earn higher returns by lending their shares to short sellers.[8] The damage caused by all three activities stems from the core problem, which is a systemic failure to provide secure, guaranteed, final settlement for trades.

The CCS system provides one more way for the broker to make money in this process. The answer lies in the notes to the financial statements for NSCC, where settlement failures are called "open positions": "Open positions are marked-to-market daily. Such marks are debited or credited to the involved participants [broker] through the settlement process."[9] So, as excessive short selling causes the price of the shares to fall, each day the CCS will credit back to the failing broker the cash collateral they put up to borrow shares from the central depository. If that broker can drive the price of the shares to zero, the CCS will further oblige them by declaring the securities "worthless," eliminating any remaining obligation from their records.

Economic impact on government bonds

With a bond, there is another idea to consider: yield. A bond will pay a rate of interest that is fixed when the bond is issued. For example, a bond issued at 10% will pay $10 per $100 for as long as the bond is outstanding (basically, until it matures). If the price of the bond falls, the yield rises because the dollar amount of the interest remains unchanged. In the example of a bond paying 10% ($10 interest paid on a bond originally sold for $100), if the price falls to $90 then the yield rises to 11% ($10 interest paid on a bond that cost you $90). When the market price of a bond falls and the yield rises, the next time the issuer (e.g. the US Treasury) wants to issue a new bond, they will have to match the higher yield (interest rate) to get anyone to buy it. That pushes up the interest expense which will, after all, eventually cost taxpayers more because taxes are the main source of government revenue.

Chapter 2. Start at the Beginning

It is hard to know where to start when writing about events that I observed at first hand. There were things that happened before the first part of the story that, while not part of it, laid the background that made the story possible. Those events are important to make sense of what comes later. In theater, there is a technique called a "plant." For example, a knife may be slipped nonchalantly onto a table at the beginning of Act One only to be used in a vengeful act against the protagonist in Act Three.

The "knife" here is my knowledge that short sales and stock loans created a situation where more than one person could claim ownership of the same share of stock. These claims showed up when it came time to receive dividend payments and to cast votes in matters of corporate governance like electing directors or approving mergers. Several people who were in the financial services industry especially in and around New York a long time before I got there in 1987 would tell me about a problem that was common knowledge even in the 1970s when the organizations for centralized clearing and settlement in the US were being created. After the paperwork crisis of the late 1960s, everyone had bigger fish to fry, as they say, than to try to balance out share ownership. Back in the 1960s, it was virtually impossible to get shares re-registered in the name of the new owner in time to settle stock trades which was allowed to be almost two weeks after the date of the trade. As long as the seller got paid, banks, brokers and regulators looked the other way when share ownership records did not keep up with the changes. The knowledge of this problem of keeping the company's share ownership records up to date as shares were traded – and the fact that the regulators knew about it yet took no action – is the knife on the table at the beginning of this story. In 2003, that knife would reappear in the hands of unscrupulous actors. This time it was sticking out of the backs of a multitude of small business entrepreneurs in North America and individual investors around the world.

A decade before that, in early 1993, I was accepted to the Ph.D. program at New York University. It meant leaving my job at the Depository Trust Company (DTC), the central depository for nearly all the shares of publicly traded companies in the US and a large portion of corporate and municipal government bonds, as well. Not long before I left DTC, I got a call from Ray Riley, a vice president at Manufacturers Hanover Trust Company, asking if I would meet with him to discuss a problem with one of DTC's programs that allows its members to lend out the shares of stock they have on deposit with DTC. Ray is retired now but during all my work on this subject, he was always my go-to expert for all things related to transfer agents and shareholder recordkeeping. I first met Ray when we worked together on the Operations Committee of the Securities Transfer Association (STA) from the time when I joined DTC. He and I were on the team that developed and implemented the Signature Guarantee Medallion Program (STAMP), a program that remains in use today as the standard for signature verification in financial transactions.

Ray approached me about the problem because he believed that only DTC could be in a position to help resolve it. Maybe he figured that since I was leaving DTC anyway, I might take on the impossible task. I like to think it also was because he trusted me after years of nearly daily business interactions. When I started working at DTC, my title was Director of Transfer Agent Services, a mid-management position in the operations division where my role was to maintain good working relationship with transfer agents in the US and Canada. Ray and I met for lunch one day while he explained the problem to me; the problem that he saw with short selling and stock lending.[10] Ray said that many of the transfer agents had noticed, that they were unable to reconcile the number of shares voted by DTC Participants with the number of shares issued and outstanding on their records, especially around record dates when they were establishing the identities of the shareholders with rights to cast votes in corporate elections. They suggested that stock lending resulted in multiple parties having electronic entitlements to the same shares. I understood what short sales were and I knew about DTC's program for stock lending, where they would arrange to borrow shares from one member to lend to another member to cover any failure to deliver shares for settlement at National Securities Clearing Corporation (NSCC). What I did not realize before Ray explained it to me was the impact those two were having on shareholder voting rights and corporate governance.

Usually when a broker, a bank or an investor sells stock, they already own it and they present those shares for delivery to the buyer's broker. In a short sale, they have to borrow the stock from some owner in order to make delivery (and receive payment) on settlement day. Sometimes, the sell order is executed before they can get the shares. In that case, DTC's partner firm, the NSCC would step in and arrange for the stock shares to be loaned from a DTC member to cover the short position at settlement.[11] One of the primary motivations for DTC to be the "lend of last resort" was to provide orderly settlement. If they did not lend the shares, then those trades would fail to settle, opening the door for a cascade of unrelated trades also to fail settlement. To a reasonable man, it would make sense to reverse the singular trade that failed: Force the buyer and seller to undo the trade. The seller who cannot deliver the shares they sold would not get paid and the buyer would not have to pay for shares they would not receive.

But DTC (who processes the final exchange of money for shares) could not order this unwinding of one trade. The reason is because of a process at NSCC known as "continuous net settlement" or CNS. With CNS, trades are matched and cleared for settlement throughout the day and final settlement only occurs once at the end of every trading day. Cleared for settlement simply means that the buyer and the seller have agreed to all the terms of the trade (price, number of shares, location of settlement, etc.). It does not mean that anyone has confirmed that the buyer has the money to pay for the shares or that the seller has the shares to deliver. The facts of ability to pay and ability to deliver do not come to light until the end of the third business day after a trade; even then it is not known with certainty until after the markets have closed for the day.[12] If it is discovered at that late hour that the seller does not have the shares to deliver to the buyer, it has become impossible to reverse the individual trade. With CNS, all the trades are settled on a "net" basis. If a broker sells 100 shares and buys 100 shares of the same stock, their "net" position in that stock is zero at the end of the day. Similarly, if the price of the sale order and the price in the buy order of the trade are the same, the broker is also in a net zero position for cash; otherwise, if they sell for a higher price than they buy, there will be a net payment of cash due to the broker during final settlement. If, for any reason, the broker with a net payment of cash due cannot make the payment, the central depository (DTC) can borrow the money (from a bank or from the Federal Reserve Bank) to make up the difference. When that happens, the broker would have an entry in their DTC account indicating that they owe the money plus accumulated interest to DTC. The borrowed money is then used to cover the payment of cash to the net sellers at final settlement.

On the other hand, when a broker does not have the shares to deliver for final settlement, there is no bank to go to for a loan.

Unlike cash, which comes from only one source (the U.S. Treasury and their agent, the Federal Reserve Bank), stocks are issued by thousands of companies. Also unlike cash, which the Treasury can autonomously order more of printed, companies have to follow state and federal rules before they can issue more stock. They often also need to get approval from existing shareholders, all of which can take months or even years to achieve. That is why shares for final settlement have to be borrowed from existing shareholder owners. When those loans are done through the central depository, the shares are borrowed from other brokers in the system. The issuer is not involved in the transaction. In fact, the issuer is not even notified that the shares have been loaned from a registered owner because, on the books of the issuer, DTC remains the registered owner. Of course, this is true even if the seller borrows the shares from another broker in a private loan in time for delivery at final settlement. However, in the case of broker-to-broker stock loans, there are too many parties involved for the issuer to ever hope of keeping track of who is holding the shares and who is actually registered on the books as the owner. DTC holds the majority of the shares of most US public companies. When he decided to approach me, Ray Riley believed it was possible for DTC to take some corrective action.

While I was working at DTC, senior management asked me to work with the transfer agents and registrars who keep the shareholder records for all of the companies in the Dow Jones Industrial Average (DJIA). They wanted to know what percentage of the shares of those companies was held in their vaults. At that time, DTC held upwards of 80% of all the shares issued by the 30 companies that made up the DJIA in 1991. For the more than 80% of shares held at DTC, it should be easier to keep track of who owns real shares than to try to track down all the broker-to-broker exchanges and loans.

When I approached DTC senior management with the issue of stock lending creating problems in corporate governance, they were aware of the impact of their programs and processes but dismissed it as trivial.

Loopholes for brokers, not for shareholders

The average person should be concerned about how well Wall Street is keeping track of corporate share ownership. Corporate stock shares (equities) make up more than 20% of household wealth in the U.S. American families have more than $20 trillion at stake. Those are direct investments in shares. More than half of all American households own some stocks.[13] That figure does not include another $22 trillion in household retirement funds, including pensions plans, 401(k)s and IRAs. Defined benefit pension funds allocate about 50% of their investments to stocks.[14]

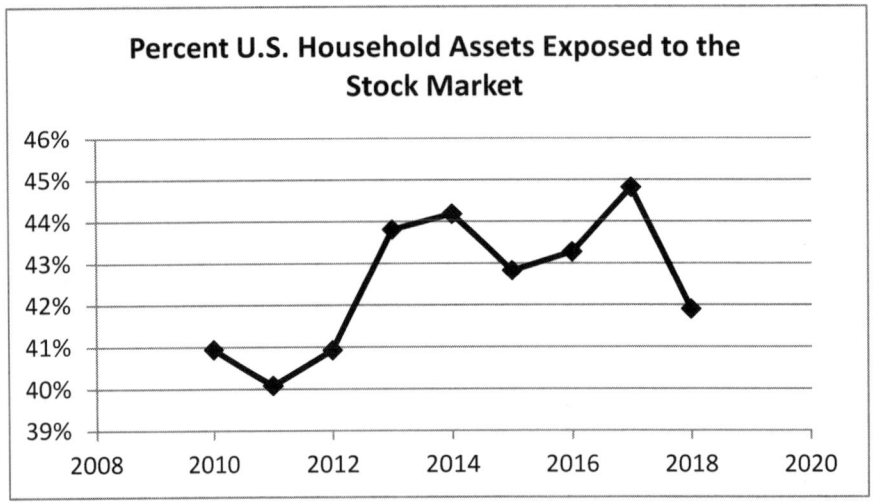

Data Source: Board of Governors of the Federal Reserve System, *Financial Accounts of the United States*, Table B.101.h Balance Sheet of Households; amounts outstanding end year. Percentage includes direct ownership plus pension funds.

The problems created by shorts, loans and fails are common knowledge in New York. One very early story was related to me by the head of a large, second-generation family-run stock transfer company in New York City. He was also a former New York City Assistant Attorney General. He was the Securities Transfer Association's (STA's) point man with the Securities and Exchange Commission (SEC) on regulatory matters in the 1980s. Transfer agents for public company shares are regulated by the SEC (among other government agencies). The head of this transfer agent was an outspoken critic of naked short selling and of the SEC's failure to "close the loopholes" by not enforcing delivery of stock shares for final settlement.[15] The SEC, in fact, put rules in place to prevent issuers from exiting DTC after the management of one company successfully convinced their individual investor shareholders to get their holdings issued in certificate form in their own names.[16]

Many corporate transfer agents long held the view that the SEC supported the short sellers as affecting some sort of "social Darwinism." Popular financial press accounts and even some academic publications praise short sellers as having some prescient knowledge about companies that are either poised for a big fall or that are over-priced for reasons unrelated to stock fundamentals. Without going into a lot of details about the theory of determining stock prices, the reality is that short sellers can, in fact, bring down prices of otherwise valuable companies.[17] If Wall Street brokers can execute enough short sales and leave them open long enough, they can have a negative impact on the ability of a small company to access capital. If that happens at a critical point in the development of the company, it can literally drive them out of existence.

Companies victimized by short sales, stock lending and settlement failures made numerous attempts over the years before 2003 to fix the problem: declaring reverse stock splits, recapitalizations, name changes, the issuance of warrants and "loyalty shares," etc.[18] All these efforts failed and eventually only made it impossible to fix the underlying regulatory failure. By calling attention to the sources of the problem, it allowed the SEC and DTC to "close the loopholes" used by public companies to get out of the system that was allowing their corporate shares to be abused.

Carl Hagberg is another of my long-time colleagues and friends from my days in New York at DTC. He is one of the most well-respected experts on individual stock ownership programs in the US. Carl has decades of experience in all areas of corporate trust (the umbrella department that handles stock transfers and other important corporate governance matters). When I first met Carl in New York, he was with Manufacturers Hanover Trust Company, the largest provider of stockholder and bondholder services in the country, at that time. He retired in 1993 to establish his own firm with the mission of helping public companies to develop their own top-notch shareholder service programs.[19]

Carl was my go-to expert for all things related to corporate governance operations then and throughout my efforts to achieve regulatory reform. Anytime I called on him, Carl was willing to share his knowledge, expertise and experiences with me. He told me when we first started to work together on these issues that he had heard from several good sources that DTC would "make deals with companies to have them issue new shares directly to DTC…to resolve large fail-to-deliver situations…and to avoid or settle threatened litigation." I asked him to explain why companies would consent to this, since it would dilute the value of all the other shares. He told me that most of the companies caught up by abusive short-selling schemes were often in need of additional capital.[20] They, of course, would almost certainly be totally unaware that DTC was *part of the problem*. Instead, those companies gladly issued additional shares to DTC to cover the open trades, in exchange for an infusion of cash. The failing broker did not suffer any consequences for failing to deliver shares for settlement because the US centralized clearing and settlement system tolerates open fails. In these cases, they actively worked to protect the failing broker from consequences.

Another close friend who would play an important role in this story is Tom Montrone. When I first met Tom, he was President/CEO of Registrar & Transfer Company (R&T).[21] Tom already had more than a decade in the securities transfer business with large trust companies and banks before I met him. He is a terrific friend who will later come to my defense when DTCC (the parent company of DTC and NSCC since 2000) attempts to silence me when I speak out against their role in the destruction of so many entrepreneurs and the ruin of investors (Chapter 16). Tom became the poster child for the ruins of corporate governance when he appeared in the cover photo for a *Bloomberg Markets* article on the problem created for corporate voting (Drummond 2006a).

Tom had long been an outspoken critic of the "over-voting" that was enabled by deficiencies in broker procedures that let both the borrowers and the lenders of stock submit votes for the same shares. The industry utility that captures ownership data from DTC and brokers would actually introduce a service to allow brokers to adjust their votes (without correcting the investor account records) by notifying them when they reported more votes than they had share rights. (We return to this issue of "over-voting" with more explanation and details in Chapter 8.)

Carl Hagberg especially considered this situation to be one more example of DTC's "breach of fiduciary duty" to the public companies whose securities are deposited with DTC with the understanding that the investors' rights of ownership – and voting power is among those rights – will be properly safeguarded.[22] Not one to shy away from controversy, Carl speculated that DTC might have been lending restricted shares which would be a real bombshell if it could be proved, even if DTC were an unwitting accomplice to the violation of an important broker rule. Carl went so far as to offer to represent any small company with a problem by camping out on the sidewalk at DTC – free of charge – to get answers! Ray, Carl and Tom would remain my go-to team for all things related to recordkeeping and shareholder rights for the owners of equity shares in US public companies. All three had, at one time or another, complained to the SEC about the problems they saw first-hand.

While I was an operations manager at DTC, my experience with SEC examiners is that they were not well-informed about centralized clearing and settlement. I remember the first time I met with an SEC examiner in my role as an operations manager. The first question they always asked was: "So, what does DTC do?" Transfer agents told me of similar experiences during SEC audits at their offices. In conversations, transfer agents like Tom and Ray found that SEC staff auditors did not even believe that DTC lent out stock, despite having "stock lending" as a listed service. Tom told me that he once had a conversation with an SEC attorney in New York who did not understand why it was important for brokers to deliver shares for final settlement. The SEC was so adamant about making the entire system work electronically that they forgot what the system was developed to do – solve the problem of delivering shares for final settlement. The SEC, like DTC, was openly hostile toward the idea that an issuer would not want their shares held in a centralized system that provided services to multiply the number of shares being traded beyond the number of shares authorized by the corporation.

Many companies did not understand what was happening to them or the role the centralized clearing and settlement system played in the problem. It would not occur to them to complain *about* DTC although many of them complained *to* DTC. When they did complain, DTC would stonewall them. DTC got the SEC to grant approval of a rule change to prohibit requests for withdrawal of certificates by issuers.[23] Small and unseasoned companies are under a lot of pressure to meet SEC filing deadlines and requirements. Many did not want to bring themselves to the attention of the SEC. The first sign of the damage being done to their company was often an unexplained drop in the market price of their shares. The second sign, getting more votes than there were legitimate shares, might only be visible to the transfer agent or the corporate secretary.[24]

Indeed, as we brought public and political attention to the issues, it became increasingly difficult to get anyone from DTC – even long-time friends and colleagues – to return our phone calls. Carl Hagberg and I would leave messages for colleagues, get referred to secondary contacts, and eventually find that contacts who had previously communicated freely with us were transferred unexpectedly to new departments. By the time I entered the fray in 2003, DTC and the SEC were already beginning to circle the wagons.

One of the primary reasons that DTCC and its subsidiaries DTC and NSCC will not or cannot take action to correct the problem is that the majority of the Board members in the centralized clearing and settlement system are industry representatives. They represent the banks and brokers who were part of the problem – not part of the solution. So the question for the stock issuing companies and their corporate trust agents was: Who at DTC would even listen? When Ray Riley approached me in 1993, he made me understand the impact of shorts sales and stock lending on shareholder voting and corporate governance. It would not be until much later, after 2003, that we would get a glimpse into the third part of the problem which was that the system allowed brokers to fail to deliver shares for final settlement.

Ray Riley was taking a big chance approaching me when he did in 1993. There was the possibility that the senior management at DTC would not listen to me about the problem, or even that they would refuse to take action. Even more serious implications came from the fact that the company he worked for had senior managers sitting on the Board of Directors at DTC and NSCC. Most transfer agent companies (except independent firms like R&T) were also banks or had a broker arm that was most likely engaging in short selling, stock borrowing and stock lending.[25] By bringing the problem to light, Ray and others could be subject to reprisal from the brokerage side of the house. When Manufacturers Hanover and other large New York banks were taken over in following years, Ray and his colleagues who spoke to me about the problem did not retain positions.

There were few other people at the time – and even later when the issues came to light – that were willing to take the career risk that would be associated with speaking out at DTC. In fact, my former colleagues at DTC made it pretty clear to me that they were not willing to have their names associated with my activities because they were not willing to jeopardize their positions (employment). Much later, I would learn that a friend tried to get DTCC management to acknowledge the impact of stock loans on share prices in 2002. That friend did not stay at DTCC long after that and, in some ways, she attributed coming forward to her being, if not pushed out then at least made to feel unwelcome.

PART II. BACK TO WHERE I LEFT OFF

Chapter 3. A Sidewalk Café in New York

When I graduated from NYU in May 2000, I had a couple of job offers. But the one that I actively pursued was doing research at the Milken Institute. My dissertation covered the mergers and acquisitions of the 1980s (and early 1990s) among the Fortune 500 firms. This was the "merger mania" period in US corporate history. It was also the period when Mike Milken's "junk bonds" were at the forefront of financing options for takeovers. I had a finding in my research that demonstrated a real economic benefit from all those takeovers: when financing was available for large mergers and acquisitions, inefficient firms were taken-over, no matter how big they were.[26] When Drexel went out of business it virtually ended the market for high-yield bonds because they were the only place that published closing prices.[27] High-yield or "junk" bonds were being used to finance most of the very big mergers and acquisitions during the 1980s. After the collapse of the market for junk bonds, brought on by the demise of Drexel Burnham and the jailing of Mike Milken, any inefficient firm could escape takeover as long as they could grow large enough. In other words, the availability of financing – even junk bond financing – meant that large inefficient firms would be subject to market discipline. Without that financing, they could operate as inefficiently as they wanted as long as they were too big to be acquired.[28]

I guessed that Milken would be interested in this result. When I found the Milken Institute's website, they were running a research contest. I submitted my paper and won an award, which Mike presented to me on stage at the American Economic Association's annual meeting in Boston in January 2000. By the end of May, after completing my PhD in economics at New York University's Graduate School of Arts and Sciences, I was living in southern California and working as Senior Research Economist in Capital Studies at Milken Institute. I was looking forward to a long career with a growing reputation for excellence in economic research.

Before long, I was sitting next to Mike Milken at planning meetings for the Global Conferences and other events. I was even invited to his house in Encino, along with the senior management of the Institute, for planning meetings. There were long days in the office, early morning conference calls and even a few one-on-one research discussion meetings with Mike. By late-2003, I was well-entrenched at Milken Institute. For example, I was completing a project done jointly with a Big Six accounting/consulting firm. No one else at Milken Institute could handle the large dataset or run the mathematical models that I could, which meant that I got to travel to London for inter-firm presentations.

Unbeknownst to me and completely separate from my work at Milken Institute, a group of investors, issuers and their lawyers were already hard at work, filing Freedom of Information Act (FOIA) requests with the SEC in search of the data they needed but which DTCC was unwilling to provide to prove the damage being done to them by the regulatory failure in US financial services. One investor in particular, David Patch, an aviation engineer with General Electric, had incredible success getting data on settlement failures through FOIA requests even before the regulatory requirement for public disclosure.[29] Dave became an advocate for market reform after he invested in some small or start-up companies that were seeing the signs of stock market manipulation.

The napkin story

In late 2003, my boss and I went to New York to reconnect with some of Mike Milken's "legacy" contacts – big-time investment firms that benefited from working with Mike in his Drexel days. I had a few individual meetings with the Milken/Drexel legacy contacts to try to offer some research work that could be performed at the Milken Institute. The ultimate goal was to encourage general contributions for research in the Capital Studies Group. Providing some one-off research reports was a way to introduce these businesses to our work. One afternoon, my boss tells me he has just come from lunch with an old friend, Gary Jewell, a Houston-based lawyer. Gary said that he was in New York looking for someone who understands post-trade clearing and settlement, possibly someone who may have worked at the Depository Trust Company. My boss recognizes the company name as part of my past work experience. He asks me to meet Gary over coffee. The two of them had run marathons in their younger days and my boss presents it to me as doing him a favor. Gary brought Wes Christian to that casual meeting.

James "Wes" Christian, is a Senior Partner at Christian, Smith, & Jewell in Houston. If not for Wes, I may not ever have become aware that the crack in the system Ray Riley brought to me in 1993 was becoming a gaping chasm in 2003. Wes was born, raised, and educated in Texas. He comes complete with a pleasant drawl that belies his non-nonsense approach to the matter. Wes would lead a team of 65 lawyers as he eventually uncovered more than 1,200 hedge fund and offshore accounts working through more than 150 broker-dealers to strip small and medium size public companies of their value.

As soon as the coffee is delivered to our sidewalk café table, Wes advises me that the discussion is confidential. I have no idea what he is about to tell me, but I agree to his requirement. Since that day, of course, I have told this story many times, including for newspaper reporters and documentary film makers. I do not know if I have all the facts of Wes' story exactly right, because I was completely blown away by what he told me that day. Anyway, here is how I remember it:[30]

Wes' story begins on a Sunday morning when he and his friend, colleague, and fellow lawyer John O'Quinn are chatting with a fellow worshiper after church services. It is the early 2000s, they are in Houston and the sting of Enron is still fresh on everyone's mind. Wes would blame it on his Texan heritage, or maybe his cowboy sense of justice, but he was not able to walk away from that chance encounter without doing all he could to make things right. I think I know how he felt, because I will have the same reaction after he tells me about it.

This fellow worshipper begins to tell Wes and John a story, one they do not initially understand. It seems to be a complex story full of technical details about Wall Street activity. Neither of them has a background in finance at this point, but something about the tale catches at them. Maybe it is the tragedy of their friend's fate in these events: his small company has been destroyed and with it his reputation and the ability to try again to start another business.

When Wall Street destroys a company, they cut off their access to capital. Mike Milken wrote a lot about the importance of what he calls "the Democratization of Capital."[31] I learned more about the importance of access to capital while working with Mike. An entrepreneur starts with only an idea. In our system of capitalist democracy, that should be all you need. Under socialism, you would also need a government connection to get access to the means of production. In old-European oligarchies, you may have had to come from old money or have a rich uncle that was also a banker. But in a capitalist democracy, where the savings of households are accumulated into the investment needed by businesses, every good idea should be able to raise money by selling shares in the stock market. It is a concept that is as American as apple pie.

Exactly the way that Ray Riley explained it to me in 1993, the fact is that the excess supply of shares created by shorts, fails and loans will have a negative impact on share prices that is greater than any outright sale of the shares by an investor. The impact can run to multiples of the issued and outstanding shares. In documented cases, the number of shares being traded – and voted – was 150% of the issued and outstanding shares of a company, even a big company like Bank of America. This happens to large and small companies, but the small companies have a harder time coming back from the damage done to their ability to access capital markets.

The fellow worshiper goes on to tell Wes and John that his employees are jobless and he regrets their loss, maybe even more than his own. He asks Wes and John for their help in addition to their fellowship that Sunday morning. They agree only to meet with him later in the week. The fellow worshiper shows up at the meeting fully prepared. He does more than just talk. He has documented a situation that O'Quinn will later refer to as the worst US economic disaster since asbestos.

Wes' practice to that point has been mostly in real estate and business organizations, plus commercial litigation including intellectual property rights and medical malpractice. John O'Quinn of O'Quinn, Laminack & Pirtle (OLP) in Houston was a plaintiff's lawyer who made his name winning billion dollar verdicts against the makers of diet drugs, silicone breast implants and tobacco. To help their friend, Wes and John would have to embark on a crash-course in the intricacies of high finance. One has to wonder if they would have agreed to move forward had they known the enormous scope of the problem that lay ahead.

Sitting in that New York sidewalk café in late 2003, Wes drew out a scenario for me on the back of a napkin. I quickly recognize that this is the same problem the corporate trust officers like Ray Riley brought to me in 1993, when fails to deliver were around $6 million. In 2003, while I am meeting with Wes in New York, the fails in equities are over $6 billion. We would not come to understand the full extent of the problem (including that it was also happening in bonds and derivatives) until years later when fails to deliver in US Treasury bonds soared into the trillions of dollars. That part of the story comes later.

Back in 2003, we are only looking at equity shares (stocks). Wes was setting out to take on Wall Street – a formidable task. I caution him that Wall Street does not just have a lot of money, they have all the money. They hold your retirement account, the money you are saving for your kids' education, your grandmother's savings account – *all of it*. If that was not a formidable enough task, Wes is also setting his sights on organized crime and offshore companies. According to Wes, one criminal can set up more than 100 offshore companies, establish a brokerage account for each one, and then buy and sell shares among them to multiply shares through shorts and fails. Unwitting investors buy what does not exist and brokers routinely turn that money over to themselves and the criminal sitting offshore. Some critics estimate that 40% of the companies that are subject to market manipulation through shorts, fails and loans may have gone bankrupt anyway due to poor business practices or other factors. But the other 60% likely would have survived, thrived and produced products and services to the benefit of the economy.

When Wes finished his description, I was simply stunned to hear that events that were first brought to me in 1993 were being brought to me again a decade later. I felt as if my failure in 1993 allowed the problem to become massive. A $6 million dollar problem had grown 1,000 times bigger in just ten years. Back in 1993, I was just a mid-level operations manager, powerless to make the required changes. After hearing Wes' story about the exact same events that had only become worse, I made a decision to commit my time to helping the companies and investors harmed by shorts, fails and loans. I wanted to make up for my inability to fix the problem while I was at DTC ten years earlier.

A few months after that first meeting with Wes Christian, he arranged for me to act as an expert witness for John's firm (OLP). Wes explained that the contract would be with OLP because John O'Quinn was bank-rolling the lawsuits. Later, O'Quinn would tell *Dateline NBC* (2005) that he was prepared to spend as much as $100 million to prove a conspiracy of manipulation in the stock market.[32] I worked for and with Wes directly on a variety of test-case lawsuits filed in the state courts. There were, at least initially, no questions about the billings – I sent them to O'Quinn and payments were prompt. After Mr. O'Quinn died in late 2009, naturally, there were some delays. When I asked about it, Wes told me that the partners at OLP were opposed to using experts in the cases so that the firm was not willing to continue with payments. I figured out that this was probably a good idea since very few of the other consultants I met working with Wes were really expert in much of anything! In any event, Wes made good on payments for all my billings.

Under contract to provide assistance in the lawsuits they planned to bring against the DTC, Wes arranged to have a couple boxes of documents sent to me for review. Most of my work was very general, not specific to any particular case or lawsuit. I organized briefing sessions for Wes and his colleagues either with me presenting to them in Houston or at meetings including some of my former associates in New York. I wrote briefing reports and revised reports written by others. Otherwise, Wes only used me as a fact witness in any court filings and my last work for Wes was in 2008 – barely five years in total.

Chapter 4. Blind Men Describe an Elephant

Soon after I signed on to work with Wes Christian, I ended up on the mailing list of several of the "experts" that Wes was using before he brought me on board. These are the consultants I referred to earlier. One was a dentist in Michigan who had, to the best of my knowledge, no experience in post-trade processing. The Michigan dentist apparently tried to figure out a lot of stuff for himself by reading articles posted to the internet and maybe talking to a few retail brokers. As one might expect, this led to some disastrous misunderstandings.

First, everyone knows that the internet has a lot of bad information. A study of the accuracy of medical information on the internet (Themistocleous, Karavolias,et. al, 2003) reported finding about 20% of the answers to some common questions were "misleading and invalid."[33] In 2010, research by Penn State University Professor Marcia DiStaso published in the scholarly *Public Relations Journal* reported finding errors in 60% of Wikipedia articles. 25% of companies with entries on Wikipedia admitted they do not check them for accuracy.[34]

Retail brokers are probably just as bad as sources for information on the existence and impact of settlement failures. They know little more than most investors about being on the receiving end of a short sale or a fail to deliver, about whether your vote is counted when you send your instructions to the firm, and about whether your received a dividend or a payment-in-lieu of a dividend. The CEO of a large online retailer found out the hard way that the retail broker – even those serving the richest clients of the firm – can only repeat what they are told by operations: the trade settled, they took the money from his cash account and credited his stock account for the shares. When he pressed the question, he found out that the trade had, in fact, failed to settle and there were no shares in his account. It took him months to get delivery after the retail broker told him the trade settled in three days.

Before you can work as a barber in the US, you need to complete more than 1,000 hours of training, pass a practical exam (where you demonstrate barbering skills), and a written exam with 50 questions in 90 minutes. All that is required to sell stocks and bonds in the US is to pass an exam set up by the Financial Industry Regulatory Authority (FINRA) – the self-regulatory organization for brokers. Since they wrote it by themselves for themselves, well, you can imagine they would not make you learn anything that would shed a bad light on the industry. The Series 7 license exam allows almost two hours for answering a series multiple choice questions.[35] The questions cover the major job functions of a broker, which FINRA considers to be:

Major Job Function	% of Questions
Provide customers with information about investments, make suitable recommendations	73%
Obtain and verify customers' purchase and sales instructions and agreements	11%
Open accounts using customers' financial profile and investment objectives	9%
Seek business for the broker-dealer	7%

In other words, FINRA considers 73% of a broker's job to be convincing you to make certain investments. You can only take the exam for the license after you are hired by a FINRA member firm – the ultimate Catch 22 designed to retain power for what one senator will call "the Black Priesthood" (Chapter 19).

Overall, working with the lawyers and their consultants, especially in the early days, was like being the sighted person who comes upon the blind men attempting to describe an elephant.

- If they were entrepreneurs of companies that went public, they saw naked-short selling by unscrupulous underwriters in league with bad brokers.
- If they were investors, they saw unscrupulous regulators failing in their duty to protect them.
- If they were regulators, they saw unscrupulous companies trying to cheat money out of the markets and rob investors.
- If they were brokers, they saw cry-baby companies who could not play with the Big Boys on Wall Street.
- If they were lawyers, they saw the potential for a big payoff for their clients when they convinced a jury that Wall Street was cheating companies and investors.

In some respects, each delusion was right, yet just like describing an elephant in parts, the whole truth of post-trade processing, which is where the actual impacts of the problem initiated, cannot be understood in parts. Each player in this drama seemed to have based their opinion of the cause of the events on their knowledge of the limited effects they could see, which did not give them a complete picture. Just as in the fable of the Blind Men and the Elephant, people believed something to be true based on their personal experiences and seldom went on to see the complete picture before coming to a conclusion about the causes. They limited themselves to only that part which they experienced, taking action as if that were the whole. In the various versions of the story of the blind men, the sighted-man resolves the argument by explaining what an elephant is. In the world of shorts, fails and loans, many of the players (consultants, CEOs and lawyers alike) rejected my suggestions for action because I challenged their small-world view of events; they preferred to stick to their own limited knowledge which elevated their importance to investors, lawyers and companies willing to pay for bad advice.

Bud Burrell was one exception. I was reading his blogs and emails, but did not get to meet him until my company organized an event in Los Angeles (Chapter 13). Bud had actual Wall Street experience, which was rare among this group of Blind Men. Bud would tell me that the lawyers, including district attorneys and FBI lawyers that he and I met with, do not want someone with an actual command of the subject matter because they would lose control of their ability to prosecute. He also suggested that "there was some Democrat political agenda that I, to this day, do not have full knowledge of." Bud believed, and some of the paid consultants even admitted to him in so many words, that the consultants who were closest to the lawsuits filed by OLP were "Democratic Operatives." Bud, on the other hand, is a graduate of West Point, with five years of service in the Army and a staunch Republican. He spent most of his early adult life after the Army working for major broker-dealers in New York. Bud's position was that they rejected us because we knew too much – our expert knowledge challenged their views in ways they could not handle.

Over the years, the non-expert consultants would burn up a lot of my time and most of the money available from law firms and mid-sized companies to fight the issue in court. Both Bud and I agree that the cases may have gone further with knowledgeable expert witnesses. One consultant, who I will refer to as BC because he is not a public figure, even told me that he had to keep writing nonsense white papers for lawyers because he needed money to finish a home remodeling project. Another, who I will call RS, admitted to me that he did not even know what a short sale was until one of the lawyers paid him to prepare an expert witness report for one of their cases against short selling! He milked both the lawyers and several victimized companies for untold sums of money, despite not having a clue about what a whole elephant looked like. It was disgraceful, but when I tried to call attention to these problems, I was told that:

(1) most of the managing partner lawyers would not work with a woman; and
(2) they believed that RS's title (from having been a minor political appointee in Washington D.C.) would carry more weight with judges and opposing counsel than actual knowledge.

The first point has always been a blind spot for me. The first two bosses when I started working were female; I was used to seeing men and women in positions of authority in the business place, so it didn't occur to me that gender would be an issue. If gender bias was present, someone had to point it out to me.

Whatever they believed, after the financial crisis of 2008 when most of those consultants could not get jobs at a car wash, I was the primary expert witness against the top lawyer in New York for the largest global investment bank. After my deposition, he made a billion-dollar settlement in a complex international case that hinged on the true nature of a transaction processed at DTC. I know exactly what an elephant is and is not!

Worse yet, these guys insisted on "mansplaining" to me everything they thought they knew; yet they were incapable of learning how things really worked. One of the companies that Wes is working with ended up on the "chill" list at DTC – a condition where DTC allows electronic movements of shares but will not allow shares to be withdrawn in the form of certificates (usually for individual shareholders who are clients of the member brokers and banks). I had multiple long phone calls with BC and reviewed multiple long documents from him where I had to correct the explanations of the reports they were getting from DTC and

NSCC. He kept running up the billable hours, but Wes kept using him. Maybe Wes wanted to help him remodel his house all along – I never figured this out. Eventually, one of the lawyers would ask me to work with BC on a paper (which I explained to the lawyer was so full of errors I think the phrase I used is that my kid sister could tear it apart on cross-examination); or to go over RS's upcoming testimony and expert witness report with him. I made it clear that the lawyer would have to pay me to talk to those guys. They did pay me and to this day I do not understand why they wasted their and their clients' money on Blind Men. I can only hope that the lawyer got what he wanted, and that it helped his clients.

The players that were the most vocal were all interested in one thing: money. Either they were chasing down opportunities to bill lawyers representing the companies who were being damaged; or they were shareholders deluding themselves into expecting to get rich quick when the brokers paid-up. As often as I could, I tried to make this clear to all of them: "The parties you are up against have all the money and they are going to use it to stop you."

It was the need to explain the whole elephant, combined with my guilt over not sticking it out at DTC in 1993 to see the problems corrected, that motivated me to keep working on making the naked, short and greedy system stop hurting America's entrepreneurs and the investors around the world who supported their endeavors.

PART III. COMMITTING TO A CAUSE

Chapter 5. Real Experts Meet

Going forward, I reviewed documents and submissions for lawsuits being filed in various state courts. My understanding is that these were designed to test claims using state law because all federal securities law is designed to be tried only in the Southern District of New York where courts are notoriously favorable toward brokers and banks and notoriously unfavorable to shareholders. It made sense to me that this should really be a big issue in the states, much more important to the states than some of them realize. Every corporation files their papers at the state level, including information about capitalization (number of shares, value, etc.). The states have an interest in whether or not there are more shares in circulation than are authorized.[36] Someone has to be held accountable for that, and yet the corporation has done nothing to increase the number of shares.

The lawyers often did not tell me where they were using the material I wrote, sometimes I did not even have the name of the litigants. As an expert witness, my job is only to keep the facts of the matter straight. I only offered opinions on what I knew, without speculation. I had no vested interest in who won or lost any particular case. The lawyers would have me review documents they received from opposing counsel. I would make lists of discovery questions, even write papers, but the lawyers pressing some of the earliest "naked short" lawsuits would not tell me how the cases were going unless I made a specific request for an update. Although Wes Christian initially brought me close after our meeting in late 2003, I think he eventually recognized that I "knew too much" and that the less-knowledgeable consultants were more inclined to write what he wanted to hear where I would only write what I could back up with facts, data and experience. It was never that Wes did not value the truth of the matter, just that his job was to remain focused on who won and who lost.

As I reaffirmed my commitment to the cause, I brought together my team of recognized industry experts for a meeting in New York to inform the lawyers and their communications people about shorts, fails and loans. Present at that meeting were Carl Hagberg, Raymond Riley and a selection of former colleagues from the Pacific Clearing Corporation and DTC plus a couple of men I knew who had experience in brokerage operations. Two of them had also come with me to work on US-AID projects to build post-trade clearing and settlement organizations in Poland and Russia. Each of them had experience keeping track of who owned shares through the maze created by DTC and the brokers. Going forward, I would recommend each of these specialists – real experts – to a variety of lawyers, investors and companies for help with their cases against brokers and banks and for help finding their true investor shareholders. Carl, in particular, would come to play an important role as I tried to save the CEO from himself at the Overstock.com, Inc. annual meeting of 2006. But that comes later.

One of the first things we agreed on was that the term "naked short selling" was too limiting. The problem was much bigger. The ultimate damaging effect was that there were more shares in circulation than the company had issued and outstanding. This condition could result from short selling not covered with borrowed shares ("naked short selling" which results in a fail to deliver), regular short selling covered with borrowed shares ("stock lending") and fails to deliver (for any reason). Again, shorts, loans and fails were all three at issue. Although fails were the most visible symptom, stock loans used to cover short sales also result in multiplied shares.

In an unfortunate turn of phrase, some lawyers and companies were calling the extra shares "counterfeits." For anyone who spent any time inside operations in the financial services industry, "counterfeits" are a much more literal problem. One of the reasons that the industry pushed for electronic recordkeeping of shareholders is that the physical certificates could be – and sometimes were – counterfeited. In the 1980s and 1990s, especially, the industry printers moved to incorporate some of the same anti-counterfeiting strategies used in currencies:[37] special paper containing colored threads, embedded holograms, etc. We knew that "counterfeit" was not going to convey the right idea to those in the industry who were in a position to make changes. A claim of counterfeit shares would be easily dismissed by regulators as a problem for criminal prosecution and not one that could be addressed by regulatory reform.

Soon after my team started, we coined the phrase "phantom shares" which we agreed to use going forward as the best way to describe the problem. Bloomberg TV would produce a special program using that word in the title, and print media would begin to apply it to the problems associated with corporate voting and other important issues.

At the end of year, Wes asked me to review a research paper on fails to deliver that was released by the SEC. RS had located the paper and wrote a long list of comments that I was expected to respond to. Most of what he wrote – again – was inaccurate, demonstrating a poor understanding of the underlying issue of settlement failures, although he was getting up to speed on "naked short selling." The paper was written by Leslie Boni who was then a visiting financial economist at the U.S. Securities and Exchange Commission (SEC). Before the visiting position at the SEC, Boni graduated from the University of Colorado and has since held teaching positions in finance at University of New Mexico and California State University, Northridge. In the 2004 paper, Boni called fails to deliver an "investment strategy." She claimed to "provide evidence consistent with the hypothesis that market makers strategically fail to deliver shares when borrowing costs are high." In other words, brokers simply fail to deliver at their convenience and for their financial advantage. There is little or no discussion in Boni, as there was in more scholarly works, of designing fines or other consequences to discourage this behavior.[38] There is certainly no discussion of the damaging effect on corporate governance from increasing the number of shares in circulation through stock lending and settlement failures.

I debated several times about what to call the "so-called experts" in order to keep the text of this narrative flowing. In my records, I have a folder labeled "players" – some of them got paid to work on the issue and some were just caught up as investors, lawyers or entrepreneurs. Patrick Byrne, then-CEO of Overstock.com (he comes into the story in Chapter 10), would dub them the "pajamahideen," a play on words that he used to refer to the freedom fighters who worked from home (in their pajamas) in the crusade against naked short selling. It was fitting since many of them were simply looking for someone or something to blame for the financial damage they were experiencing – also since most of them did all their research on the internet, wrote online blogs and sent out multiple long email tirades against the regulators, the brokers and anyone who disagreed with them.

Although the pajamahideen have been relentless in their pursuit, the "bad guys" they are chasing are poorly identified, ranging from prime brokers, regulators and members of congress to elusive off-shore criminal enterprises. It is true that organized crime was identified, pursued and prosecuted for abusive stock manipulation.[39] But what the crusaders are missing is the essential point that it does not take a conspiracy to create phantom shares and that stopping it will take real regulatory reform. The regulatory crisis continues to unfold as the pajamahideen are chasing one red herring after another. This is not to say that they are not having a real impact on the problem. Quite the contrary. They successfully push through requests for data from the SEC using the Freedom of Information Act (FOIA). They get the media talking and writing about "naked short selling," sometimes by putting their own reputations on the line to call attention to the issues.

Throughout the summer of 2005, Wes asked me to work with the "Blind Men" consultants who had been part of his team for three or four years. one of them even admitted to me that he kept pushing the work with Wes because he needed money to finish remodeling his kitchen. Every time I was on a phone call with him, I heard hammering and sawing in the background. Wes and John are experiencing setbacks in the courtroom with reports like the "proxy project." I tried to make Wes understand that the report was not only not good writing or research but in fact there were so many things wrong that it would hurt Wes' chances of success. For a long time, though, Wes remained committed to using these so-called White Papers. At one point, when I tried to explain the problems to Wes, he just said, "I need you to fix it."

The several men that Wes Christian and John O'Quinn kept around and paid to write reports for them did not care about the issues as a cause but, more importantly, none of them knew much about post-trade clearing and settlement which is where the problems were being sustained and where regulatory reform could be pressed. After multiple defeats in a few test cases, the lawyers become increasingly reluctant to take on DTCC.

I continued to reach out to my contacts from the Securities Transfer Association, where I used to sit on the Operations Committee. These are the agents of the publicly traded companies. They see the over-voting and the problems in dividends that are created when shares are sold and not delivered, when the phantom shares build up in the system to the point where there are more shares in customer accounts at brokers than the companies ever issued in the first place. These are the industry insiders who know exactly what the problem really is.

Chapter 6. STA White Paper

In stark contrast to Boni's Ivory Tower utterances, the Securities Transfer Association, Inc. (STA) issued a white paper in December 2004 on the role of short sales in over-voting for corporate elections. The STA had met with the SEC earlier in the year to discuss the over-voting that happens when shorts, fails and loans create more voting rights than there are shares. (See box, STA meets with SEC May 2004.) When their concerns were ignored, they decided to issue a White Paper to get the topic out in the public eye. Titled "Treating Shareholders Equally," the paper discussed the way that voting rights are processed when stock shares are held by brokers who in turn deposit the shares at DTC. Their conclusion is that some unauthorized parties are being allowed to vote while real owners unknowingly lose their voting rights. The STA was able to identify practices that allowed brokers to ignore the votes cast by real shareholders. (An excerpt of the white paper is available in Chapter 8 as an attachment to my comments to the SEC on proposed regulations.)

> **STA meets with SEC May 2004**
> The Securities Transfer Association meets informally with the SEC at least four times each year to go over current topics of interest, updates on regulatory rule-making, etc. At one such meeting between members of the STA Board of Directors and a Senior Associate Director from the Division of Market Regulation, one of the topics they discussed is what they see as "Street Over-Voting" which results when brokers ("the street") turn in votes for the Phantom Shares in their customer accounts. Although there are no formal notes from the meeting, one of the Board members shared this exchange with me:
>
> "A rule-making petition received by the SEC from the Business Round Table, as well as a letter of concern from David Smith of the

> American Society of Corporate Secretaries, brought [proxy over-voting by the street] into the limelight. Charlie Rossi [then-President of the STA] indicated that a STA sub-committee, to be formed in June [2004], is to review procedures regarding the handling of over-voting. This committee will be comprised of proxy experts from many transfer agents. It is not expected to provide a cure, but merely procedural guidance and case studies. The attendees pointed out that the street does not take the same approach to balancing the files that it takes in regard to dividend disbursements. For example, the omnibus file [list of Participant share balances] received from DTCC often fails to balance to the transfer agent's position for CEDE & CO. This is happening despite the daily balancing of the FAST position [DTC's automated program for stock transfers] by the transfer agent. We also suspect that stock lending by brokers that have discretionary lending authority due to margin accounts and the failure of these brokers to reduce voting authority of their customers or recall the loans are contributing to the phenomenon."

Far from attempting to legitimize long term short sales with stock lending and especially fails to deliver as investment strategies that needed to be coddled and supported by the SEC, the STA knew that those processes and procedures were hurting shareholders and, as a result of not protecting shareholder voting rights, it was hurting America's entrepreneurs, too.

Just four months after the STA's white paper is released, the Securities Industry Association (SIA) sends a letter to the NYSE describing how they can hide over-voting caused by shorts, fails and loans. (The letter is available in Chapter 8 as an attachment to my comments to the SEC on proposed regulations.) Five months after that, the NYSE would remove the mandatory buy-in rule, which could have been used to force a seller to deliver shares by allowing the buyer to purchase the same shares on the open market and to charge the cost back to the original seller. By removing that rule, the NYSE made it virtually impossible to demand delivery of stocks post-trade. When the STA surveyed their members about the corporate voting experience around the time of the SIA letter, it showed that over-voting occurred in more than 90% of corporate elections. (An excerpt from the STA Newsletter describing over-voting in 2005 corporate voting is in Chapter 8 as an attachment to my comments to the SEC on proposed regulations.)

The next year, the STA found over-voting in every corporate election surveyed. A new service was implemented that year which provided brokers with feedback between the time they received the number of shares on deposit at DTC and before they submitted votes from their investor clients. For the transfer agents and corporate trust professionals aware of the issues at stake, the new service gave brokers the opportunity to toss out votes before over-voting occurred. In doing so, according to the STA, "the service helps to perpetuate a system that could potentially defraud legitimate shareholders of their voting rights. In most instances, shareholders are unaware that their votes may be tossed out or may be diluted by votes cast by persons that don't hold shares and don't have the right to vote" (STA 2006; Montrone 2006; see excerpt in Box below). The next year, 2007, the STA joined with the Society of Corporate Secretaries and Governance Professionals in calling for "a complete review and overhaul" of the corporate voting process under federal proxy rules (STA 2007a). Even after Wall Street brokers started using the new service to pull out the phantom votes, the STA found that more than one-third of companies received up to 25% more votes at their annual meetings than there were shares outstanding (STA 2007b). There was still a lot of work to be done if we were going to hope to improve the situation for shareholders.

Short Selling and Stock Lending Make "A Mockery of Shareholder Democracy"

"[M]illions of phantom share records may be created through the practice of stock lending. These shares result in brokers authorizing voting positions when there are no actual shares backing the positions on the shareholder meeting record date. Market players may look to borrow or lend shares for any number of reasons [including] to get voting rights without actually purchasing the shares, to hedge or increase beneficial interests due to speculation on a corporate merger or other investment strategies. ... In mid-January [2006], 8.5 billion shares were loaned out on NYSE companies or more than two percent of the outstanding stock for these companies. While shares are out on loan, the original and secondary lending party's accounts will still show the shares in position at the brokerage, creating what some call 'phantom shares.' Voting rights are supposed to travel with the shares when they are loaned. However, it has been confirmed that many brokers cannot adjust their clients' voting rights to account for the loaned shares. Consequently, proxy materials are mailed in large quantities to entities that do not actually have shares held in position over the meeting record date, but merely 'show' shares on the account records of their brokerage firm. These entities do not have the right to vote at the shareholder meeting and shouldn't be getting material. Adding insult to injury, corporate issuers have to pay the postage, printing and service fees for these mailings.

This process may be further exacerbated by trade fails over record date. An investor could sell a position, but fail to deliver the shares by settlement date. If the trade was executed before the meeting record date, both the buyer and the seller might vote the shares because their account positions would not have been adjusted to account for the fail. Some have argued that the dollar volume of fails is small relative to the total dollar volume of trades and thus, fails are an inconsequential event. However, small percentages applied against large numbers can be significant. If only 1% of DTC trades fail and DTC settles $1 Quadrillion of trades a year, then $10 Trillion worth of trades fail a year. This is not a small number. DTC indicated that 85%

of all fails are settled within 10 business days. If fails occur in a random market, the dollar value of fails that exceed 10 days would be $1.5 trillion. Fails may be sufficient to potentially create a swing in voting rights on the critical record date for a shareholders meeting. ...

Recently a major bank was fined $1 million for failing to exercise due diligence. The firm had allowed their over-voting service subscription to lapse and had failed to adjust votes to prevent over-voting in 12 out of 15 instances tested, according to an announcement by the NYSE. The emphasis here appears to be more on form: to prevent over-voting, than on substance: making sure each legitimate shareholder's voting rights are preserved and protected by reconciling shareholder records *before* proxy material is distributed." (STA 2006)

Chapter 7. Tax Consequences

As I continued to look at fails to deliver not only in equities but also in bond trades, it came to my attention that there is favorable tax treatment for dividends on equities as well as interest on government bonds. The federal government does not tax interest earned on municipal bonds (bonds issued by states, cities, counties, etc.). State governments (where there have income taxes) do not tax interest earned on US government bonds (the commonly called "Treasuries" but also bonds issued by other federal agencies). After researching the consequences to government coffers, I wrote to the IRS and the Treasurers in several states to call attention the situation. Congress had made changes to the tax code in the early 2000s to collect taxes on "dividends in lieu" when an investor's shares had been loaned. What they were not aware of, I believed, was that there were also significant tax consequences if a seller failed to deliver shares for settlement. Furthermore, the buyer (especially retail investors) would be receiving payments in lieu of federal and municipal bond interest as well as dividends for stocks that could be going undeclared because the scenario including settlement failures is not described in the regulation.

In addition to contacting state and federal tax authorities, I did several press interviews on this subject that resulted in published articles, including one (without attribution) in Barron's.[40]

Bond trades

On November 12, 2008 the Treasury Market Practices Group (TMPG at the Federal Reserve Bank of New York) presented recommendations to correct widespread settlement fails in US Treasury securities (UST). In 2009, the TMPG developed legal documents and market conventions that permitted counterparties to agree that a buyer of UST who fails to receive securities from a seller on the originally scheduled settlement date can submit a claim against the seller. Although settlement fails have been a problem since 2001, the TMPG was being forced into action by the sheer magnitude of the fails experienced in the fall of 2008: failures to deliver peaked at more than $2.5 trillion and stayed over $1 trillion for seven straight weeks.

In the interim, for every day that the UST went undelivered, there could be an investor on the buying end who received an "entitlement," sort of an electronic IOU, showing the UST in their account. When that happens, the buyer's broker-dealer would provide the investor with "payments in lieu" of interest on UST. Currently, the broker-dealer does not provide the investor with a break out of real UST interest versus payments in lieu of interest. Therefore, these investors would report the income to the states as tax-exempt interest on UST.

For *every day* that $2.5 trillion of UST went undelivered, nearly $208 million worth of payments in lieu of interest could be made to investors (using a conservative 3% interest payout and assuming the fail crosses over the interest payment date). For the average state tax rate of 5%, that translates into nearly $4 billion in lost revenue to the states for 2008.

Estimation of costs to taxpayers and investors
I completed a research paper on this subject in 2007 (with an update in 2008): *Trade Settlement Failures in U.S. Bond Markets* (available at http://papers.ssrn.com/Author=272819). Based on the data and my estimates, I can calculate the specific costs for uncollected state taxes and for the loss of use of funds to investors. These are direct costs.[41]

Payments in lieu of interest on US Treasury securities

Forty-three states have either income taxes or taxes on dividend and interest payments. The calculation for lost revenue to the states is similar to that for the federal government. The Treasury will only pay actual interest to investors who are owners, i.e. those who receive securities at settlement. Investors who are given "entitlements" to these securities therefore receive "payments in lieu" of interest. Broker-dealers do not differentiate these payments for tax reporting purposes so that investors take the tax exemption on these payments.[42] Investors who receive payments in lieu of interest when their broker-dealer fails to receive purchased bonds will deduct those payments from their income on tax returns. Because these payments are not actual interest income on Treasuries, investors should be paying ordinary income tax on them. Therefore, the state treasuries are collecting less tax than they should be. The calculation is summarized in the table below. I estimate that the states are losing about $271 million per year in tax revenue.

$180,394,571,429	Fails to deliver in US Treasury securities
$5,411,837,143	3% interest paid on US Treasury securities
$270,591,857	5% average state tax rate
$270,591,857	Annual lost revenue to states

Average state individual income tax rate calculated from data available from the Federation of Tax Administrators for tax year 2008. The fails to deliver are for April 2008, before the fails in US Treasuries surpassed $1 trillion. In the fall of 2008, these fails passed $2.5 trillion, representing significantly higher revenue losses to the states.

Investors' loss of use of funds

In addition, states may be losing tax revenues because investor income is less than it should be as a result of settlement fails (in other financial assets, in addition to Treasuries). In the period between when the investor paid for the bonds and when the bonds are actually received, the investor could have used the money for other investments. The buyer's broker-dealer gains this time-value of the trade's cash over the fail interval by investing any end-of-day cash into investment vehicles such as overnight repurchase agreements that allow them to earn interest on idle cash balances. Individual investors do not share in this compensation. The value of the fails can vary wildly from day to day, but we believe this estimate needs to be more conservative than the tax consequences because we are assuming that the same value remains failed throughout the year. We use our overall failure to deliver figure for year end 2007 of $251.9 billion to calculate the loss of use of funds to investors. We also use the federal funds rate, which is extremely conservative given the fact that this principal risk primarily comes from broker-dealers.[43] Based on the mean 2.9% federal funds rate in the period of this study, the loss of use of funds to investors from settlement failures in US bond markets is $7.3 billion per year. Again using the average 5% state tax rate, this additional investor income could contribute an additional $365 million to state revenue if investors were able to recover these losses.

Stock trades

During the period that the shares are not received, the investor will receive payments in lieu of dividends. These payments are excluded, under IRS rules implemented in 2004, from the favorable tax rate afforded to dividends.[44,45] It was only stock lending that tipped off the IRS, but in fact all fails to deliver have the same effect on dividends and interest. NSCC reported that shares valued at $5,761,192,000 failed to be delivered for settlement as of December 31, 2007. The difference between the tax rate on qualified dividends and the tax rate on ordinary income is between 10% and 20%.[46] Assuming these shares pay an average 1% dividend yield, then investors paid between $5,761,192 and $11,522,384 in excess taxes each year.[47] Further, research shows that many firms initiated dividends following the dividend tax cut in the Jobs and Growth Tax Relief Reconciliation Act (JGTRRA) of 2003.[48] Therefore, it is likely that the monetary benefit to investors from a reduction in settlement failures would increase across time.[49]

Further, investors incur economic damages when they are denied the use of funds between trade date and actual delivery date. Using publicly available data on failures to deliver in NYSE and NASDAQ "threshold securities" alone, I calculate that loss to have been $762 million in 2007.[50] This is not a one-time loss but an ongoing monetary loss to investors that will not diminish as long as the system tolerates failures to deliver.

PART IV. SUCCESS SEEMS POSSIBLE

Chapter 8. Regulation SHO

The culmination of the efforts of the pajamahideen to capture and kill the red-herring of naked short selling seemed finally as if it would come to fruition with the implementation of Regulation SHO, the SECs first effort to solve the problem of fails to deliver.[51] Sadly, it fell far short of what was needed to correct the real underlying problem. The media and regulatory focus stayed directed at "naked short selling" which was and is a way to marginalize anyone who complains. This proved most true when the SEC started passing new regulations without enforcement teeth as a means to pacify those complaining about naked short selling. For decades it has been common knowledge that brokers can sell stock they do not own and simply "forget" to report the trade as a short sale. Yet the new rules were all directed at regulating short sales.

On July 28, 2004, the SEC adopted the initial rule to address the problem of failures to deliver. Called "Reg SHO" for short, the rule became effective September 7, 2004 with the first release of fails data from NSCC set to begin in January 2005. For most of the people crusading against "naked short selling," it was a long time coming. For some of the companies that saw the number of their shares in circulation multiplied many times over, it was too-little-too-late.

Reg SHO required brokers to mark trades as either "long" (meaning the seller owned the shares and would deliver them for settlement) or "short." Reg SHO also suspended temporarily the price test that prohibited any short sale after a share's price started falling for stocks "in which a substantial number of failures to deliver have occurred." "Substantial" would be defined as 10,000 shares or 0.5% of the number of shares outstanding. The "substantial number" was set as a threshold and any stock that had more than the threshold number of failures to deliver for five consecutive settlement days would be put on a "Threshold List" and be referred to as a "threshold security."

Reg SHO also required short sellers to locate shares to borrow before selling. The failure to locate shares to borrow before selling should have been an important way for the SEC to pressure brokers into complying with Reg SHO. In reality, it simply created an opportunity for enterprising entrepreneurs to open new businesses designed to locate shares that could be lent. That particular business was fraught with problem for decades before Reg SHO. Here are just a few examples to indicate the breadth of the problem.

The first example is a 1984 case involving a night supervisor at Depository Trust Company.[52] The investigation grew out of the 1982 collapse of Drysdale Securities. It was a scheme involving fraudulent stock loan transactions and the embezzlement of over $700,000 from DTC. The owner of a stock loan finder business, along with two vice presidents from a New Orleans brokerage firm and a night supervisor at DTC all pleaded guilty in the end. They had the DTC employee transfer as much as $20 million worth of stock to dormant accounts. The shares would stay there for several days, allowing the stock to be lent before the DTC supervisor would "discover" the transfer as an "error."

In 1986 a Merrill Lynch supervisor pleaded guilty to three felony charges related to a stock borrow scheme. Another stock-loan abuse probe in 1989 resulted in guilty pleas from employees at Shearson Lehman. Thomson McKinnon settled a civil case with the

SEC in 1989 for letting the stock loan department use securities that should not have been lent.[53]

In June 2006, the NYSE announced that they were preparing to launch a series of investigations, including investigating the improper use of "finders," hired by brokers to help them locate securities to complete short sales, the same problem that occurred in 1984 and 1989. NYSE was also again investigating instances where stock loan departments used securities they had no right to lend. There is no reason to believe that this decade's regulations and enforcement will be any better than it was in the last two decades.

What made the crusaders most happy was that Reg SHO was going to impose delivery requirements on brokers for trades in shares on the Threshold List. Once a fail occurred, brokers were given almost three weeks to close it out – a very generous timeframe. If the selling broker did not deliver shares three weeks after the broker took the investor's money, the only punishment was t hat they were not allowed to short sale that stock again without borrowing in advance of the sale. As we would see in the weeks and months after Reg SHO was implemented – and especially as the financial crisis of 2008 took hold – brokers regularly ignored the requirement to deliver shares even after three weeks. If they had made good on delivering shares for settlement, then the list of stocks on the Threshold List should have become shorter every day until it was empty. Instead, the number of stocks on the NYSE Threshold List increased by 32% in the first three years of reporting.[54] Even in 2019, brokers are failing to deliver shares for settlement on trades in about 6,000 companies every day.

In my view, some of the best comments from the crusaders were submitted by David "Dave" Patch. I first met Dave at a public forum in Washington DC that was organized by an association of state-level securities administrators in the US, Canada and Mexico.[55] Dave was an engineer with an international infrastructure and aviation supply company in the US. Dave had initiated dozens of FOIA requests for data long before Reg SHO reporting was even proposed. He wrote well-informed articles for Stockgate Today ("An online newspaper reporting the issues of Securities Fraud" hosted on the now defunct investigatethesec.com website). Dave understood, better than most other non-financial industry individuals whose comment letters I read, that the first problem that should have been corrected was the failure to deliver shares for settlement. Rules covering short sales "would not ensnare [a trade that] was not a 'Short Sale' on the books" of the broker.[56] My point was and always would be: why short when you can fail? The centralized clearing and settlement system in the US allows any trade to remain in the system unsettled if the seller fails to deliver shares. Even respected researcher James J. Angel, Associate Professor of Finance at the McDonough School of Business at Georgetown University, did not recognize this fundamental point. He is so well-known in this area that Dr. Angel's research on short sales was quoted in the proposal for Reg SHO. Although he would come to understand the reality of the issue later, during the initial comment period he wrote: "The failure-to-deliver problem is an artifact of the lack of supply of lendable shares. The SEC should work with the Fed to resolve this problem." I think he realized later that the "Fed" (Federal Reserve Bank) could not produce shares.

Although I was not aware when Reg SHO was initially proposed, I made comments on several of the amendments to Reg SHO and on other relevant rules. Like Dave Patch, I recognized that the failure to deliver shares at settlement was the ultimate problem. It turned out that I was aware of the problem just a little longer than Dave. In his November 2003 comments, Dave wrote:

> In the late 1990s, the SEC sought the advice and comments of Investors and Institutions regarding shorting abuses. This comment period yielded better than 2,000 comments addressing a common issue of illegal 'Naked' shorting. In response to this, the SEC took meager actions and is again, 4-5 years later, seeking additional comments[,] this time admitting [that] those 2,000+ letters were correct and illegal 'Naked shorting' exists. ... The SEC has failed in using 5+ years of data to seek out the root and to cut it off.

My first contact with the problem was in 1993. My subsequent research on this issue found that the problem was older than either of us could have known at the time. Dave may not have been aware that the problem of settlement failures at the central clearing and settlement organization appeared in SEC reports going back to the beginning of NSCC and DTC. In fact, NSCC and DTC were created to solve exactly the problem of Wall Street's inability to get shares delivered in time for settlement. Trade settlement failures had been a fixture in US equity markets for decades. Originally, settlement failures were thought to have been caused by the necessity of moving paper securities which had to be re-registered into the name of the buyer to effect settlement (in exchange for paper representations of money, too). In the late 1960s, activity literally ground to a halt – trading was suspended one day per week to allow the paperwork to catch up for settlement (SEC 1968 Annual Report). In less than 25 years, DTCC had immobilized most share certificates (DTCC 1999, p.27). According to a research study by the Securities Industry Association (SIA), certificates are involved in "just over one-tenth of 1% of all trade transactions processed daily" (cited in DTCC 2004, p. 23). Yet, the percentage of trades that fail to settle today is not substantially different than it was in 1968 (SEC 1973) when it was used to justify the creation of a central depository that separated investors from companies.

My comment letters to the SEC on Reg SHO and related rulemaking explain this and other important elements of the problem, much of which was missed by those who allowed short selling or naked short selling to capture their imaginations. By ignoring the fundamental problem of settlement failures (or "fails"), the regulatory changes would stop short of requiring real settlement – the final exchange of shares for money. This chapter presents copies of my four most important comment letters on the topic. For the reader not already familiar with Reg SHO, each letter is introduced with a non-technical description of the proposed rules. For a complete discussion of Reg SHO, including Rule numbers and links to *.pdf versions of all the Final Rules as published, please visit the SEC's webpage at:
https://www.sec.gov/divisions/marketreg/mrfaqregsho1204.htm
[Last Modified 10/15/2015; Accessed 6 July 2019].

All SEC Final Rules, including comments and links to proposed rules, can be found at https://www.sec.gov/rules/final.shtml. Alternatively, the interested reader can search the Release and File numbers from the following on the homepage of the SEC's website.

- Reg SHO amended to eliminate the "grandfather" provision; approved August 7, 2007; effective October 15, 2007 (Release No. 34-56212; File No.: S7-12-06).

When Reg SHO compliance began in 2005, any fail to deliver that was open before the effective date was excluded from the close-out requirements (i.e. brokers were not required to deliver shares to settle the trades). Recognizing that there were still persistent fails to deliver two years after the original compliance date, the SEC modified Reg SHO "by eliminating the grandfather provision" and narrowing some other exemptions. It provided a generous "35 settlement day phase-in period following the effective date" which they decided would be needed by the brokers who already had two years to settle those failed trades.

My comments on this amendment to Reg SHO include the economic impact on capital markets, the structure of incentives, and corporate governance. In it, I also argue for the role of the States in protecting investors and entrepreneurs.

August 29, 2006

Ms. Nancy M. Morris, Secretary
Securities and Exchange Commission
100 F Street, NE
Washington, DC 20549-0609
Via www.sec.gov

Re: File No. S7-12-06

Secretary Morris:

Introduction
I am a Ph.D. economist doing research and consulting in finance and economics. I am formerly Director of Transfer Agent Services for Depository Trust Company in New York, and Operations Manager for Pacific Depository Trust Company and Pacific Securities Clearing Corporation in San Francisco. I also was Senior Advisor for KPMG on the USAID Capital Markets Project to design and implement trade clearing and settlement operations during privatization in Russia. Over the last three years I have been a paid advisor to companies, investors and law firms on the issues addressed by Regulation SHO. My comments will reflect my expertise in economic analysis of law and market efficiency, plus securities processing operations.

I support the Commission's efforts to keep from creating new grandfathered fails when an issue briefly comes off the Threshold list. Although many people were aware of failures to settle that existed either before the Regulation was effective or before the issue qualified for the Threshold list, it was careful review by Commission staff that revealed this additional source of unattended settlement failures.

I also applaud your request for comments from transfer agents on the impact on proxy voting rights and processes. These gentlepersons have been trying for many years to bring attention to the damage done to proxy voting rights through short sales and stock lending. Since my expertise extends to the securities transfer industry, I will address comments to that issue as well.

In the first two sections, I begin with a discussion of the impact of settlement failures on capital market efficiency and the impact of Regulation SHO on economic incentives. In Section III, I address the relationship of short sales and stock lending to proxy voting rights. Section IV offers a specific discussion of the systemic causes of the problems generally attributed to "naked short sales" by the vocal group of companies and investors now demanding action. In Section V, I outline a primary argument for the roles States can play in protecting investors and companies. Sections VI and VII argue in favor of increased transparency at DTCC and SEC, respectively. Finally, Section VIII points out a grammatical error in the proposed text and some factual errors in the subject file.

I. Fails Disrupt Market Efficiency

Not only the Commission, but also exchanges, and SROs are charged with a duty "to remove impediments to and perfect the mechanism of a free and open market."[1] Economic efficiency is violated when trade settlement fails. At the risk of being pedantic, I believe it is useful to point out some required elements for efficiency in capital markets. In economics, efficiency means that 1) Resources are allocated where demand is highest; 2) No seller

---

[1] Exchange Act (1934), Section 3(f)

effects prices, so each seller has the incentive to cut costs in order to raise profits, thereby providing for the efficient use of allocated resources; and 3) Every buyer pays the same price, thereby achieving efficient distribution.

The three elements of economic efficiency are violated by settlement failures in this way: 1) The supply of shares is allowed to exceed the demand: when purchased securities are not delivered, an entitlement to the same share may be sold a second time either through intentional manipulation or poor record keeping; 2) sellers have no incentive to reduce transaction costs because they are not required to complete transactions; and 3) a buyer who purchases shares that go undelivered at settlement has paid a price that is out of synch with the market; that is, when payment occurs on t+3 and share delivery is at t+13 (or worse) there is a temporal distortion in profit and incentives.

Investors have no way to purchase equity securities except through a broker-dealer who may be allowed to fail at settlement. A key element in free-market efficiency is that no one is forced to accept the sellers' terms or go without. When that happens, efficient allocation and distribution are harmed, resulting in the introduction of price differentials so that investors buy less than they would at equitable prices. In consideration of the promotion of efficiency and competition (section VIII, p. 40) [2], the proposed amendments will promote price efficiency but only to the extent that the original regulation left the door open to inefficient market operations through the institutionalization of failures to settle.

Beyond the ethical implications of imperfect knowledge between bargaining parties, it is a requirement of efficient capital markets that all participants are using the same information set. When one participant is allowed to fail to deliver securities on selected trades, then that participant has private information that is not

---

[2] Page numbers throughout this document refer to the .pdf version available at SEC's website.

available to the rest of the market. By providing any exceptions to close out requirements, the Commission is institutionalizing inefficiency in the capital market.

This is not to say that market makers should not be permitted "to sell short threshold securities in order to hedge options positions," as the Commission expects the market to work. Rather, the problem of fails being permitted strategically to one participant and not to another, whether the failure is the result of short, long or hedge transactions, creates an additional imbalance in the information sets that are required to be identical for all participants in efficiently functioning capital markets.

Regarding the length of the phase-in period ("e.g. 60 days instead of 35", p. 11) the economic tradeoffs associated with any delay in implementation are the reduction of economic efficiency which suffers when fails are permitted and which suffers further when fails are permitted to persist. The shorter period is always desirable from the standpoint of efficiency.

In the context of options positions, the file discusses "a sufficient amount of time to allow a fail to remain that results from a short sale by an options market maker to hedge a pre-existing options position that has expired or been liquidated" (p. 20). Although I have no practical experience with options markets, I am a trained economist. My argument against allowing fails for these instances is similar to that for all fails: Every market transaction requires completion for the analytical framework to fully obtain. The counterparty to any market activity is operating under the assumption that the trade will be fulfilled, including the delivery of securities at settlement. The counterparty in an options transaction is specifically dependent in their financial analysis on the impact that the market maker's activities will have on supply, demand and price for the option and the underlying security. In this case, the damage to the counterparty goes beyond the lack of information about fails. They incur further damage when expectations of market reaction to the market maker's activities do not occur due to the fact that the transaction was not completed as agreed.

I agree with the Commission that new data processing and communications techniques should create the opportunity for more efficient, effective, and safe procedures for clearance and settlement. However, one might be tempted to equate automation with efficiency; and this would be a grave error. Our problems will not go away with improved technology and shorter settlement cycles; they will only get worse. Today already, a trade riddled with inaccuracies can be passed right down through clearing and settlement without any human intervention. This must obviously be the case if the Commission equates fails with trade errors. For capital market efficiency to exist in the U.S., someone will have to enforce trade settlement, including securities delivery.

I think that allowing "the cost of closing out the fail [to] be a part of the economic cost of making a trading error" (p. 14) is a brilliant suggestion on the part of Commission staff. If I purchase a service, I will pay for it. But if the service provider makes an error, they should not come back to me (the investor in this case) to pay for their mistakes. Enforcing the cost of closing failed trades to the erring party will add to real economic efficiency as those firms that make too many trading errors will be driven out of business, and those that are better at executing trades (all the way through to settlement) will survive.

II. Poorly aligned economic incentives under Regulation SHO

An additional reason for eliminating fails by making the cost of closing out the fail part of the economic cost of making a trading error is to better align economic incentives. The existing penalty for not closing a fail is prohibiting the participant from failing on a future short sale by requiring what amounts to pre-borrowing the securities before the trade is accepted.[3] This does nothing to penalize the offending party. Therefore, it provides no

---

[3] Rule 203(b)(3)(iii).

disincentive to creating fails in the first place. On the other hand, if the service providers know the cost of errors will be theirs to bear, there can be additional economic gains that extend from assuring that the most efficient firms survive in a competitive marketplace.

The Commission asks: "Can the close-out provision of Rule 203(b) be easily evaded?" (p. 17). The obvious answer is: any provision that has no penalty will be evaded by simply doing nothing. What can be accomplished as long as trades are not required to be settled and no federal rule is violated when trades fail? In the Commission's own words:

"CNS is essentially an accounting system that indicates delivery and receive obligations among its members (i.e., broker-dealers and banks). These obligations *do not reflect ownership positions until such time as delivery of shares are actually made.*"[4]

Therefore, money changes hands while ownership does not. Investors are being cheated of ownership rights and privileges while being denied use of the funds taken from their accounts in payment. With no real teeth, with no enforcement mechanism, and as long as neither the Commission nor the SROs will force settlement of trades, these amendments will be no more effective than the original Regulation SHO.

I'm highly confident that systems are in place to be sure that customers deliver money on time.[5] Automated systems could and should track when customer shares are not delivered on time for settlement. It does not seem reasonable that the broker could "make a notation on the order ticket at the time an order was taken which reflected the conversation with the customer as to the present location of the securities" (p. 18). Electronic trading now makes it possible for the customer to never meet or talk to a broker. While it would be a good argument against requiring

---

[4] From http://www.sec.gov/divisions/marketreg/mrfaqregsho1204.htm (Updated 05/06/05) Question 7.1: Do naked short sale transactions create "counterfeit shares?" Emphasis added.

[5] For more on this point, see comments submitted by Wayne Jett.

documentation of the contact, this also argues in favor of not allowing fails in the first place. Trading systems should be able to detect the presence and absence of securities prior to execution. Regardless of how it is achieved, any limit on the duration of a fail is meaningless without an enforcement mechanism.

The Commission asks (p. 12) if "eliminating the grandfather provision make[s] it more difficult for short sellers to provide market discipline against abusive practices on the long side?" If short sellers cannot count on trades being completed, then the analytical model they are working with is useless.[6] This is not unlike the analytical problem described above for the counterparty in an options contract. The proper alignment of incentives for short sellers, if the Commission desires to encourage their activity, is to assure complete and final settlement of all market activity on time. Section 23(a)(2) of the Exchange Act requires the Commission to consider "the impact any such rule or regulation would have on competition"; and in fact, grandfathered positions do damage to competition by allowing some broker-dealers and not others the advantage of additional time to effect the change of ownership required for trade settlement.

III. One share, one vote[7]: Missing from U.S. Capital Markets

I welcome the opportunity to comment on the relationship of proxy over-voting to the topic of short selling and stock lending. As I examine the issues, it becomes abundantly clear that the problem here is much more than "naked short selling." The real problem stems from a three-fold arena: shorts, loans and fails. When a stock is sold, regardless of whether the trade is marked "long" or "short," if the shares aren't presented at settlement,

---

[6] For an example with a detailed explanation of how short sellers are damaged by settlement failures, see the recent lawsuit filed by Electronic Trading Group against the prime brokers.

[7] For a comprehensive and unbiased review of this problem and its relationship to short selling and stock lending, read "Corporate Voting Charade" by Bob Drummond, April 2006, Bloomberg Markets.

there are problems created in the customer's accounts when they are given what are known as "entitlements." If the failed trade (or even a legal short sale) is covered with borrowed shares, the situation is made worse when a voting or dividend record date passes because no one seems to be able to keep track of who owns what shares. I refer to the April 2005 letter from the SIA to the NYSE[8] (attached as Exhibit A) and the subsequent report of the NYSE's audit of proxy procedures[9] (attached as Exhibit B). In combination, these present a dire picture of the ability of the broker-dealer community to keep track of ownership; DTCC further enables this irresponsible behavior by inserting stock lending into settlement procedures.

The Commission notes "When Regulation SHO was proposed, commenters noted difficulties tracking individual accounts in determining fails to deliver" (p. 15). How tragic that the problem has gone this far; that not only do the broker-dealers not know whose shares are bought, sold and lent, they can't even tell if a selling customer has delivered shares. I am highly confident that they keep track of whose money has been received; there is no excuse for not extending the same level of fiduciary care and diligence to the securities side of transactions. The Commission also asks, "Should we consider requiring customer account-level close out?" Unfortunately, the Commission is not "requiring" any close outs, since even the t+13 settlement requirement is being willfully ignored as evidenced by increasing numbers of fails in threshold securities and reports from investors of delays in securities delivery that extend for months. The suggestion (further on p. 15) of a prohibition on "all short sales in [a threshold] security by an account" that has previously failed to settle could help stem the intentional creation of phantom shares, though it does little to address the underlying problems.

---

[8] April 26, 2005, Securities Industry Association letter to Anand Ramtahal, New York Stock Exchange.
[9] Obtained from an anonymous source.

The Commission admits that "large and persistent fails to deliver can deprive shareholders of the benefits of ownership, such as voting and lending" (p. 8). In fact, lending can deprive shareholders of their voting rights. As is made obvious in Exhibit A, many investors are *unknowingly* deprived of the right to vote. I emphasize "unknowingly" because many people believe that their vote is counted just because they send the proxy instruction card back to their broker. Very few, including state and national senators I have spoken to personally, realize that the broker-dealer may be using a lottery to determine whose votes are counted.

Next, the Commission asks would "borrowing, rather than purchasing, securities to close out a position be more effective in reducing fails to deliver, or could borrowing result in prolonging fails to deliver?" (p. 17).[10] Purchasing the securities is the only effective way to close out a failure to deliver. Borrowing shares only moves the failure from one participant to another, leaving in place the problem of either duplicating voting rights or distributing them at random. The Commission itself admits that entitlements *do not reflect ownership positions until such time as delivery of shares are actually made.*[11]

In the Nanopierce Amicus[12], the Commission quotes Section 17A of the 1934 Act, in which Congress gave:

"direction to the Commission to be followed in administering the statute. Congress found that (A) The prompt and accurate clearance and settlement of securities transactions, *including the transfer of record ownership* and the safeguarding of securities and funds related thereto, are necessary for the protection of

---

[10] DTCC has implied that borrowed shares are included in fails until the loan is paid back. In this section, I will discuss the question as asked. In Sections VI and VII, I emphasize my growing concern over the impact of DTCC's obfuscation on the ability of the Commission to effectively regulate the industry.

[11] See footnote 4 above for reference.

[12] Nanopierce Technologies, Inc., et. al. V. DTCC et. al., Nevada Supreme Court Case No. 45364, District Court Case No. CV04-01079, Brief of the Securities and Exchange Commission, Amicus Curiae, on the Issue Addressed. Emphasis added.

investors and persons facilitating transactions by and acting on behalf of investors."

Yet by the Commission's own admission, transfer of record ownership *does not occur* under fails or under stock loan. Trades settled with borrowed shares, which are subject to recall, leave open a failure to receive.

The Commission makes much of the options market maker exemption and rules. While I applaud the effort to close an obvious gap in the original Rule, I question whether the Commission or some SRO has sufficient information to judge compliance with this rule. If the broker-dealers cannot keep track of which customer's shares have been lent (see Exhibit A) or reconcile long and short positions (see Exhibit B), I find it highly unlikely that the options market makers have the record keeping for compliance with this rule.

To fulfill the request for empirical data, I attach Exhibit C, which contains information collected by STP Advisory Services on proxy over-voting from the current year. Furthermore, I refer the Commission to the newsletter of the Securities Transfer Association, which regularly carries articles addressing the impact of short sales and stock lending on over-voting.[13]

The fact is that the Securities Transfer Association and the Business Roundtable have been fighting the proxy side of this battle for decades. They started at the stock exchanges, who told them that the omnibus proxy wasn't their problem, it was DTCC's program. So they went to the DTCC, who told them that they were only following the rules approved by the SEC. When they talked to staff at the SEC, as recently as 2004, they were told: "Who cares who votes the shares as long as you don't see it." The SEC's philosophy has been to intercept *over-reporting* before the issuer

---

[13] By way of example, excerpts on the subject are included here from their December 2004 White Paper & Concept Release (Exhibit D) and Newsletter 2005 Issue 4 (Exhibit E).

sees the *over-voting*. In other words, the Commission is denying there's the rhino behind the couch.

IV. Source of the problems: Shorts, Fails and Loans

If the problem were just "naked short sales," then the dilution of share value and shareholder rights would be corrected when the shorts were covered and the market price moved toward the real value of the firm. But when settlement failures are added to the picture, then the shorts have no incentive to cover.[14] The trade is allowed to remain unsettled indefinitely; there is no margin call because there is no loan. Finally, even where stock lending takes place, the problems are only compounded as explained above (Section III).

To be perfectly clear, the source of the problem is three-fold – short sales, settlement failures, and stock lending. The short sellers do harm to a company's reputation and damage to the share price, both of which limit the firm's ability to access capital, both private capital and market-based capital. Investors bear the brunt of the damage from the settlement failures because they are not getting delivery/ownership of shares after making payments. Institutional investors likely stand on both sides of the problem: as investors, they see the value of their portfolio shares eroded by the short sellers, and then they relinquish their voting rights in the pursuit of higher returns by lending their stock to short sellers. The damage caused by all three issues stems from the core problem, which is a failure on the part of management at the DTCC to provide secure, guaranteed, final settlement for trades.

---

[14] Therefore, there is no "de minimis amount of fails that should not be subject to a mandatory close out" (page 13).

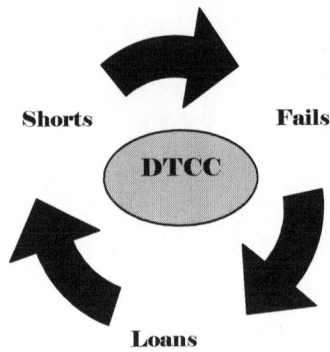

Trades settled with borrowed shares leave open a failure to receive. The distinction between deliver and receive is probably made clearest in NSCC's Annual Financial Statements:

"The failure of participants to deliver securities to NSCC on settlement date, and the corresponding failure of NSCC to redeliver the securities, results in open positions. ....[15] At the close of business on December 31, 2005, open positions due to NSCC approximated $3,423,028,000 ($4,346,655,000 at December 31, 2004), and open positions due by NSCC to participants approximated $2,445,326,000 ($3,328,295,000 at December 31, 2004) for unsettled positions and $977,702,000 ($1,018,360,000 at December 31, 2004) for securities borrowed through NSCC's Stock Borrow Program."

What this says is that there were $3,423,028,000 in *fails to deliver* and $2,445,326,000 in *fails to receive* for total open fails of $5,858,354,000. Including the $977,702,000 in *fails to receive* that were covered by stock borrowing, the total *level of fails* was $6,846,056,000 at December 31, 2005.

---

[15] The missing text is not relevant to this point. However, it describes the process by which the miscreants are able to recover any settlement monies presented to DTCC for failed trades. "Open positions are marked-to-market daily. Such marks are debited or credited to the involved participants through the settlement process." If they can drive the price of the security to zero, the DTCC will further oblige the scheme by declaring the securities "worthless," which allows them to eliminate any remaining obligations.

Furthermore, the Nanopierce Amicus[16] explains the purpose of a clearing agency: "to be so organized, and have the capacity, to be able to: facilitate the prompt and accurate clearance and settlement of securities transactions," and that they must be able to "enforce compliance by its participants with the rules of the clearing agency." So how is it that DTCC is unable to enforce the settlement of trades? They are explicitly given the means to do so in the Exchange Act:

"A registered clearing agency may summarily suspend and close the accounts of a participant who ..., (ii) *is in default of any delivery of funds **or securities** to the clearing agency...*"[17]

If the DTCC neglects to take action against participants who are in default of delivery of securities, and the SEC neglects to take action to discipline the DTCC, then where can investors turn for protection?[18]

The Commission asks, "Should we consider including or specifically excluding an exception for DVP trades ...?" This question demonstrates a misconception that is at the core of the problems generally referred to as caused by "naked short selling." In reality, shares on deposit should be eligible for trading only if there is a way to know that they have not been previously promised for loan, pledge, etc. This is particularly true for DVP trades where no SRO is present to enforce delivery and settlement. DTCC must ensure settlement for all trades at t+3 and not allow failures beyond t+4. If a trade fails at settlement, the delivering participant should be able to fix it the next day.

V. States need room to take action

I applaud the efforts of Governor Huntsman in Utah plus Securities Administrator Lambiase and Attorney General

---

[16] Nanopierce Technologies, Inc., et. al. V. DTCC et. al., Nevada Supreme Court Case No. 45364, District Court Case No. CV04-01079, Brief of the Securities and Exchange Commission, Amicus Curiae, on the Issue Addressed

[17] Section 17A.a.5.(C). Emphasis added.

[18] The phrase *"protection of investors"* is mentioned 186 times in the Exchange Act of 1934.

Blumenthal in Connecticut. They bravely stepped into a place where property rights are not being protected by the United States to provide for some protection for shareholders, investors and companies in the States. The inherent advantages of the States are of importance in this topic. Since States have the right to register corporations, and to well regulate corporations and their securities, then the federal government can defer to the States' determination of whether and how to protect those corporations and the citizens who invest in their securities.

The following are examples of statements made by the SEC, NASD and DTCC indicating that there are no existing rules at the Federal level to protect investors from settlement failures:

- "failure to deliver securities on T+3 does not violate the rule." Footnote 2 of the file.
- "Should a member ... fail to deliver the security on settlement date, the NASD deems such conduct inconsistent with the terms of [the] Rule ..." NASD Rule 3370(b)(4)(C). Therefore, fails are not a violation of a rule and there are no consequences for failing.
- "NSCC is not a regulator, nor does it exercise enforcement powers." Larry Thompson, DTCC General Counsel, Euromoney Letters to the Editor, June 2005.

Since neither the SEC nor any SRO can force the settlement of a trade, then it must be left to the States to protect investors who want delivery of securities they have purchased.[19] In fact, it would appear from the above that the States are the *only* place that investors can get protection in these matters. If there is a trade-off between the protection of corporations and investors and economic integration, it is one that the State governments can develop more effectively than if there were one Federal rule. The States have the ability to work out therapeutic approaches to an issue that continues to elude Federal regulators.

---

[19] I respectfully request that the SEC no longer submit amicus briefs in which the SEC supports the defense that these are matters outside the jurisdiction of the States in lawsuits brought by shareholders and issuers in the States against the DTCC and other parties in matters relevant to settlement failures.

Surely, since there apparently is no rule in place at the Federal level to enforce the delivery of ownership of securities to the purchaser, then the SEC should not stand in the way of the States when they try to enforce delivery of a product for which an investor has paid. Further, corporate issuers should not be intimidated into believing that they are violating "short squeeze" prohibitions when they try to help investors get the product for which they have paid.

It is well understood in development economics that autocrats face incentives to provide selective benefits and, as such, they may attempt to maximize control over economic activity. In order to motivate investors to depend on government officials to place and protect investments, autocrats may overlook or even encourage opacity, corruption or inadequate protection at the federal level. Commercial transaction costs for private citizens will be better reduced when democratic leaders face incentives to provide such protection broadly. The incentives for correct behavior in these cases are clearly with the States.

VI. Call for Transparency @ DTCC

The Commission specifically asks commenters to "provide analysis and data to support their views." This is exceedingly difficult to do since DTCC is obfuscating the real magnitude of the problem by using poor metrics and biased statistics. For example, in footnote 3 (p. 3) of the file there are NSCC statistics on average daily failures to settle as a percentage of dollar value. It is deceptive to use a figure based on dollar value to support the statement that "the majority of trades settle on time" because a statistic describing the majority of "trades" should be by number, not by value.

Again, in footnote 18 (p. 8), the Commission offers NSCC statistics from two unequal time periods to support the statement "that Regulation SHO appears to be significantly reducing fails to deliver." Data for the *9 months* from April 1, 2004 to December 31, 2004 are compared to the *17 months* from January 1, 2005 to

May 31, 2006. Comparing statistics from periods of *different lengths* is bad math, at best. Furthermore, it is well known that market data exhibit seasonal variation.[20] It is particularly deceptive to include January in one and not the other, since the "January effect" is especially well-known and studied.

Footnote 18 continues giving a list of statistics from NSCC that are presented with inconsistent measurement units. In most cases, NSCC does not reveal if percentages are by value, by transaction or by number of shares. At best, this is a sloppy presentation of statistical data. At worst, it is an attempt to deceive.

The statement in footnote 19 (p. 8) is blatantly biased. It offers the number of Threshold securities as a percentage of equity securities "including those that are not covered by Regulation SHO." Including equity securities not covered by Regulation SHO in the denominator of a statistic meant to depict the scope of the problem identified with Regulation SHO only serves to obfuscate. These biased statistics serve to deceptively minimize the problem and exaggerate the progress made by Regulation SHO.

Unfortunately, DTCC's obfuscation may be damaging the Regulation SHO Threshold lists themselves. In the Final Rulemaking on Regulation SHO, the terms "fails" and "fails to deliver" are used interchangeably, without reference to "fails to receive."[21] For example, in the Final Rule a threshold security is

---

[20] For example, see Porter, R. Burt, "Measuring Market Liquidity" (October 2003), which provides evidence of a strong January seasonal effect on liquidity, and which summarizes recent research suggesting that aggregate market liquidity varies over time. Available at SSRN: http://ssrn.com/abstract=439122. See also Kamstra, Mark J., Kramer, Lisa A. and Levi, Maurice D., "Winter Blues: A SAD Stock Market Cycle" (October 2003), which demonstrates seasonal differences in market behavior using international data. Available at SSRN: http://ssrn.com/abstract=208622. For additional evidence, see DeGennaro, Ramon P., Kamstra, Mark J. and Kramer, Lisa A., "Seasonal Variation in Bid-Ask Spreads" (March 2006). Available at SSRN: http://ssrn.com/abstract=624901.
[21] The following terms do not appear anywhere in the final rulemaking: "fail to receive", "fails to receive" or "failure to receive" or "failures to receive". The

described as one where "there are aggregate *fails to deliver* at a registered clearing agency of 10,000 shares or more per security; that the *level of fails* is equal to at least one-half of one percent of the issuer's total shares outstanding;..." (emphasis added); and in the accompanying footnote, "For example, if an issuer had 1,000,000 shares outstanding, one-half of one percent (.005) would be 5,000 shares. An aggregate *fail to deliver* position at a clearing agency of 10,000 shares or more would thus exceed the specified *level of fails*."[22]

Compare that to the language used by DTCC's Larry Thompson when he refers to "...about $1.1 billion of the 'fails to receive,' or about 20% of the total fail obligation." These figures belie his revelation that "...fails to deliver and receive amount to about $6 billion daily,..."[23]

One is left to wonder if the DTCC is taking literally the SEC's instructions that "[a]t the conclusion of each settlement day, NSCC will provide the SROs with data on securities that have aggregate *fails to deliver* at NSCC of 10,000 shares or more." Does DTCC report both the *level of fails* and the number of *fails to deliver*? The SEC's instructions to the SROs are: "For the securities for which it is the primary market, each SRO will use this data to calculate whether the *level of fails* is equal to at least 0.5% of the issuer's total shares outstanding of the security." Taken as written, using DTCC's distinction between fails to deliver and fails to receive, the SROs should be doubling the reported number of shares failed in order to arrive at the level of fails used to calculate the 0.5% threshold.

If one needs additional examples of DTCC's obfuscation, I offer the following:

---

word "receive" appears 36 times, primarily in the context of where the SEC has "received" comments.

[22] Page 48016, in Part V. Rule 203. B. 1.

[23] $1.1 billion is only 18% of $6 billion. Naked Short Selling and the Stock Borrow Program, @dtcc interview with Larry Thompson, March 24, 2005. Available at http://www.dtcc.com/Publications/dtcc/index.htm

- In a June 2005 Letter to Euromoney, Larry Thompson says that "a small minority of delivery failures (0.25%) are filled by shares borrowed through the SBP" [Stock Borrow Program]. In an earlier interview he said that "about 20% of the total fail obligation" was solved through SBP. If believed, this would mean that 20% of the value of fails is found in 0.25% of the shares? Yet the DTCC and the SEC want us to believe that the problem exists primarily for small and mid-sized companies.[24] Of course, no reasonable person could believe all three things at the same time.
- In the @dtcc interview, Thompson describes "fails to deliver" as a number of transactions and "fails to deliver and receive" as a dollar amount,[25] thereby making comparison and statistical analysis impossible.
- DTCC presents the value of fails as a percentage of *all* transactions processed. But there are numbers presented in various annual reports which indicate that netting eliminates the need for settlement in over 90% of transactions processed.[26] Therefore, the fail rate could be significantly higher than they claim. Furthermore, there is a distinction between value and volume where trades are concerned. The difference can be as high as 5 percentage points between the two.[27]
- DTCC makes clear in their statistics that borrowed shares are included in fails until the loan is paid back. A failure to receive is closed out with borrowed shares but a failure to deliver is retained by the DTC (who has an open debit on their books awaiting the return of the loaned shares from NSCC). This

---

[24] See, for example, statements at http://www.sec.gov/spotlight/keyregshoissues.htm

[25] "Currently, fails to deliver are running about 24,000 transactions daily"; "fails to deliver and receive amount to about $6 billion daily."

[26] For example, from the 1998 NSCC annual report, "Total value of transactions processed was $44.6 trillion." and "Netting eliminated the need to settle $42.6 trillion in trading activity." Therefore, only $2 trillion actually went to settlement.

[27] For example, from 1998 NSCC annual report: "And on a peak day, November 16, of $2.8 trillion entering the system for netting and settlement, GSCC reduced the obligations of participants by 94 percent for all transactions and 89 percent of the dollars." Similar numbers are not released for NSCC's equity activity, which would clear up a lot of questions.

distinction is made explicit by Thompson in the 2005 interview @dtcc: "The Stock Borrow program is able to resolve about $1.1 billion of the 'fails to receive,' or about 20% of the total fail obligation." The Commission asks, "Would borrowing, rather than purchasing, securities to close out a position be more effective in reducing fails to deliver, or could borrowing result in prolonging fails to deliver?" (p. 17). Obviously, borrowing will not eliminate a failure to deliver.

So what is the reality? According to an article by Bob Drummond in Bloomberg Markets (September 2006) "On an average day in March, [those] unsettled trades amounted to more than 750 million shares in almost 2,700 stocks, exchange-traded funds and other securities...."[28] Further, the article reports: "At the end of 2005, about 23,000 trades hadn't settled ...." If these numbers are right, then the average failed trade was for about *32,600* shares, compared to the *300* shares or less DTCC says comprise 70% of all transactions.[29] This is my final and most recent example of the kind of information that DTCC is hiding by releasing vague and misleading statistics.

VII. Call for Transparency @ SEC

Unfortunately, obfuscation has not been limited to DTCC. Statements by the Commission also raise questions. In footnote 2 (p. 11) of the file: "Between the effective date of Regulation SHO and March 31, 2006, 99.2% of the fails that existed on Regulation SHO's January 3, 2005 effective date have been closed out. This calculation is based on data, as reported by NSCC, that covers all stocks with aggregate fails to deliver of 10,000 shares or more." If only 0.8% of grandfathered fails are still open, then why does anyone think eliminating this small piece will make a difference? How big are these 0.8% of grandfathered fails that eliminating them will serve to achieve the intended objective of these

---

[28] According to Depository Trust & Clearing data obtained by Drummond from the SEC through Freedom of Information Act requests.

[29] "...[A]pproximately 70% of equity trades currently [2006] submitted to NSCC are for 300 shares or less." DTCC Important Notice A# 6218, P&S# 5788, March 15, 2006.

amendments ("to reduce the number of persistent fails to deliver attributable primarily to the grandfather provision …")?

In the request for comments, the Commission puts forth "the premise that a high level of fails to deliver for a particular stock might harm the market for that security." And then asks, "In what ways do persistent grandfathered fails to deliver harm market quality for those securities, or otherwise have adverse consequences for investors?" Without the routine release of the number of fails per company, how can anyone support comments on this matter with data? The primary party with an interest in researching this is the company itself. At a minimum, the numbers (of transactions, shares and value) should be released to the issuer for analysis. To require FOIA requests from every issuer is simply obstructionist.

I am one who seeks greater transparency, including requiring "the amount or level of fails to deliver in threshold securities to be publicly disclosed." Information about settlement failures would put investors on notice that they need to follow up on the delivery of paid-for shares from their brokers. Ideally, much as was intended by the Utah law passed this year, the disclosure should be made by each broker of the aggregate fails to deliver (trades, shares and value) for each security. Having the broker make the disclosure would further protect shareholders as they would be aware if there is a particular problem with their broker.

Providing the investing public with access to information about settlement failures by individual brokerage firms and on individual stocks would *not* increase the potential for manipulative short squeezes. As I said earlier, a short squeeze would occur if investors were driven to purchase the stock in the first place, not if they are driven to demand delivery of that for which they have already paid.

VIII. Clarifications and Corrections

- A grammatical correction is required in the following text on page 49:

- (ii) The provisions of this paragraph (b)(3) shall not apply to the amount of the fail to deliver position in the threshold security that is attributed to short sales by a registered options market maker, if and to the extent that the short sales are effected by the registered options market maker to establish or maintain a hedge on an options position that ~~were~~ [was] created before the security became a threshold security;
- The definition of settlement found in footnote 2 is misleading. It represents settlement as a one-sided process where the delivery of payment is divorced from the receipt of the securities that the investor has purchased. In fact, this is core to the problem in the capital markets today: investors are paying for securities, and then not getting delivery.
- The file describes CNS in footnote 11 as a system which "nets the securities delivery and payment obligations of all of its [NSCC's] members." This should read "nets the securities delivery obligations for each of its members in each security and nets the payment obligations for each of its members." To state this otherwise is a profoundly misleading statement, one that leads to confusion among the commenters. Some have taken this wording to mean that there is one net position in each security at the end of the day.
- It is unfortunate that the Commission is using "short squeeze" in footnote 16 in the context of requiring brokers to deliver to investors that which they have purchased. The phrase "illegal short squeeze" should be reserved for intentional acts of manipulation that drive investors to buy the stock in the first place, not actions taken AFTER the purchase in an attempt to gain delivery of bought and paid for shares.

Closing

In closing, I hope the Commission will let go of the romantic illusion that correctly marking trades is an alternative to a strong and proficient settlement system. Capital market efficiency can only be enjoyed after enduring the cost of repairing the formal system.

Thank you for your consideration of my comments. Please feel free to contact me at 310 285 8153 if I may be of assistance.

Sincerely,

Susanne Trimbath, Ph.D.
CEO and Chief Economist

Exhibits:
A. SIA Letter to NYSE
B. NYSE Audit Report
C. Proxy Problem Summary
D. STA White Paper (excerpt)
E. STA Newsletter (excerpt)

Securities Industry Association
120 Broadway · 35 Fl. · New York, NY 10271-0080 · (212) 608-1500, Fax (212) 968-0703 · www.sia.com, info@sia.com

April 26, 2005

Mr. Anand Ramtahal
Vice President
Member Firm Regulation
New York Stock Exchange
11 Wall Street
New York, NY 10005

Dear Mr. Ramtahal:

The members of the SIA Ad-Hoc Committee on Proxy Over Reporting (the "Committee") wish to express their gratitude for the NYSE's participation in the highly productive and interactive meeting held on March 4, 2005 at SIA's New York office. Since the NYSE and the SEC have been looking into the process of over reporting, we thought it would be beneficial to convene a meeting to discuss the methodologies used by firms to accommodate the proxy process. As stated at the onset of the meeting, our goal was to review the generic proxy flows, reach consensus on the different processes, and create industry best practices that are approved by the NYSE. Our members are seeking greater clarity regarding best practices in order to ensure compliance with NYSE and SEC regulations.

Over Reporting

SIA, together with its Corporate Actions and Securities Operations Divisions[2], have been reviewing the proxy over reporting issue since mid-2004. This issue was raised by tabulators and several transfer agents. Certain SIA member firms also alerted us that it had become a focus of recent NYSE examinations.

Over reporting occurs when ADP or a financial institution submits to an issuer's tabulator a voting position on behalf of a broker-dealer (or bank) that exceeds the record date position for that broker-dealer as determined by DTC and securities registered in that broker or bank's nominee name. The potential for over reporting may exist for a number of reasons associated with improper position reconciliation, such as: margin account securities on loan; fails to receive; and, shares registered in the broker's own name.

One of the conclusions SIA reached from our research was that broker-dealers should provide the tabulators with a street name vote that reconciles with the voteable record date position. In this regard, we believe that ADP offers a critical tool for achieving this goal - the ADP Over Reporting Prevention Service that works in conjunction with DTC and broker-dealers to avoid over reporting. In September 2004, I wrote to ADP proxy service subscribers strongly encouraging them to use this service.

It is relatively simple for broker-dealers to subscribe to ADP's Over Reporting Prevention Service. Firms need only to send a letter to the DTC Proxy Department, with a copy to their ADP Client Service Representative, requesting them to release their firm's stock record date position to ADP on its nightly transmission. The service compares a participant's reported position to its DTC position, flags any differences, and enables the participant to make appropriate adjustments. To date, more than 100 brokers have subscribed to this service, representing 90%[3] of the street positions. As NYSE requested, ADP and SIA representatives are actively working on contacting the other firms that account for the remaining 10% of street positions to urge them to use the service.

March 4, 2005 Meeting Recap

At our March meeting, the Committee noted its support of the industry's use of the ADP Over Reporting Prevention Service, particularly as it offers a reconciliation process to counter the potential for over reporting. In recent studies performed by ADP, they were unable to find any existence of an over vote when using this service.

Regarding margin accounts, which are allowed to vote their entire position even if their shares have been hypothecated[4] pre or post reconciliation (see Appendices A and B), it is our understanding from the discussions at the March meeting that no rule exists to give us guidance in this area. Therefore, firms have been relying on their margin agreements, which allow a firm to reduce customer votes based on that firm's determination that the shares have been hypothecated.

The Committee agrees with the NYSE's recommendation made at the March meeting to include additional disclosure language in each proxy mailing, reminding customers that their beneficial voting rights may be reduced by shares that are hypothecated.

---

[3] Source: ADP

[4] Hypothecation of Securities: pledging of securities to brokers as collateral for loans made to purchase securities or to cover short sales, called margin loans. When the same collateral is pledged by the broker to a bank to collateralize a broker's loan, the process is called rehypothecation.

We also understand from discussions at our meeting, that NYSE Market Regulation and Enforcement has concluded that as long as a firm performs a reconciliation - be it pre or post mailing - and there is no over voting, then the firm's process does not conflict with any NYSE rules. The Committee supports firms having the option of performing either a pre or a post reconciliation, and believes that such flexibility should be retained. This position is supported by the results of the Committee's review of pre and post workflows.

As we also mentioned in March, the Committee believes that it is important that firms exercise some form of "in-house" due diligence in reconciling client positions for the purpose of evaluating the voteable shares, instead of relying completely on a third party vendor. The Committee also believes that whatever methods are used to reconcile client positions (such as an impartial lottery or proration, as explained in Appendices C2 and C3), they should be proportional and equitable among all clients.

As part of its review of the proxy process, the Committee compared it with the dividend payment-in-lieu process (see Appendix C). The Committee found that there are significant differences between the processes, which include:

- All beneficial owners, regardless of their margin status, are entitled to receive dividend payments, but they may not be entitled to vote their shares.
- There are differences between making investors whole with cash on a payable date, and making investors whole with voting rights on record date.
- The dividend process adopted is a result of regulation. Proxy regulation does not require a specific allocation process.
- While aspects of the logic used in dividend processing may be applicable to some of the allocation methods used in proxy processing, there are other allocation methods that are in place that meet the requirements.

A Comparison of the Pre and Post Mailing Reconciliation Processes

In our March meeting, you requested that we prepare a summary of the pros and cons of both the pre and post mailing reconciliation processes. We offer such a summary below, and both scenarios assume the firm is using the ADP Over Reporting Prevention Service. The NYSE rules governing proxies require broker-dealers to perform due diligence by reconciling their positions but, as mentioned earlier, do not express a preference for either the pre or the post mailing reconciliation process.

A. Pros Common to both the Pre and Post Mailing Reconciliation Processes

- The balancing of the stock record to offset shorts, loans and fails is in keeping with street practice – the right to vote is decided by who possesses and controls the security.
- The broker-dealer's risk of over voting is minimized.
- The allocation process is equitable and proportional since an impartial lottery, proration, etc. are used to reduce shares of margin accounts when needed.

- ADP receives the DTC position and provides its clients with the comparison for review.
- Regardless of the method used, adjustments can still be made due to potential over voting.

B. Additional Pros re: the Pre-Mailing Reconciliation Process

- Since shares are reduced systemically based on need, very little intervention is required by the proxy department.
- Share reduction is accomplished in a proportional and equitable manner utilizing standard acceptable street processes such as an impartial lottery or proration.
- Client disclosure of the adjusted share quantity is documented on the voting card.

C. Additional Pros re: the Post-Mailing Reconciliation Process

- Clients are allowed to vote their entire position and no reduction to any client's position takes place unless there is a potential over vote situation.
- There will be minimum client impact in the proxy process.
- Potential over vote situations are reported to the broker-dealer by ADP's Over Reporting Prevention Service and share reductions are made only when required.

D. Cons re: the Pre-Mailing Reconciliation Process

- Since shares are reduced from clients' positions before the vote is cast and, since on average only 35% of clients usually vote, clients whose positions have been reduced may not vote their full position.
- This process requires internal programming work to account for impartial lottery or proration, etc. allocation methods.
- If an entire position is reduced (i.e., due to a fail to receive or the shares being hypothecated), a client may be excluded from receiving a proxy mailing that includes information about their investments.

E. Cons re: the Post-Mailing Reconciliation Process

- The number of votes cast may not be consistent with what the client has received on the proxy card.
- Timing of votes and concentration of meetings may provide the proxy department with a very short window of time to reconcile an over vote situation.
- If a proportional and equitable proration is performed, a large number of client positions may be reduced.

Record Retention

The NYSE record retention rules in this area[5] were adopted when broker-dealers performed the entire proxy process themselves, including receiving and mailing proxies, tabulating votes, issuing a nominee's final vote on an omnibus proxy, and billing for the

---

[5] See Appendix D.

mailing. Firms maintained detailed records on the solicitation, issuer requirements, receiving and mailing proxies, NYSE opinions on the nature of the proposals, signed proxy cards, tabulating tapes, master ballots, and invoices (supported by the expenses incurred).

Over the past several years, an increasing number of broker-dealers have outsourced the proxy process to ADP Investor Communications. At this time, we believe a majority of firms are doing so. By contracting with ADP for such services, broker-dealers have access to ADP's ProxyPlus system and can monitor ADP's processing of its proxies. In addition, ADP is required by contract with the firm to maintain the applicable records up to and in some cases exceeding seven years (NYSE Rule 452.20 requires three years), including - in our view - samples of the proxy material mailed to the beneficial clients. We believe that ADP maintains adequate records to support their process. Deloitte & Touche performs independent annual audits to verify this is the case, and presents certifications to each broker-dealer that are maintained by the firms as a record of compliance.

The Committee believes that the record retention requirements for the broker-dealer should reflect the work performed by the proxy department in today's enviornment, i.e. client proxy support, monitoring of ADP's proxy function, and the international proxies. It is the Committee's understanding that, in accordance with NYSE rules, the housing of a broker-dealer's proxy processing and voting records at ADP adheres to the requirements of accessibility within a reasonable timeframe for retrieval.

In conclusion, the Committee wishes to express its appreciation for your time and interest in this important project. Our understanding is that we have been able to reach agreement with the NYSE on the use of either pre or post reconciliations as a tool for reconciling proxy voting, as well as on the additional disclosure language for proxy mailings. We welcome the opportunity to meet with you in the near future to discuss the contents of this letter and to bring closure to any open issues. Our ultimate goal is to produce an industry wide SIA document on Proxy Best Practices that is supported by the NYSE and facilitates the proxy process for the benefit of investors and all industry participants.

Yours truly,

Donald D. Kittell
Executive Vice President

cc: Tony Alberti, NYSE
Michael Alexander, Charles Schwab
Larry Bergmann, SEC
Richard Bommer, SIA
Jerry Carpenter, SEC
Bernadette Chichetti, NYSE
John Colangelo, DTCC
Arthur Cutter, UBS
Richard Daly, ADP
Don Donahue, DTCC
Diana Downward, DTCC
James Duffy, NYSE
Richard Ketchum, NYSE
Catherine Kinney, NYSE
Phil Lanz, Bear Stearns
Patricia Mobley, DTCC
Ronnie O'Neill, Merrill Lynch
John Panchery, SIA
Simon Swidler, NYSE
Lew Trezza, FMR
Steve Walsh, NYSE

Appendix A, (Example Only - Does not represent all B/D processes)

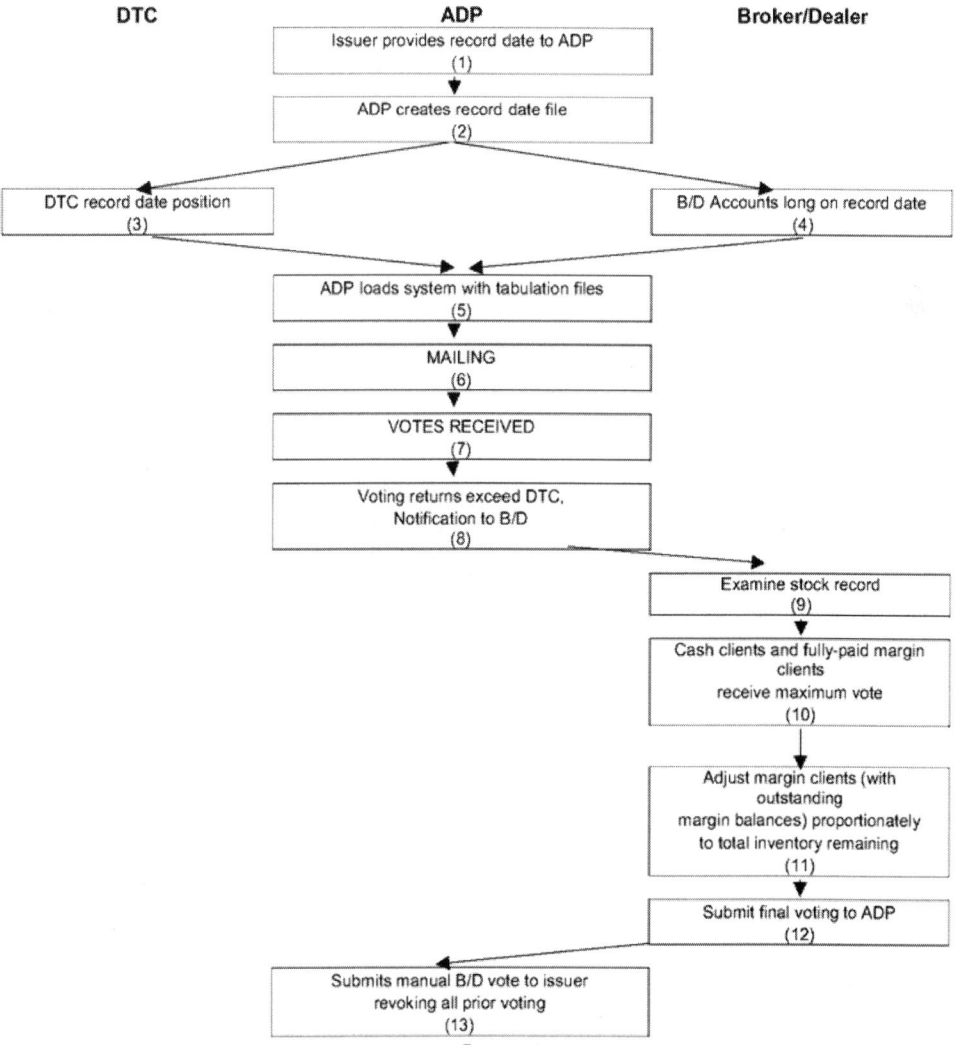

Appendix A, (Example Only - Does not represent all B/D processes)

NOTES:

(1) Issuer contacts ADP requesting material quantities. Search request contains other information, including record date

(2) ADP transmits file to B/D and DTC containing CUSIPs of interest for current record date

(3) DTC transmits participant listings with record date securities positions for which DTC has received authorization from its participants (B/D signs letter of authorization for DTC to release this information to ADP as a part of Overvote Service enrollment process)

(4) B/D systems adjust stock record to eliminate non-voteable shares, such as Delivery versus Payment accounts, shares held in customer name, intercompany offset accounts, triparty accounts and proprietary long and short positions. Margin accounts receive full voting on long shares. Reported shares may exceed DTC and registered inventory

(5) ADP loads both files to tabulation system.

(6) ADP mails proxy materials to clients. Margin account Voting Instruction Form reflects full long position.

(7) Clients return voting instructions to ADP via hard copy, telephone, internet, or Proxy Edge (ADP Institutional Voting System)

(8) If voting returns exceed DTC position, B/D is notified via e-mail, PostEdge (ADP Web Portal) or hard copy report

(9) B/D examines stock record, to identify additional voteable shares (i.e. registered positions), if any, and to segregate cash clients, fully paid margin clients, and non-fully paid margin clients

(10) Vote tabulation is adjusted manually so that cash and fully paid margin clients receive maximum voting

(11) After satisfying cash and fully paid margin clients voting instructions, non-fully paid margin client voting instructions are tabulated. These instructions are prorated to inventory available after step (10)

(12) The voting results in steps (10) and (11) above are combined and transmitted to ADP

(13) ADP submits manual voting result calculated in (12) above to issuer

B/D uses various reconciliation methods to ensure the accuracy of ADP's process

Appendix B, (Example Only - Does not represent all B/D processes)

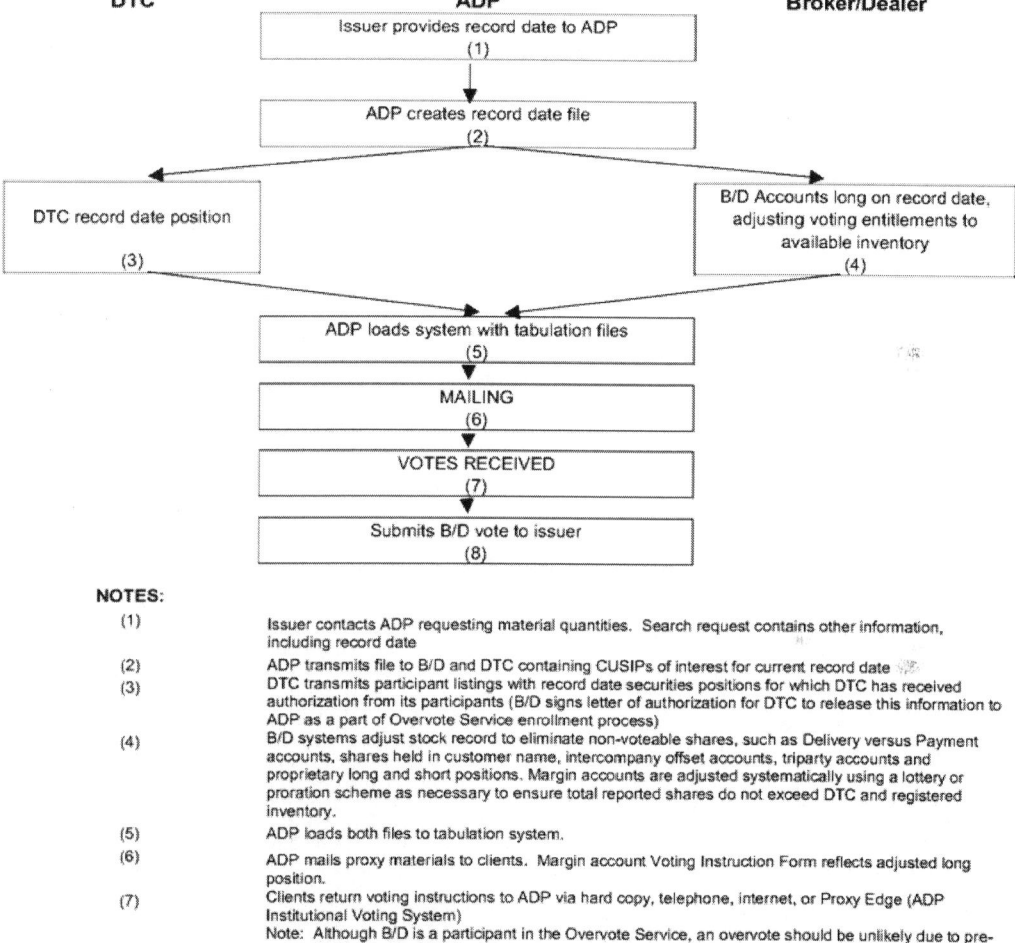

NOTES:

(1) Issuer contacts ADP requesting material quantities. Search request contains other information, including record date

(2) ADP transmits file to B/D and DTC containing CUSIPs of interest for current record date

(3) DTC transmits participant listings with record date securities positions for which DTC has received authorization from its participants (B/D signs letter of authorization for DTC to release this information to ADP as a part of Overvote Service enrollment process)

(4) B/D systems adjust stock record to eliminate non-voteable shares, such as Delivery versus Payment accounts, shares held in customer name, intercompany offset accounts, triparty accounts and proprietary long and short positions. Margin accounts are adjusted systematically using a lottery or proration scheme as necessary to ensure total reported shares do not exceed DTC and registered inventory.

(5) ADP loads both files to tabulation system.

(6) ADP mails proxy materials to clients. Margin account Voting Instruction Form reflects adjusted long position.

(7) Clients return voting instructions to ADP via hard copy, telephone, internet, or Proxy Edge (ADP Institutional Voting System)
Note: Although B/D is a participant in the Overvote Service, an overvote should be unlikely due to pre-reconciliation in step (4). If an overvote should occur, the process would continue as in step (9) of the Post-Mailing Reconciliation model

(8) Voting results are conveyed to issuer

B/D uses various reconciliation methods to ensure the accuracy of ADP's process

9

NAKED, SHORT AND GREEDY 97

Appendix C, Example of the Lottery Process for Dividend Payments in Lieu*

§1.6045-2(f)(2) *Payments in lieu of dividends other than exempt-interest dividends--*(I) *Requirements and methods.* A broker that receives substitute payments in lieu of dividends other than exempt-interest dividends on behalf of a customer and is required to furnish a statement under paragraph (a) of this section must make a determination of the identity of the customer whose stock was transferred and on whose behalf such broker receives substitute payments. Such determination must be made as of the record date with respect to the dividend distribution, and must be made in a consistent manner by the broker in accordance with any of the following methods:

(A) Specific identification of the record owner of the transferred stock;

(B) The method of allocation and selection specified in paragraph (f)(2)(ii) of this section; or

(C) Any other method, with the prior approval of the Commissioner.

A broker must keep adequate records of the determination so made.

(ii) *Method of allocation and selection--*(A) *Allocation to individual and nonindividual pools.* With respect to each substitute payment in lieu of a dividend received by a broker, the broker must allocate the transferred shares (*i.e.*, the shares giving rise to the substitute payment) among all shares of stock of the same class and issue as the transferred shares which were (1) borrowed by the broker, and (2) which the broker holds (or has transferred in a transaction described in paragraph (a)(1) of this section) and is authorized by its customers to transfer (including shares of stock of the same class and issue held for the broker's own account) ("loanable shares"). The broker may first allocate the transferred shares to any borrowed shares. Then to the extent that the number of transferred shares exceeds the number of borrowed shares (or if the broker does not allocate to the borrowed shares first), the broker must allocate the transferred shares between two pools, one consisting of the loanable shares of all individual customers (the "individual pool") and the other consisting of the loanable shares of all nonindividual customers (the "nonindividual pool"). The transferred shares must be allocated to the individual pool in the same proportion that the number of loanable shares held by individual customers bears to the total number of loanable shares available to the broker. Similarly, the transferred shares must be allocated to the nonindividual pool in the same proportion that the number of loanable shares held by nonindividual customers bears to the total number of loanable shares available to the broker.

(B) *Selection of deemed transferred shares within the nonindividual pool.* The broker must select which shares within the nonindividual pool are deemed transferred for use in a short sale (the "deemed transferred shares"). Selection of deemed transferred shares may be made either by purely random lottery or on a first-in-first-out ("FIFO") basis.

(C) *Selection of deemed transferred shares within the individual pool.* The broker must select which shares within the individual pool are deemed transferred shares (in the manner described in the preceding paragraph) only with respect to substitute payments as to which a statement is required to be furnished under paragraph (a)(2)(ii) of this section.

(3) *Examples.* The following examples illustrate the identification of customer rules of paragraph (f)(2):

Example (1). A, a broker, holds X corporation common stock (of which there is only a single class) in street name for five customers: C, a corporation; D, a partnership; E, a corporation; F, an individual; and G, a corporation. C owns 100 shares of X stock, D owns 50 shares of X stock, E owns 100 shares of X stock, F owns 50 shares of X stock, and G owns 100 shares of X stock. A is authorized to loan all of the X stock of C, D, E, and F. G, however, has not authorized A to loan its X stocks. A transfers 150 shares of X stock to H for use in a short sale on July 1, 1985. A dividend of $2 per share is declared with respect to X stock on August 1, 1985, payable to the owners of record as of August 15, 1985 (the "record" date). A receives $2 per transferred share as a payment in lieu of a dividend with respect to X stock or a total of $300 on September 15, 1985. H closes the short sale and returns X stock to A on January 2, 1986. A's records specifically identify the owner of each loanable share of stock held in street name.

From A's records it is determined that the shares transferred to H consisted of 100 shares owned by C, 25 shares owned by D, and 25 shares owned by F. The substitute payment in lieu of dividends with respect to X stock is therefore attributed to C, D and F based on the actual number of their shares that were transferred to H. Accordingly, C receives $200 (100 shares x $2 per share), and D and F each receive $50 (25 shares each x $2 per share). A must furnish statements identifying the payments as being in lieu of dividends to both C and D, unless they are exempt recipients as defined in paragraph (b)(2) of this section or exempt foreign persons as defined in paragraph (b)(3) of this section. Assuming that A has no reason to know on the record date of the payment that the dividend paid by X is of a type described in paragraph (a)(3)(ii)(A)-(D) of this section, A need not furnish F with a statement under section 6045(d) because F is an individual. (However, A may be required to furnish F with a statement in accordance with section 6042 and the regulations thereunder. See paragraph (h) of this section.) By recording the ownership of each share transferred to H, A has complied with the identification requirement of paragraph (f)(2) of this section.

Example (2). Assume the same facts as in example (1), except that A's records do not specifically identify the record owner of each share of stock. Rather, all shares of X stock held in street name are pooled together. When A receives the $2 per share payment in lieu of a dividend, A determines the identity of the customers to which the payment relates by the method of allocation and selection prescribed in paragraph (f)(2)(ii) of this section. First, the transferred shares are allocated proportionately between the individual pool and the nonindividual pool. One-sixth of the transferred shares or 25 shares are allocated to the individual pool (50 loanable shares owned by individuals/300 total loanable shares = 1/6; 1/6 x 150 transferred shares = 25 shares). Assuming A has no reason to know by the record date of the payment that the payment is in lieu of a dividend of a type described in paragraph (a)(3)(ii)(A)-(D) of this section, no selection of deemed transferred shares within the individual customer pool is required. (However, A may be required to furnish F with a statement under section 6042 and the regulations thereunder. See paragraph (h) of this section.) Five-sixths of the transferred shares or 125 shares are allocated to the nonindividual pool (250 loanable shares owned by nonindividuals/300 total loanable shares = 5/6; 5/6 x 150 transferred shares = 125 shares). A must select which 125 shares within the nonindividual pool are deemed to have been transferred. Using a purely random lottery, A selects 100 shares identified as being owned by C, and 25 shares identified as being owned by D. Accordingly, A is deemed to have transferred 100 shares and 25 shares owned by C and D respectively, and received substitute payments in lieu of dividends of $200 (100 shares x $2 per share) and $50 (25 shares x $2 per share) on behalf of C and D respectively. A must furnish statements to both C and D identifying such payments as being in lieu of dividends unless they are exempt recipients as defined in paragraph (b)(2) of this section or exempt foreign persons as defined in paragraph (b)(3) of this section. A has complied with the identification requirement of paragraph (f)(2) of this section.

*Source: IRS letter ruling number 8546032 dated 8/19/85

Appendix C2
Proxy Proration Example*

	Long	Short	Vote Yes	Vote No
DTC		13,000		
Cust A	1,000		1,000	
Cust B	2,000			2,000
Cust C	3,000		3,000	
Cust D	4,000		4,000	
Cust E	5,000		5,000	
Cust F		2,000		

Customers Long 15,000 shares
DTC box 13,000 shares
Total Yes Votes 13,000
Total No Votes 2,000

We need to reduce our total votes by 2000. That is 13.33 per cent of our overall total votes.
We would reduce the Yes votes by 13.33 % (1,733)
We would reduce the No votes by 13.33 % (267)
*Assumes all clients have margin accts (no cash accts) with outstanding balances,
so all accounts are subject to proration.

Appendix C3
Impartial Lottery Example*

	Long	Short	Voteable Shares Pre lottery	Voteable Shares Post Lottery 1	Voteable Shares Post Lottery 2	Voteable Shares Post Lottery 3	Voteable Shares Post Lottery 4
DTC		13,000					
Cust A	1,000		1,000	0	0	1,000	1,000
Cust B	2,000		2,000	2,000	2,000	2,000	2,000
Cust C	3,000		3,000	3,000	3,000	3,000	3,000
Cust D	4,000		4,000	3,000	4,000	2,000	4,000
Cust E	5,000		5,000	5,000	4,000	5,000	3,000
Cust F		2,000	0	0	0	0	0
Total Votes			15,000	13,000	13,000	13,000	13,000

New client positions after running four separate lotteries

Customers Long 15,000 shares

DTC box 13,000 shares

We need to reduce our total votes by 2000

Shading shows amount of new voteable share positions
*Assumes clients A, D and E have margin accounts (no cash accts) with outstanding balances and clients B,C and F do not participate in the lottery because they are short or fully paid with no margin balances

Appendix D, Summary of the current NYSE rules governing records and record retention

Proxy Records –
NYSE 452.16 Records covering the solicitation of proxies show the following:
    1. The date of receipt of the material from the issuer or person soliciting the proxies
    2. Names of customers to whom the material is sent together with date of mailing
    3. All voting instructions showing whether they are verbal or written
    4. A summary of all proxies voted by the member organization clearly setting forth total shares voted for, against or not voted for each proposal to be acted upon at the meeting

Retention of Records –
NYSE Rule 452.20 - All proxy solicitation records, original of all communications received and copies of all communications sent relating to such solicitation, shall be retained for a period of not less than three years, the first two years in an <u>easily accessible place.</u>

CAD SUMMARY OF NYSE SPECIAL PROXY EXAMINATIONS

The NYSE provided a draft of the Special examinations, to me, John Panchery SIA and Don Kittell SIA that were conducted of eight (8) member organizations. The NYSE conducted these examinations to determine the adequacy of member organizations written supervisory procedures and monitoring efforts with respect to proxy voting.

The member organizations' books and records were reviewed to determine the accuracy of proxy voting relating to annual shareholders' meetings of the companies selected for review. The actual member organization names were not disclosed. However, the names of the Companies Annual Meetings were included in the findings provided.

The NYSE stated that the objective of the examinations was to determine the member organizations' compliance with various Rules including the NYSE Rules listed below.

The examinations disclosed deficiencies at each member organization and the following 9 Rules were cited in the various examination reports, and in varying degrees of non compliance.

- NYSE Rule 342 (Offices – Approval, Supervision and Control)
- NYDE Rule 401 (Business Conduct)
- NYSE Rule 451 (Transmission of Proxy Material)
- NYSE Rule 451.90 (Schedule of Approved Charges by Member Organizations in Connection With Proxy Solicitations)
- NYSE Rule 452 (Giving Proxies by Member Organizations)
- NYSE Rule 452.20 (Retention of Records)
- NYSE Rule 440 (Books and Records)
- SEC Reg. 17a-3 (Records to be Made by Certain Exchange Members, Brokers and Dealers)
- SEC Reg. 17a-4 (Records to be Preserved by Certain Exchange Members, Brokers and Dealers).

The following is a summation of the findings as stated in the NYSE Audit Summary.

1. Member Organizations could not provide written & documented procedures.
2. Supervisory review of the proxy process was not found.
3. The NYSE states that Member Organizations can not outsource their responsibilities.

4. Record retention: All documents must be easily accessible, and presented upon request.
5. Independent Audit Reviews, internally and externally of their internal records, controls & procedures. No evidence of review.
6. Position Balancing and Adjustments. Reconciliations were not conducted
7. Securities / Share on loan can not be included in the voteable position.
8. Independent Audit Reviews of the Proxy Service Provider, (ADP) was not conducted.
9. Billing Control's, & Procedures with ADP, no reconciliation was completed.
10. Reconciliation of records to assure that beneficial Owners Votes were accurate prior to the stock record being sent to the Service Provider.
11. Supervisory Review of the Service Provider (ADP), to ensure compliance with Proxy Rules & Regulations was not maintained.
12. Proprietary Long Positions were not netted against, Proprietary Short Positions, and Securities Borrowed was included in Long Positions. Thus resulting in over voting.
13. Member Organizations entire long positions, net of securities borrowed was used for voting purposes. There were no other attempts to modify the proxy summaries to adjust for beneficial owners, which resulted in overvoting.
14. No Independent Supervisory review of proxy voting results complied by ADP, It's Service Bureau, Rule 342.
15. Firms did not net customers long positions against related short positions prior to voting the long shares.
16. Pledged Margin Option Positions can not be voted.

Overvote Analysis from 2006 Proxy Season
Reports gathered by STP Advisory Service, LLC

Agent #1:
Number of Meetings 1/1/06 – 6/9/06: 146
Number of Meetings 1/1/06 – 6/9/06 with at least one overvote occurrence: 140
(90% of the occurrences of over-voting were traced to DTC Participants.)

10 Examples of True Overvotes

CO#	NOMINEE	R/D CEDE POS.	ADP VOTE	OVERVOTE
1	GS Int'l	70,008	287,390	217,382
2	Nat'l City Bank	47,782	48,138	356
3	Scottrade	223,580	528,152	304,572
	Stifel Nicolaus	0	25,000	25,000
	UBS Fin'l	0	182,892	182,892
	UBS Securities	0	11,660	11,660
	USAA Brokerage	0	14,015	14,015
	Wedbush Morgan	0	123,200	123,200
4	Interactive Brokers	1,196	18,396	17,200
5	Interactive Brokers	11,675	13,008	1,333
	Nat'l Fin'l Serv	4,995,444	5,142,434	146,990
6	Terra Nova	2,000	5,000	3,000
	UBS Securities	4,550	53,800	49,250
7	Interactive Brokers	71,692	75,492	3,800
	UBS Securities	0	149,600	77,717
	USAA Brokerage	94,985	99,985	5,000
8	Northern Trust	164,413	190,626	26,213
9	Huntington Banks	69,221	84,000	14,779
10	Bear Stearns	2,434,159	2,486,727	52,568

(R/D = Record Date)
(CEDE = DTCC Nominee Name)
(ADP = Automated Data Processing, industry utility for proxy vote submission)

Agent #2
# of Meetings since 1/1/06 - 6/09/06: 51
# of Meetings with over-voting: 30
# of over-voting occurences: 48

We did have two large over-votes (3.9 million and 1.3 million shares) posted by Credit Suisse, in a company for which they did not have a position at DTCC.

Inspector of Election #1

It seemed statistically certain to me that most of the company's individual investors did NOT receive the proxy materials from ADP in timely fashion. ADP certainly seemed "over-stressed" this year. They tried to tell me that there were "problems with slow delivery of 'standard mail' "- but upon further inquiry, it turned out that they had used a special UPS service to deliver directly to postal-distribution centers around the country, which normally assures faster delivery not slower. Packages seem to have disappeared at ADP. Yet another client told me that while ADP "began mailing" in timely fashion, they didn't finish until nearly three weeks had passed.

Full Text available at www.stai.org

WHITE PAPER & CONCEPT RELEASE

Treating Shareholders Equally:
Alternatives for Street Proxy Distributions
December 2004

Excerpt from page 4: "In retrospect, while the current system works for some, it does not work for all. ... Some intermediaries, when generating the beneficial shareholder-voting file, have apparently not factored into their control environment failed trades, stock loans or other short conditions. As a result, a number of requests for voting instructions are mailed to parties that should not be authorized to vote. At times, this can result in votes being discounted and **the real owners unknowingly losing their voting power** or, in some cases, they are ignored.

EXECUTIVE SUMMARY

The focus of this White Paper is to illustrate the fundamental challenges associated with distributing shareholder meeting voting rights and materials to beneficial shareholders, and to provide a potential solution for the equitable treatment of both shareholders and issuers. Also provided is a summarization of earlier studies and current experiences that clearly demonstrate a need for change. Studies by tabulators and corporations alike have identified the following issues associated with the current proxy distribution system:

- Inaccurate reconciliation practices of securities held in street name resulting in over-voting for virtually every annual meeting.
- Unequal treatment of beneficial shareholders at the shareholder meeting.
- Issuer access to Non-Objecting Beneficial Owners (NOBOs) for distribution and tabulation of proxies is not permitted.
- Corporations are required by law to cover street proxy distribution costs; however, they have no control over pricing, leading to a monopolistic environment which includes pricing abuses and lack of a complaint review process.

The United States continues to recognize a process that consists of substandard voting rights for beneficial shareholders and non-negotiable pricing. The next section will outline, in greater detail, the conditions that exist in the current proxy distribution process, and a solution, similar to one recently adopted in Canada, will be provided as an alternative. This White Paper is intended to identify the flaws that exist in the current process and offer solutions utilizing models from both the Canadian market experience and existing market elements already in place in the United States. The proposed solution will provide the following:

1. Processes that ensure that beneficial positions are reconciled in order to prevent over-voting.
2. Procedures and practices that ensure accurate, timely distribution of materials and equitable voting rights for beneficial shareholders.
3. A structure wherein the issuer has responsibility for selecting its proxy material distributor and tabulator.

Over the decades, numerous requests have been made for a review of the current proxy system. These requests have been met by ad hoc committee reviews that have reduced prices for the largest companies, while doing little to improve the integrity of the system and provide broad-based, open market competition. Ad hoc committees cannot overhaul the street proxy process. The United States must address the archaic process of restricting issuers access to street name positions for distributing voting rights to beneficial shareholders, if it wants to be a leader in the areas of corporate governance and open-market practices.

Excerpt provided courtesy of STP Advisory Services, LLC   www.stpadvisors.com

STA Newsletter

2005 – Issue 4

The Securities Transfer Association, Inc.   A PUBLICATION OF THE SECURITIES TRANSFER INDUSTRY

Established 1911

Excerpt

Street Proxy Tabulation Results:
Over-Voting Still Pervasive

During the 2005 proxy season, one major transfer agent conducted a thorough review of all street proxies submitted for banks and brokers through ADP. The objective of the review was to ensure the accuracy of the voting and to assess the progress in addressing over-voting and other voting conditions. The agent tabulated 341 U.S. equity issuers. Attempted over-voting of street positions occurred for every tabulation! The following is a summary of causative factors observed:

...

<u>Simple Over-Votes</u>: The agent continued to see over-votes cast by DTC participants, who, when contacted, simply explained that the excess voting is attributable to the brokers stock loan services or other trading-related situations.

Discussion - Over-voting continues to be a problem. The SIA letter indicated that a resolution for this situation was a lottery or pro-ration of voting rights when commingled shares are on loan. This solution has clearly not been implemented across the board. ADP's over-voting service, in its weakest implementation, resolves the issue by simply capping a participant's vote at its DTC record date position. This neither effectively addresses the issues regarding integrity of voting rights nor the excess issuer cost caused by mailing of materials to holders not entitled to vote.

...

Summary and Conclusions

Street voting problems continue to abound, The over-voting services provided by ADP clearly do not address the issues created by stock lending, trade fails and other record date brokerage record deficiencies. The street proxy system lacks audit accountability required of meeting inspectors and is still too costly and difficult for issuers to effectively communicate with their shareholders. Some improvements were made, but the basic integrity of the system is still questionable. After a year plus of industry proxy committee meetings, the underlying issues appear to remain.

Excerpt provided courtesy of STP Advisory Service, LLC   www.stpadvisors.com

- Naked Short Selling Antifraud Rule; approved October 14, 2008; effective October 17, 2008 (Release 34-58774; File No. S7-08-08).

This rule was proposed in March 2008, as the financial crisis began to unfold. The SEC admits in the introduction to the proposal that "naked short selling" is not defined under Federal law but that "[a]ll sellers of securities should promptly deliver, or arrange for delivery of, securities to the respective buyer and all buyers of securities have a right to expect prompt delivery of securities purchased. Thus, the proposal takes direct aim at an activity that may create fails to deliver. Those fails can have a negative effect on shareholders, potentially depriving them of the benefits of ownership, such as voting and lending. They also may create a misleading impression of the market for an issuer's securities." Three years after Reg SHO was implemented, fails to deliver continued to grow. It would not be until the summer of 2008, when the banks that were the source of fails to deliver in the shares of thousands of small companies began to see massive numbers of fails to deliver *in their own shares* that the SEC would put a short-selling ban in place – but *only for the shares of those banks!*[57]

The stated purpose of the rule was to correct something that I and people like Dave Patch had been writing to the SEC about for years – trades that fail are not always marked "short" and the shares sold in any trade that passes through the centralized clearing and settlement system in the US are allowed to go undelivered indefinitely. In DTCC's Continuous Net Settlement System (CNS), settlement failures are resubmitted "on a perpetual basis."[58] This SEC proposal was to make it "unlawful for any person to submit an order to sell a security if such person deceives a broker-dealer, participant of a registered clearing agency, or purchaser regarding its intention or ability to deliver the security on the date delivery is due, and such person fails to deliver the security on or before the date delivery is due." In other words, it would be illegal to lie about delivering shares for settlement. Obviously, this rule was necessary because brokers and other sellers had been lying about delivery for decades.[59] The wording, however, suggested that the brokers were telling the SEC that it was their customers who were lying, not the brokers themselves.

My comments were in favor of establishing liability for fails to deliver. The 13-day close out requirement in Reg SHO was completely ineffective, largely because there were no real consequences for failing to deliver. The fails to deliver reported by NSCC virtually doubled between December 31, 2006 and December 31, 2007. My comments include calculations of the economic damage being done to investors both through the loss of favorable tax treatment for dividends, which they would get if they were not receiving payments in lieu of dividends as the buyer-side of a seller's fail to deliver, and for the loss of the use of their investment money while waiting for the delivery of shares they bought. (Similar calculations are included in Chapter 7.)

May 30, 2008

Ms. Nancy M. Morris, Secretary
Securities and Exchange Commission
100 F Street, NE
Washington, DC 20549-1090

Re: File Number S7-08-08

Dear Secretary Morris:

I write in support of proposed Rule 10b-21 to establish liability for settlement failures ("fails to deliver"). The term "settlement" means the delivery and receipt of funds *and* securities. Indeed, whether a particular transfer qualifies as a settlement payment depends on whether it involves an exchange of consideration and securities in connection with the completion of a securities transaction. If securities have not been delivered, then settlement clearly has not occurred. Settlement finality is a key component of market integrity. It provides assurances to both buyers and sellers that a trade will be completed.

Settlement finality is essential to the securities market. A systemic crisis could occur when settlement fails in one market segment cause widespread volatility in the financial system as a whole.

[1] Further, investors are harmed if they make payments in securities transactions and do not receive securities. The markets and investors need the assurance of Rule 10b-21 that securities transactions will be settled especially in times of financial market volatility.

---

[1] For example, my research shows that failures to deliver occurred in 15% of mortgage-backed securities (MBS) trades in 2005 and 8.9% in 2006. By the time the settlement fail rate in MBS receded to the level of other bonds in 2007, the entire credit market was in turmoil. For the calculation of fail rates see *Settlement Failures in Bond Markets*, available from the Social Science Research Network at http://ssrn.com/abstract=1016873

While I find Rule 10b-21 timely, I have a few concerns regarding the assumed effectiveness of Rule 203(b)(3) plus the potential for moral hazard behavior under Rule 10b-21 and the departure from the standard of ordinary care expected from broker-dealers.

General concerns

Relying on close-out requirements under Rule 203(b)(3)(iii) of Regulation SHO, the Commission discusses the requirement for "immediate action to close out a fail to deliver position in a threshold security in the Continuous Net Settlement (CNS) system that has persisted for 13 consecutive settlement days by purchasing securities of like kind and quantity." Statistical evidence indicates that this rule is not effective. From December 2006 to December 2007, fails to deliver at the National Securities Clearing Corporation (NSCC) increased by 99%.[2] At the same time, the value of transactions entering CNS increased by only 62%.[3] While I agree completely that broker-dealers need the "additional encouragement" of Rule 10b-21 to "deliver shares by settlement date," enforcement of Rule 203(b)(3)(iii) should be the first line of defense against failures to deliver.

In the discussion of proposed Rule 10b-21, the Commission makes further reference to Regulation SHO and the responsibility of the broker-dealer "for determining whether there are reasonable grounds to believe" that a seller will settle.[4] If proposed Rule 10b-21 assigns liability only to the seller, then this could allow the broker-dealer to take no responsibility for their decision to accept the sell order. Because the broker-dealer will be paid a commission only if the trade order executes, the combination of circumstances establishes a situation whereby

---

[2] Fails to deliver at NSCC were $3,749,160,000 at year-end 2006 and $7,454,648,000 at year-end 2007. Source: NSCC Annual Financial Statements, 2007.

[3] Includes equity, bond and ETF transactions. Source: Depository Trust and Clearing Corporation, Annual Report, 2007. The systemic risk also continues to rise: NSCC's Clearing Fund at year-end 2007 was only $4,866,576,000, an increase of just 60% over the previous year.

[4] Page 15377, File S7-08-08.

moral hazard behavior is induced on the part of the broker-dealers. Their economic incentives are aligned in favor of accepting sell orders that have some risk of delivery failure. The only way to mitigate this effect is to place at least some of the liability on the broker-dealer for executing the order.

The possible motivation for a broker-dealer to be less than strenuous in defining "reasonable grounds" leads to my final concern. The discussion in proposed Rule 10b-21 allows that a broker-dealer may be deceived by a seller "making misrepresentations" about shares that are difficult or expensive to borrow. Shouldn't a broker-dealer be themselves in possession of such basic knowledge about securities they are dealing in? To allow that the broker-dealer would not know enough about the security to know if there are shares available for borrowing and/or delivery would, in my opinion, be a departure from the standards of ordinary care that investors have come to expect from broker-dealers and, in fact, from all financial intermediaries in US securities markets.

Specific comments requested
- Proposed Rule 10b-21 should apply to all securities, not just sales of "threshold securities." In fact, the value of settlement failures in the bond markets is many times that of equity markets. My research shows that bond trade fails also increased from 2006 to 2007, though not at the rate of increase seen in equity trades. While some progress was made to reduce bond market settlement failures from about 8% of all trades to less than 5% from 2005 to 2006, bond trades failed at an increased rate of 5.4% in 2007. Preliminary data for 2008 indicate that this will be a record year for settlement failures.[5] Therefore, I encourage the Commission to reject consideration of any limitations on the application of Rule 10b-21.

---

[5] Nearly 9% of US Treasury trades resulted in a failure to deliver in the first 5 months of 2008, compared to 1.2% in the same period last year. This figure is for trades involving Primary Dealers only and may be substantially higher for all trades.

- The proposed rule will have a positive impact on liquidity and market quality in securities traded. Settlement finality requires not only the payment of consideration but also the delivery of securities in order for trades to be completed. Without strict rules against settlement failures, a systemic crisis could occur where investors are reluctant to engage in trades in US markets because settlement finality is in question. The markets and investors need the assurance of Rule 10b-21 that securities transactions will be settled.

Impact on the economy

There is a monetary benefit to investors from enforcing delivery on settlement date. During the period that the shares are not received, the investor will receive payments in lieu of dividends. These payments are excluded, under IRS rules implemented in 2004, from the favorable tax rate afforded to dividends.[6,7] NSCC reported that shares valued at $5,761,192,000 failed to be delivered for settlement as of December 31, 2007. The difference between the tax rate on qualified dividends and the tax rate on ordinary income is between 10% and 20%.[8] Assuming these shares have an average 1% dividend yield, then investors are paying between $5,761,192 and $11,522,384 in excess taxes each year.[9] Further, research shows that

---

[6] Section 6045(d) reflected the changes to information reporting for payments in lieu of dividends effected by the Jobs and Growth Tax Relief Reconciliation Act of 2003 (JGTRRA). Implementation was delayed to 2004 at the request of broker-dealers who commented that they needed additional time to implement system changes.

[7] Conversely, broker-dealers may not be reporting these payments as "in lieu." In that case, the investor does not suffer a monetary loss. Instead the loss accrues to the federal government (i.e., taxpayers). If "payments in lieu" are reported as bona fide dividend payments, the IRS will collect less revenue (income tax payments) than they would have had the payments been properly reported as "in lieu."

[8] The tax rate on qualified dividends is 5% or 15% (depending on the individual's income tax rate). If the individual has a regular income tax rate of 25% or higher, then the qualified dividend tax rate is 15%. If the individual's income tax rate is less than 25%, then qualified dividends are taxed at the 5% rate.

[9] The mean dividend yield for the S&P 1500 was 0.9% in 2003. See Jeffrey R. Brown, Nellie Liang and Scott J. Weisbenner, *Executive Financial Incentives and Payout Policy: Firm Responses to the 2003 Dividend Tax Cut* (December 2004).

many firms initiated dividends following the dividend tax cut in the Jobs and Growth Tax Relief Reconciliation Act (JGTRRA) of 2003.[10] Therefore, it is likely that the monetary benefit to investors from a reduction in settlement failures will increase across time.[11,12]

Further, investors incur economic damages when they are denied the use of funds between trade date and actual delivery date. Using publicly available data on failures to deliver in NYSE and NASDAQ "threshold securities" alone, I calculate that loss to have been $762

Available from the Social Science Research Network: http://ssrn.com/abstract=631182. Their calculation of the average dividend yield includes firms that do not pay dividends, making the calculation relevant even if there are non-dividend paying companies among those whose shares were not delivered to NSCC. The question of whether the failure to receive occurred on a dividend record date is less relevant because the value of shares that investors fail to receive has never been zero. In fact, most academic research on the subject shows that the activity leading to payments in lieu of dividends actually increases around record dates.

[10] "[A]mong S&P 1500 non-dividend-paying firms, the fraction that initiated dividends jumped from only one in a hundred firms in 2001and 2002 to nearly one in ten firms in 2003." See Jeffrey R. Brown, Nellie Liang and Scott J. Weisbenner, *Executive Financial Incentives and Payout Policy: Firm Responses to the 2003 Dividend Tax Cut* (December 2004). Available from the Social Science Research Network: http://ssrn.com/abstract=631182.

[11] A significant percentage of households reporting dividend income are either retired or earn less than $50,000 per year. Speaking in support of JGTRRA, James W. Struckert, Chairman of the SIA Regional Firms Committee, said "According to the most recent IRS data, 34.1 million tax returns (or 26.4 percent of total tax returns, representing 71 million people) reported some dividend income in 2000. Of all taxpayers that claimed some dividend income in 2000, nearly half (45.8 percent) earned less than $50,000 in adjusted gross income (including dividends). ... Importantly, almost half of all savings from the dividend exclusion would go to taxpayers 65 and older, thereby giving retirees an additional reliable, long-term source of income to supplement their social security earnings and other retirement savings. The average annual tax savings for the 9.8 million seniors receiving dividends would be $936." Testimony before the Subcommittee on Economic Policy of the Senate Committee on Banking, Housing, and Urban Affairs, May 22, 2003.

[12] Furthermore, interest paid on municipal bonds in the US is exempt from federal taxes. When bond trades fail the investor gets a payment in lieu of interest. Unlike dividends, these payments are not differentiated by the broker. As a result, the US government is missing out on $1.54 billion per year in tax revenue.

million in 2007.[13] This is not a one-time loss but an on-going monetary loss to investors that will not diminish as long as the system tolerates failures to deliver.

Concluding Remarks

The clearance and settlement system depends on guarantees by all participants that they will perform their obligations. Uncertainty about the final status of entitlements could lead participants to engage in certain types of activities that are detrimental to the 50.3% of American households who own US equities.[14] Confidence in the securities markets is diminished when investors and others cannot rely on the receipt of securities in trades. During the time that there is uncertainty in the securities markets about the receipt of securities in settlement, investors' confidence will diminish. Tolerance for settlement failures seriously undermines the protections that should be afforded all investors in US securities markets.

Sincerely,

Susanne Trimbath, PhD

cc: Internal Revenue Service, Administrative Provisions and Judicial Practice; General Accounting Office, Financial Markets and Community Investment

---

[13] Calculations for 2006 are available in the appendix to *Settlement Failures in Bond Markets*, available from the Social Science Research Network at http://ssrn.com/abstract=1016873. An updated paper, including calculations using data through mid-2008, is forthcoming.

[14] Source: *Equity Ownership in America, 2005*, Investment Company Institute and Securities Industry Association. According to Federal Reserve data, nearly three-fourths (73 percent) of Americans' liquid financial assets are invested in securities-related products.

- Surprise Custody Audits; approved December 30, 2009; effective March 12, 2010 (Release No. IA-2968; File No.S7-09-09)

Although this was not an amendment to Reg SHO, my comments point to the fact that audits should have been confirming that actual shares were in investors' accounts, and not just some sort of electronic IOU. The rule would "require registered investment advisers that have custody of client funds or securities to undergo an annual surprise examination by an independent public accountant to verify client funds and securities." They would also be required to "obtain a written report from an independent public accountant that includes an opinion regarding the qualified custodian's controls relating to custody of client assets."

The proposal listed several examples where the SEC took action against investment advisors and brokers for fraudulent conduct, including the one against Bernie Madoff (February 9, 2009). My comments were less about situations similar to Madoff's or those where the broker mis-used client funds but more about the situation where brokers debited client accounts for cash weeks and often months before they received shares. The NYSE Proxy Examination attached to my August 2006 comment letter revealed "no evidence" of independent audit reviews of internal records, controls and procedures at the brokers, setting up the conditions where corporate votes were submitted without regard to any rules.

August 3, 2009

Ms. Elizabeth M. Murphy, Secretary
U.S. Securities and Exchange Commission
100 F Street, NE
Washington, D.C. 20549-1090

RE: Proposed rule Custody of Funds or Securities of Clients by Investment Advisers

RE: File No. S7-09-09

Dear Ms. Murphy:

This proposed rule represents a major opportunity for the Securities and Exchange Commission to press for the elimination of "phantom shares" in investor accounts. By reinstating the requirement (removed in 2003) for all investment advisors to have an annual "surprise examination by an independent public accountant" to confirm client cash and securities, investors will be assured that their broker is holding all of the shares showing on the investor account statements – and that they have not been on the receiving (buying) end of any naked short sales or fails to deliver.

We agree with the Commission's proposal to have an independent public accountant confirm all securities held by the custodian and to reconcile all such securities to the books and records of client accounts. We suggest that this examination be designed to include revealing evidence that investors are holding securities entitlements for more than T+3 days when in fact their purchase was the subject of a failure to receive securities (the other side of a failure to deliver). This examination should also be designed to reveal evidence when securities lending has resulted in multiple records of ownership for shares, i.e., records of ownership that exceed the shares actually in custody. Such an examination should include reconciliation of the number of shares reported on investor accounts with the total number of shares available at the investment firm, including shares in the "free" account (not short, not on loan, etc.) at the Depository Trust Company.

We are in agreement with comments submitted by Ernst & Young and others for clarification of the Commission's reference to "client assets." In particular, we seek to have specific reconciliation of all exchange listed common stock shares. Although investors need assurances that other classes of securities are also reconciled, we believe that the equity securities of US public companies are most vulnerable to the dangers of "empty shares." (On this, see the work of Professors Henry T.C. Hu and Bernard S. Black of the University of Texas at Austin - School of Law on empty voting and empty creditors). Phantom shares, resulting from naked short selling, are implicated in the demise of Lehman Brothers, Fannie Mae, Freddie Mac and Bear Stearns.

We are concerned about corporate governance and shareholder voting rights. We have seen the damage done to investor confidence when individual investors find that they cannot withdraw their shares from a brokerage account because the trade — which they believed settled on time with shares that they fully-paid for — failed to settle. These investors thought they owned shares that were held by their investment advisor. This proposed rule has powerful potential to restore investor confidence in US capital markets.

Thank you for the opportunity to comment on this important proposal.

Sincerely,

/signed/

Susanne Trimbath, Ph.D.
Chief Executive Manager
STP Advisory Services, LLC

- Reg SHO amended to create a short sale circuit breaker; approved February 26, 2010; effective May 10, 2010 with compliance scheduled to begin November 10, 2010 (Release No. 34-61595; File No. S7-08-09).

This amendment established a "short sale-related circuit breaker." Specifically, it required the exchanges to "establish, maintain, and enforce written policies and procedures" to prevent short sales at a price "less than or equal to the current national best bid" when share prices fell 10% or more from the previous day's closing price. Once triggered, the short sale restriction would stay in place "for the remainder of the day and the following day." This process was called a "short sale price test" or "short sale price test restriction."

The proposal received many comments in seven different form letters. CNBC buffoon-commentator Jim Cramer signed a letter that was sent to the SEC 5,608 times. Cramer (and three other original signers) asked the SEC to return to the 1930s price test that was removed in the original Reg SHO.[60] The circuit breaker was very different from the earlier price test because it suspended trading in stocks that might be the subject of manipulative and/or abusive stock market activity. The earlier price test only stopped the next trade, not trades for the rest of the day and the next.

In my comments, I made a clear economic argument against short selling. At least until the point where there were significant fails to deliver in bank stocks, most academic researchers were writing in favor of short selling. Their main arguments were that short selling improved price discovery, liquidity and risk management. It is, in fact, the disappointment of expectations that alerts true entrepreneurs/investors to take action by selling shares they own. Short sellers disrupt markets by increasing the supply of shares in circulation, often beyond the legal number of shares the company authorized and issued. As long as short sellers were being coddled by the regulators and adored by academics they would never have an incentive to close out by repaying the stock loan and delivering shares to cover the short sale.[61]

June 5, 2009

Ms. Elizabeth M. Murphy, Secretary
U.S. Securities and Exchange Commission
100 F Street, NE
Washington, D.C. 20549-1090
Via www.sec.gov

RE: File No. S7-08-09

"To restore investor confidence, myths about short selling must be dispelled - short selling is a legitimate, integral and critical part of the price discovery, which aids liquidity, and contributes to capital formation and risk management processes for the U.S. markets."

Chicago Board Options Exchange, *Short Selling Principles*, April 23, 2009, attachment to Apr. 28, 2009 Memorandum from the Office of Commissioner Aguilar regarding an April 23, 2009 meeting with representatives of the Chicago Board Options Exchange and Rich Feuer Group

Secretary Murphy:

Short selling may be an investment strategy, but it is in no way critical to price discovery. Quite the contrary. It is when investors want to purchase shares that are not available, or to sell shares that are not in demand, that price discovery occurs. Enabling investors to sell shares they do not own – which is what short-selling does – makes no contribution to price discovery.

I am a Ph.D. economist engaged in independent research in economics and finance. I received my training in economic analysis of law under Professor Mario Rizzo at New York University. I am a recipient of Bradley Foundation grants in support of studies in Austrian Economics (1994-1997). As a regular part of the Austrian Colloquiums held in the Department of Economics at New York University, I gained immeasurably from my learning experiences with Professor (Emeritus) Israel Kirzner, a modern leader in the Austrian School of economics.

In his 1997 book, *How Markets Work*, Dr. Kirzner explains quite elegantly the process of price discovery through disequilibrium: "Disequilibrium prices generate direct disappointment of plans.... Such disappointment can be expected to alert entrepreneurs to the true temper of the market." (The Institute of Economic Affairs, London, Second Impression, 2000, p. 45). Market makers in general and short sellers in particular disrupt this process by altering the appearance of supply and demand for the shares of companies. Each time a market maker steps in to purchase shares that no one wants to buy or sell shares that no one wants to divest, they send disinformation into the market.

Likewise short sellers do a disservice to market prices by increasing the supply of shares in circulation. If they deliver borrowed shares then the lender holds a "marker" for the extra shares; if they fail to deliver shares at settlement ("naked short selling") then the buyer holds a "marker" for the extra shares. In either case, until the short position is closed, there will be extra shares in circulation in the market.

The only way for SEC rules to permit short selling without having this deleterious effect on the market for securities is to require that short selling investment strategies be finite in duration. I know of no financial model for investment strategies that does not include "time" as an element. If short selling is to be allowed, then it must conform to financial theory in order to be effective. Short-selling as an investment strategy requires some potential point in the not-too-distant future when actual shares are purchased in the open market for repayment of the stock loan. In today's financial system, there is no due date for a stock loan. Until this condition is remedied, then all arguments for adjustments to short-selling rules (up-tick, pre-borrow, etc.) will be ineffective.

This change would be an enormous leap forward in restoring trading in financial products to market conditions. The alternative proposals regarding price rules, circuit breakers and, especially, the "short exempt" rule only serve to add complexity – which is no substitute for innovation. That these regulations have become overly-complicated can be evidence by the increasing size of the associated rulemakings (as published in the Federal Register). The current revisions (73 pages) are almost double the size of the original proposed rule (39 pages) and 3 times the size of the final regulation SHO (25 pages). My proposal, though highly innovative, would make short-selling very straight forward: never fail to deliver and always have a close-out date.

I strongly urge SEC to take the bold step of making meaningful changes to short selling rules so that those who wish to partake of the contrary investment strategy may do so – and may do so in a way that is not disruptive to the core principal of capital markets which is to provide the means for entrepreneurs to finance productive capacity. Thank you for your attention.

Sincerely,

/signed/

Susanne Trimbath, Ph.D.
Chief Executive Manager

Chapter 9. Criminal Cases Reveal Evidence

As I explained earlier, the lawyers pursuing some of the most visible cases in this area did not use me as an expert witness. A witness who is qualified as an "expert" on the subject could be called on to help a judge (or jury) to understand the more technical points of the case. Expert witnesses are qualified to offer opinions. I did provide "Fact Witness" affidavits for two lawsuits filed on behalf of companies and their shareholders against the DTCC and its subsidiaries DTC and NSCC.[62] A fact witness is considered to be knowledgeable about the facts involved in the case through direct participation or observation of the problem. Fact witnesses are called on to testify without an opinion.

Cases against DTCC or any of the other self-regulatory organizations that govern Wall Street tend to be required to take place in the Southern District of New York; a venue that is notoriously favorable to banks and brokers. In my role as Director of Transfer Agent Services I had contact with companies all over the US and Canada. By about 2000, DTCC was and remains the only centralized clearing and settlement organization in the US. Therefore, their members are active in every state (and most countries). Still, they were able to argue successfully to have many cases dismissed on jurisdictional issues. The cases I provided affidavits for and others where I provided document reviews were easily dismissed on that basis. It was at this point, I believe, that Wes Christian and most other lawyers attempting to help the companies that were victimized by the system stopped pursuing cases against DTCC. It was just too difficult to make the arguments necessary to get a case heard in state courts outside New York where judges and juries might be inclined to consider arguments favorable toward entrepreneurs and investors.

Although the decision to forgo seeking regulatory reform from the center may have seemed easy at that point, what came next was not really simple. The cases were very complex, intersecting with criminal cases against various parties. Some were exempted by jurisdiction while others took plea deals in criminal matters, becoming cooperating witnesses and informants. The criminal actions could cause delays in the civil cases; plea deals were not always made public so that parties who might be important defendants could be shielded from civil litigation. Again, my expertise is in post-trade clearing and settlement. Not being a lawyer, it is difficult for me to give any comprehensive coverage to the criminal or civil litigation surrounding the issue. However, I feel I cannot ignore the criminal proceedings. There are a couple of cases often pointed to as having criminal prosecutions that led to the discovery of important facts and data that supported the original allegations of the business' founders.

One of those was Eagletech Communications, Inc. I got to know the founder, Rod Young, personally. I will try to tell his story based on interviews he and his lawyers did for documentaries and television news programs, plus some discussions I had directly with Rod. In one of the documentaries (*Wall Street Conspiracy*, 2012), a former FBI special agent talks about the criminal cases surrounding Eagletech. Although there would be felony guilty pleas in the criminal cases, in the end it was all too little too late for Eagletech. In a nutshell, what Rod Young experienced was a classic asset grab: the perpetrators deprived Eagletech of access to the capital he needed to take his product fully to market. Once they drive the company into bankruptcy, they are able to "grab" the asset, like the product Rod invented, for their own benefit.

As Rod explained it: "One of the biggest problems in [my] business [as a homebuilder and contractor] was communicating with people. Inefficiency and the money lost from a failed communication could sometimes amount to thousands of dollars." Rod created "proprietary unified communications products and services" that "makes it possible for mobile professionals to maintain real-time contact with one phone number while also providing telephone access to messages and Web control over the unified system." In 1999 that was a very revolutionary innovation, years ahead of its time! Based on information provided by a stock promoter in the documentary *Wall Street Conspiracy*, it appears that the unscrupulous financiers grabbed the asset after destroying Eagletech and then helped make the technology available for commercial use in Europe. When Google Voice was launched in 2009 it was based on patents originally held by Eagletech. Rod did not receive any recognition or compensation for his invention.[63]

Former FBI Special Agent Don Clark called Eagletech "the stepping stone case in stock fraud investigations" because it presented evidence of organized crime involvement with Wall Street (*Wall Street Conspiracy*). In the FBI case, 15 members of New Jersey organized crime were arrested on February 15, 2004 for racketeering. Bankers who were involved in manipulation of Eagletech stock were named as co-defendants. That case, in particularly, gave Wes Christian access to evidence that revealed the mechanics of the fraud.

Shortly before his death, a "stock promoter" named John Serubo appeared in the documentary *Wall Street Conspiracy*. Serubo and his partners introduced Eagletech to Salomon Smith Barney. Rod was naturally impressed, at the time, to have a major Wall Street firm take an interest in his business. Salomon Smith Barney's checkered history of financial scandals would lead Citigroup to abandon the use of the name in 2003. Rod, of course, was not aware of that history at the time he flew to New York for the first meetings.

According to the SEC complaint,[64] the primary perpetrators in the Eagletech criminal cases were Tonino Labella and John Serubo. Labella owned 75% of Valley Forge Securities, Inc. and acted as its Chairman and CEO. He also controlled a number of domestic and offshore securities and investment entities that he used to manipulate Eagletech's stock. This was exactly in line with the criminal conspiracy that Wes Christian outlined to me in 2003.

Labella and Serubo solicited investors to buy shares even before they approached Eagletech about going public. They pretended to sell shares to investors for a total of $1.4 million – before they had any actual shares to sell. Subsequently, they approached Eagletech and got them to issue a large block of shares (10 million) in exchange for an infusion of $1.2 million cash capital. The stock was then transferred to a brokerage account and sold into the public market. At the time, Eagletech shares were selling for $8. Fifteen other brokers, in exchange for generous kickbacks of up to 50% of the value of the trade, generated $12.7 million of sales on the initial block of shares for which Eagletech only received $1.2 million.

These and other activities took place between August 1999 and December 2000; the SEC litigation was filed in February 2005 by which time the stock was selling for just 6 cents a share. In addition to the SEC complaint, the U.S. Attorney for the District of New Jersey obtained indictments against four individuals for criminal securities manipulation activities in Eagletech stock.[65]

After Labella and Serubo took their profits from the transactions, there remained a significant number of retail investors who were on the buying end of the $12.7 million of sales – sales of phantom shares of Eagletech stock. Eventually, Rod was directed to Wes Christian and John O'Quinn by the CEO of another company that thought Eagletech stock was being attacked by securities manipulators in the same way that they attacked the stock of his own company. Wes would later admit that the case benefited from some "lucky breaks" when the FBI started an investigation on the criminal side. Rod was shocked by what he found out in the 24 boxes of paper records, 50,000 pieces of paper, and computer disks with 43,000 trade records that came out of the criminal cases. Years later, when I visited him at his home in Florida he offered to let me go through the documents. I declined because I knew that I was not in a position to understand all the details of the criminal activities. In those records Rod found that the members of his Salomon Smith Barney financing team and their options market-makers in Chicago were selling shares and then failing to deliver at settlement, even before they signed the investment agreement.

The evidence revealed in those files was exactly what I described as the "schematic for the nuke." Basically, two or more brokers flip short sales, stock loans and fails to deliver between accounts. With each repeated flip, the number of shares in circulation can be multiplied. The scenario Wes described and the one proved in the FBI case is done without using the central depository. The same scenario can take place completely within the rules of the central securities depository and US securities regulations (see diagram). The difference between the two scenarios is minor, yet only the criminal version was pursued in the US. The SEC failed to pursue the matter from a regulatory standpoint. Eventually they forced the deregistration of Eagletech's stock over a technicality (failure to timely file paperwork). Due to the downward pressure put on the price of shares of Eagletech by the excessive number of open market sales orders (which could not be fulfilled because no shares existed), Eagletech no longer had access to capital and was unable to afford to bring their communication patent to fruition.

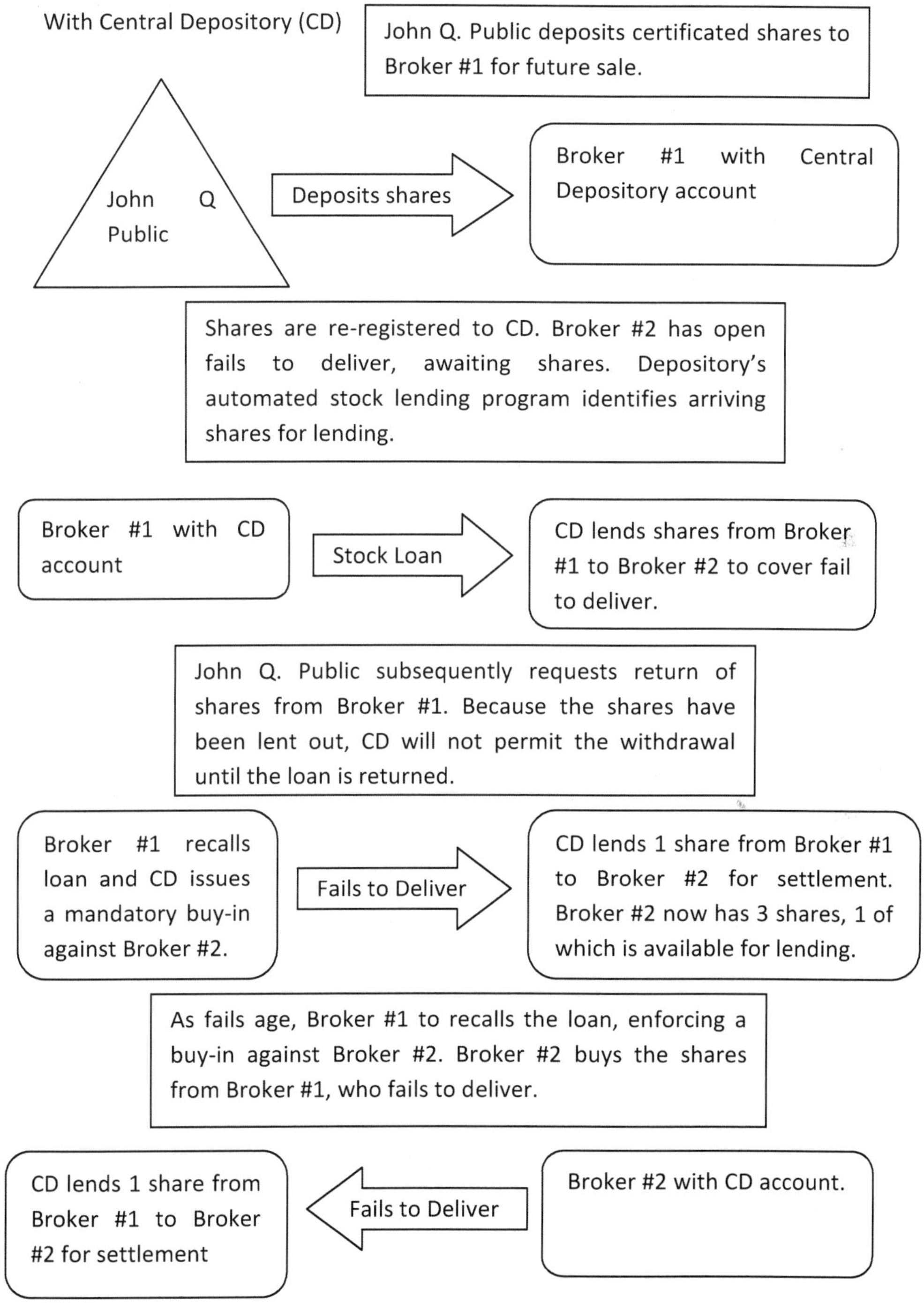

With Central Depository (CD)

John Q. Public deposits certificated shares to Broker #1 for future sale.

John Q Public → Deposits shares → Broker #1 with Central Depository account

Shares are re-registered to CD. Broker #2 has open fails to deliver, awaiting shares. Depository's automated stock lending program identifies arriving shares for lending.

Broker #1 with CD account → Stock Loan → CD lends shares from Broker #1 to Broker #2 to cover fail to deliver.

John Q. Public subsequently requests return of shares from Broker #1. Because the shares have been lent out, CD will not permit the withdrawal until the loan is returned.

Broker #1 recalls loan and CD issues a mandatory buy-in against Broker #2. → Fails to Deliver → CD lends 1 share from Broker #1 to Broker #2 for settlement. Broker #2 now has 3 shares, 1 of which is available for lending.

As fails age, Broker #1 to recalls the loan, enforcing a buy-in against Broker #2. Broker #2 buys the shares from Broker #1, who fails to deliver.

CD lends 1 share from Broker #1 to Broker #2 for settlement ← Fails to Deliver ← Broker #2 with CD account.

NAKED, SHORT AND GREEDY

Rod Young was granted permission to present his case before the SEC commissioners on February 13, 2006, and told them:

I believe that the SEC, DTCC, the Federal Reserve and members of Congress all share responsibility for failing to respond to tens of thousands of complaints of wrongful conduct from victimized companies and their shareholders. ... I contend that if you had spent but a fraction of the resources that you have spent on this proceeding on investigating just one complaint of manipulation you would have saved some innocent shareholder the loss of his pension savings or his child their education fund. I have just one question to ask you, 'when are you going to do your job?'

On July 5, 2006 Eagletech's status as a public company was revoked permanently. In their 2009 review of the SEC, the U.S. Government Accountability Office (GAO) would confirm what Rod said before the Commission three years earlier: the SEC received thousands of complaints from investors and companies like Rod's and never investigated any of them.

Chapter 10. The Battle Goes Public

The battle between Wall Street and Main Street became more public throughout 2004. Without action from Congress or the regulators, we needed to increase national exposure. In May, I helped create briefing documents to help Wes Christian and John O'Quinn prepare for an appearance on *Dateline NBC* (*Dateline: Broken Dreams*, 2005). At the end of August, I was also writing document request lists for Wes and John to use in pursuing the case for Eagletech Communications, Inc. before the criminal case broke open. The story of Eagletech is one of the most complete we have.[66] Eagletech would become the centerpiece of the *Dateline* story that Wes and John were preparing for.

Dateline began piecing together an exposé that everyone expected would "blow the roof off" the issue. After more than four months, interviews with 25 people, and gathering over 75 hours of film, the episode was first scheduled to air in March 2005. According to Gayle Essary, who was then the publisher of FinancialWire from Investrend Information, the episode was postponed just after DTCC published a letter from its general counsel, Larry Thompson, on the front page of their website that appeared to answer criticisms they expected to come up in the much-anticipated Dateline episode.[67]

After several more postponements, the episode finally aired on July 31, 2005 with the segment title *Broken Dreams* (Dateline 2005). The original story outline called for an exposé of the criminal issues surrounding the manipulation of Eagletech's stock. After viewing the episode, Rod Young said: 'It was so watered down the most scathing comment in the whole piece was that "naked short selling may be illegal and it's a very complicated story, in fact, too complicated to tell here." It was a joke' (WSC 2012).

The Dateline episode opened with a brief teaser about "Hard work, initiative and maybe a little luck" making dreams come true in America. TV personality Ron Insana began telling Eagletech's story as a "cautionary tale every investor should hear before buying another share in a small company stock." He missed the point that this is also a cautionary tale that every entrepreneur should hear before deciding to take their small company public! For the Dateline segment, they interviewed an investment advisor in Fremont, Nebraska by the name of Todd Benson. Benson not only researched Eagletech, he flew to Florida to meet with Rod personally before recommending the investment to his clients. Despite Benson making it clear that he saw all the technology working, Insana continued to lay out this story as a cautionary tale for investors, still largely ignoring the danger to entrepreneurs like Rod.

No matter how much good news there was for the company, the price of the stock of Eagletech started and continued to fall. Two years after debuting, the company was growing but the stock price kept falling. Not even the bursting of the dot.com bubble could explain what was happening. The most telling element of the stock price collapse was that it enabled Salomon to renege on their promise of long-term financing to support Eagletech. Despite having a useful product that worked (something many of the dot.com's lacked), and a sound business plan, without access to capital, Rod was forced to shut down Eagletech.

Insana would say that the lawyers representing Rod were looking at "a pattern targeting thousands of small companies like Eagletech under the radar of federal regulators like the SEC." Of course, he was wrong. The SEC knew about it. At worst, they condoned it at the behest of Wall Street and its self-regulatory organizations in order to protect their revolving-door options. At best, the SEC was incompetent.

John O'Quinn recognized that, from the start, the managing directors and their other partners at Salomon planned a scheme to drive down the stock price and make huge profits from market manipulation. Insana told viewers that the brokers were "using a kind of stock market trade called naked short selling. It's seriously complicated business to explain." While that may have been true, the idea that brokers are allowed to sell stock then not deliver it is very straight forward. As John O'Quinn would say many times, in his distinctive drawl, "It's just stealin'; that's all it is." John told Insana that he saw evidence that this was happing to at least 1,000 companies, creating market losses of more than $400 billion. By 2005, O'Quinn and the consortium of law firms he led had filed more than two dozen lawsuits in at least seven states. In court papers, Salomon Brothers claimed that the financing team working over Eagletech was acting on their own, writing that "those employees engaged only in private acts for their private benefit." Still, Insana would continue to suggest in this Dateline story that all companies like Eagletech "just got caught in the down draft in the stock market" and that they were "just victims of market forces, not of manipulative forces."

A public forum in Washington DC

Finally, something happened that seemed like it really could change our fortunes for the better. For the first time, success seemed like a real possibility. On November 30, 2005 the North American Securities Administrators Association (NASAA) hosted a public "NASAA Listens" Forum in Washington D.C. to explore the problem of market manipulation through naked short selling. The NASAA is "the oldest international organization devoted to investor protection."[68] Its members include the securities administrators in all 50 states. The state administrators regulate and enforce state level laws to protect Main Street investors from Wall Street fraud. States have been regulating securities longer than the SEC was in existence. In addition to licensing brokers and investment advisors, state administrators also play a role in the public stock offerings of companies. (See the Primer in Chapter 1 for more on the important role of the States for company stocks.)

I was one of the panelists who spoke at the Forum, along with:
- James J. Angel, Associate Professor of Finance, McDonough School of Business, Georgetown University.
- James Brigagliano, Assistant Director, Division of Market Regulation, U.S. Securities and Exchange Commission.
- Peter J. Chepucavage, General Counsel, Plexus Consulting Group, LLC (Washington, D.C.).
- John Finnerty, Professor of Finance, Fordham University Graduate School of Business Administration; Principal, Analysis Group, Inc. (New York).
- Anand Ramtahal, Vice President, Division of Member Firm Regulation, New York Stock Exchange.
- Robert Shapiro, co-founder and chairman, Sonecon, LLC (Washington, D.C.).
- Cameron K. Funkhouser, Vice President, Market Regulation, National Association of Securities Dealers.

Although the NASAA invited DTCC to send a representative to the forum, they declined. Having worked at the depository, I could see that from their standpoint, it is problematic to release information about the full extent of fails-to-deliver. Once people know the magnitude of the problem, once they know that the shares they think they are being held at a broker are not there and not being voted the way that they think they are, then this becomes problematic in the sense of having the potential to undermine faith in the system. At the Forum, I make the point quite clear that the existing self-regulatory system of post-trade clearing and settlement enables stock manipulation:[69]

In the last proxy season, one transfer agent reviewed 341 equity issues to see if there was attempted over-voting, which would indicate that more than one person was trying to vote the same shares. And they found that to be the case in every issue they examined. ... One [reason the STA] understands that this is happening ... is as a result of stock loan services and trade-related situations. What happens [is this]: two people end up thinking they own the same shares. As the number of shares multiplies, the seriousness of the problem increases. When individuals leave shares with the broker, they believe they are giving the broker their voting instructions and that the broker turns in the vote to the company for a corporate election. If the broker only has 1,000 shares on deposit and sometimes they get 2,000 votes from their account holders, the broker may or may not even divide up the percentage for and against certain proposals. ... The problem is not necessarily created by immobilization [in the centralized clearing and settlement system] but it's enabled by immobilization. So you have a system that accepts accidents and views fails as innocent. That's a system that enables manipulation.

In other words, the NYSE's long-standing rule for one-share/one-vote is violated. Each exchange has a similar rule, which is based on the principle that all shareholders should have equal voting rights in public companies so that every share is equivalent to one vote. In the best case scenario, if a broker receives for example 1,000,000 votes but only has 500,000 actual shares, they may just allocate the votes for and against in proportion to the votes they received. Essentially, in that example, the shareholder only gets one-half vote per share in their account.[70] When pressed on the question, Mr. Anand from the New York Stock Exchange stutters out his reply:

[The one-share/one-vote rule is] still in place but there is a special committee and I'm not too familiar with it... Our rules, I think they are 451/452, are business side rules.[71] And there is a committee working right now to look at our [shareholder voting] rules and with the possibility of amending those in the future.[72]

The NASAA moderator, Ralph Lambiase, then-Connecticut Securities director, was outraged over this, and shocked that he had not read anything about it:

Fundamentally that's wrong. ... I really hate to sound like I'm a little indignant about it but we fight wars over the concept of wanting people to have a vote. You want a vote, so when you take away half of my vote or some percentage of my vote, shouldn't somebody be telling me that upfront, that I may lose a percentage of my votes? What about all that I read about in corporate governance, where people talk about corporations or institutions trying to sit on the Board? There are a substantial number of financial institutions that want to make their voice heard on matters of corporate governance. You're saying that all their votes don't all count equally? ... Let me thank you [Dr. Trimbath] for bringing that up. I'm just a tad disappointed with the industry right now. ... [they] undermine the capital market system, the entire economy.

I commented that I hoped someone in the audience would write the story that needed to be written. Bob Drummond, from Bloomberg Markets was there and did an exposé in the March 2006 issue of the magazine under the title "Corporate Voting Charade" (Drummond, 2006a).

Bob's article started out by explaining the processes that create phantom shares and hence phantom votes in corporate governance matters, like electing the Board of Directors or approving mergers. Drummond found an 81% increase in the volume of stock lending in the past five years. He approached some banks and brokers to get their side of the story. They told him that as long as the brokers adjusted the votes downward before turning them in, "it's a tempest in a teapot." They showed no concern that voting rights may be given to unauthorized persons and that legitimate votes may be thrown out. After doing the yeoman's job of ferreting out data on short sales, stock lending and over-voting, Drummond was able to point to specific examples where the effect was enough to tip the scales on voting results in major corporate mergers, including Mony Group's acquisition by Axa in 2004. In the case of El Paso Corporation, the potential phantom votes were more than three times the number needed to re-elect incumbent directors over opposition, including dissent from the company's biggest individual shareholder. Drummond concluded, "[the] solution would be for Wall Street brokerages to clearly disclose who can and can't vote in corporate elections. Until this happens, double and triple voting on one share will continue to make a mockery of shareholder democracy."

Patrick Byrne, then-CEO of Overstock, was also in the audience at the NASSA Forum. I had not met him personally, but called on him with a specific challenge: buy shares of his own company and then demand proof that the shares were delivered by the selling broker at settlement. After leaving the meeting that night, Patrick placed an order to purchase 50,000 shares of the company he founded. Two weeks later, on December 14, 2005, he inquired with his bank about the finality of settlement. His banker replied that his shares, "originally confirmed to have settled on Dec 5th and in the process of being converted from DTC shares to paper, have in actuality not settled and no shares have been received by Wells Fargo from Lehman Brothers. The $1.8m for the purchase of the shares has been debited from your [bank] account…and the funds are being held in a [bank] holding account." Mr. Byrne asked: "Can you buy-in the fails?" The bank responded: "It would seem that Lehman did not have the shares when they sold them to us. … Talking with my traders they feel that we will run into the same problem [settlement failure], no one seems to have enough of the shares to deliver. … [T]hey are finding it just about impossible to find shares to borrow or buy."[73]

It took two months for Patrick to get the shares despite the fact that the broker debited his account for the full purchase price three days after the trade. At the then-current federal funds rate, he lost more than $12,000 in potential earnings for not having access to his money while he waited for the shares.

After this meeting and Patrick's direct experience with being on the receiving end of a fail-to-deliver, he spearheads an effort to change the SEC rules. I end up on several email distribution lists with the people surrounding Patrick in his efforts. That's when he named them the "pajama-hideen" – freedom fighters who work from home in their pajamas.

PART V. ESCALATING COMMITMENTS

Chapter 11. Byrne's War

After the purchase of his own shares results in settlement failure – with no buy-in possible – Patrick Byrne engaged in a crusade that a Utah magazine called "Byrne's War": "Although the heat is turning up even higher for this maverick 43-year old executive, he couldn't care less what anyone thinks. ... Byrne professes this war ... is driven by his upbringing, distaste for injustice and his conscience..."[74]

He started with the Republican U.S. senators from Utah and also pushed for state-level legislation (*Wall Street Conspiracy*, 2012). After talking to some colleagues of Patrick's, California state-Senator John Harmer took up Patrick's concerns with the US Senate Banking Committee, who have oversight of the SEC.[75] Senator Bennett (R-Utah) also took an interest in the problem, especially since it was impacting Utah-based Overstock.com. Together, they argued that the small businesses that were most easily hurt by naked short selling are the economic engine of the nation, creating most of the new jobs, and therefore deserving of protection. Stock price manipulation was choking off access to capital. Senator Bennett was committed and began drafting legislation. Senator Shelby (R-Utah) and a few other Banking Committee members were interested in holding hearings to let investors and entrepreneurs be heard. The hearings did not come to fruition. The Committee did hold a hearing on "The Role of Hedge Funds in Our Capital Markets" in May 2006; the panelists were from Treasury, SEC, Federal Reserve and an economist from the Commodity Futures Trading Commission. The pajamahideen called it "a whitewash." Later, Harmer would tell a documentary film maker that DTCC was sabotaging their efforts (*Wall Street Conspiracy*, 2012).

Still, as Patrick pulled together the pajamahideen and worked at organizing his efforts, things were starting to look up again. Ever optimistic, we were getting some national attention, and getting some action from Congress. It seemed as if we might be able to get real regulatory reform. On May 26, 2006, Utah Governor Jon Huntsman signed state senate bill S.B. 3004 into law, to institute "state fines for brokers who accumulate too many unsettled trades in any company's shares." (Associated Press May 26, 2006). One of Patrick's supporters sent out an email with the first line: "Good 1, Evil 0." I sent a letter to the Utah Governor (see Box).

> **My letter to Governor Huntsman in support of S.B. 3004**
>
> Governor Jon Huntsman, Jr.
> East Capitol Complex, Suite 220
> Salt Lake City, UT 84114
>
> Governor Huntsman:
>
> I am writing in praise of SB3004, which I believe will correct a problem that is disrupting our financial systems at the core: the failure on the part of management at the DTCC to provide secure, guaranteed, final settlement for trades. I am a professional economist with 20 years experience in financial services operations, including 10 years in trade clearing and settlement of which 6 were with the Depository Trust Company in New York.
>
> There are existing laws, including federal SEC regulations, which are intended to protect investors (laws and rules against fraud, deception, etc.). Investors bear a significant share of the damage from trade failures because the broker has failed to provide not only the trade execution service that was paid for, but has also failed to deliver the product (shares). However, we know that seeking redress under securities laws is hard for a single investor, especially because transaction costs weigh against damages. Moreover, lawsuits

representing investors often are in the nature of class actions where attorney fees may consume up to half the recovery.

SB3004 provides a more efficient solution. Indeed, the company is also aggrieved when trades fail to settle: when failure results from manipulative behavior it does harm to the company's reputation and damage to the share price, both of which limit access to capital – private as well as market-based capital. Using remedies available through SB3004, the company is in a better position than the investor to benefit from what can be learned in repeated enforcement efforts under the law.

Economic models of efficiency in the law depend on parties having ongoing interests in disputes of a certain sort, rather than merely for one occasion of the matter at hand. SB3004 gives support to that interest which resides with the companies and arms them with information they can use to better protect their shareholders. Because the SB3004 penalty monies go to the company, they are more likely to act than investors. The company's action would confer benefit not only on itself, but also on all its shareholders. Unlike existing laws and regulations designed to protect investors, SB3004 has the potential to align economic incentives with best potential outcomes.

At its heart, SB3004 is about information not penalties. Inefficient laws, like those in place at the federal level presuming to protect investors, can create asymmetric stakes. That is, an inefficient rule creates a loss to one party that is greater than the gain to the other. Thus, litigation becomes more likely when rules are inefficient. This inefficiency, I believe, may be at work in the large number of shareholder suits against companies and brokers that we see in the US now. Mario Rizzo, noted Austrian economist who specializes in analysis of law at New York University, argues that the amount of information needed for judges to achieve efficiency is excessive. SB3004 puts information in the hands of the companies who can more efficiently provide shareholder protection by being on the front line.

Shortly after the passage of SB3004, the SEC proposed amendments that would eliminate the Reg SHO "grandfather" provision, and narrow the options market maker exemption for certain arbitrage activities. As initially proposed and implemented, any fails to deliver that were in existence before the effective date were excluded from the close out rules.[76] Patrick Byrne also believed the market-maker exemption from the close-out requirement was being abused.

He was instrumental throughout this period in getting national attention for the issue because he was not afraid to, as he often put it, "set your hair on fire." Many people came to think of him as their knight in shining armor, which they could depend on to fix everything. I routinely tried to tell them not to sit back and expect one person to do it all. My affection for Patrick and his "tin-foil hat brigade" began to grow but knowing that everyone else is going to sit back and watch is what really motivated me to escalate my own commitment.

My growing concern was that the pajamahideen would remain passive if everyone thinks that Patrick and Patrick alone can solve the problem in the capital markets. Not only me, but everyone who understood the issues needed to escalate their commitment to making real changes in the financial regulatory system. Patrick understood one thing very well and was in a financial position to use that knowledge: if Wall Street could "buy" journalists, regulators and even Congressmen, so could he.

In March 2006, Patrick gathered a group of friends, colleagues and experts (myself included) to present the issue to members of the US Senate Judiciary Committee. Unfortunately, we were not invited to address the committee despite his best efforts. In the coming months, a variety of Wall Street specialists and Washington cronies would have the chance to tell Congress not to "look behind the curtain" because the Wizards of Wall Street were going to take care of everything.

Undaunted, Patrick hired a D.C. firm specializing in "legislative strategies" to arrange a media event for the team to present some specific allegations of criminal activity behind the naked short sellers besetting Overstock.com's stock prices. Patrick really enjoyed naming the groups he organized; this one is dubbed "Team Scorpion." One aide from the Department of Justice was at the event, but no one from the legislative offices came. The event was poorly attended and not widely reported. The focus on criminal activity in stock manipulation pushed aside any talk of regulatory reform. Patrick's obsession with the criminal side of the issue will come back to haunt him; eventually his accusations will get too far ahead of his evidence.

Online interview for The Sanity Check

In March, April and July 2006 I was interviewed by "Bob O'Brien," a pseudonym used by the anonymous author of an online blog called "The Sanity Check." The website, www.thesanitycheck.com is no longer active. Portions of the interview were reposted on various message boards. For example, several questions were posted to The Motley Fool.

The rest of the interview questions are harder to find online. What follows are the questions I received from Bob O'Brien and my written responses, which were posted in their entirety to his website as a three-part serial. The interview provides a window into the thinking typical of the "crusaders" or "pajamahideen" and their general approach to seeking answers. My relevant expertise is in post-trade clearing and settlement. Since I was being presented to the readers of Sanity Check as an expert in this interview, I declined to answer questions that went outside the scope of my direct knowledge and experience. Some of the questions have technical elements; I tried to address enough of the technical information in the Primer and throughout the remainder of the text to avoid adding too many editorial notes to this material. I apologize if some of it is still opaque but, again, I want to provide the reader with some insight to the thinking that was driving the pajamahideen.

I agreed to this interview for two reasons. First, Patrick Byrne was providing content to the website (e.g. slides that he used to explain naked short selling and systemic risk; he called it the "Dark Side of the Looking Glass" slideshow series). His focus remained, naturally, on the events as he saw them from the CEO's chair at a public company. I hoped to expand the dialogue to include the inadequacy of the regulatory regime to address settlement failures. The second reason was my growing affection for the motley crew of the pajamahideen – for all the misinformed opinions, and often foul rants and rages against the brokers, they were actively attempting to correct an intractable problem. Among them were the ultimate investors and shareholders who truly believed that they were taking part in the capitalist process that rewards American entrepreneurs.

-------START FIRST SERIES OF INTERVIEW QUESTIONS------

(1) **Some have expressed the sentiment that you are a whistleblower, and that it is high time a whistleblower came forward. Do you consider yourself a whistleblower?**

Legal protection for whistleblowers is reserved for those who take on the government. Otherwise, you would at least be employed by the party you are decrying. I would not meet either of those qualifications. Since I have never left a share of stock with a broker (once you've seen how the sausage is being made, you never eat it again), I cannot claim to have been individually harmed by the activity. Of course, if DTCC attempts to withhold my pension because I talked about their role in this mess, then I might have a claim to "whistleblower" status. We'll have to wait an undisclosed number of years before I am eligible to test the matter.

I am on my second career, working full time as an independent researcher and consultant in economics and finance. Although capital markets and corporate finance are in my research portfolio, I addressed the specific topic of NSS at the request of paying clients beginning in late 2003. Since that time, I have worked and will continue to work as an advisor and consultant on NSS for a variety of firms. What it comes down to is that someone pays me to give them direct advice on NSS; when I make public statements it's usually not for hire but rather in the interest of civic education. Part of my marketing strategy is to be sure all the constituencies interested in NSS know that I can help them. I apply a similar strategy to my other areas of specialization such as international finance and economic analysis of law.

(2) **Given your background there, what do you make of the current FTD [fails to deliver] issue – let's start with, why does the DTCC keep all the data secret?**

As the saying goes, "Macy's doesn't tell Gimble." DTCC keeps certain data private so that, for example, Shearson will not be able to figure out Merrill's business strategies. All the Participants compete with each other, so DTCC is careful about data that might reveal firm-specific holdings or transactions. That said, there is much aggregate data that the DTCC could release that would not reveal any trade secrets but that would identify the real magnitude of the problem.

(3) **Some refer to the SBP [stock borrow program] as a "self-replenishing, anonymous lending pool." Would you agree with this characterization?**

Yes. It is definitely anonymous (unless rules are being broken). And since nothing prevents the buyer who receives a borrowed share for settlement from depositing shares into the lending pool at the Depository, it is self-replenishing.

(4) **The DTCC takes great pains to make it clear that the SBP doesn't allow a broker to lend the same share twice via the SBP. My**

contention is that they certainly allow the same share to be lent by different brokers, thus their rhetoric is disingenuous. Do you agree, or disagree?

It's a word game. The stock borrow program does not track who lent the share (only who borrowed it). So the stock borrow program does not allow *any* shares to be lent…only borrowed, get it? They play the same word game when they say they do not make money on the stock borrow program. They don't. What they *do* make money on is the stock *lending* program. OK, so the same shares aren't lent twice by the same broker because the lender's account is reduced by the number of loaned shares until the loan is repaid. Fine. What they aren't saying is that the shares are a "fungible mass," and no one keeps track of which share was used to settle which trade. So, a Participant who receives 100 shares of OSTK [Overstock.com] at settlement could be getting 50 borrowed shares. And it is those 50 shares that can be loaned a second time.

(5) **I believe that most of the current FTD issue is caused by two things – the de-linking of clearing and settling, and the allowing of access to the proceeds from a failed delivery over and above collateralization requirements. Would you agree, or disagree, and care to comment on any other issues you feel are contributors to this?**

It depends. Are you referring to the release of collateral on borrowed stock as the price of the shares is driven into the ground? Are you referring to the fact that the seller gets paid for a failed delivery because of net settlement and the ever present "fungible mass"? I see the FTD issue as additive to the NSS issue and the stock lending issue. In other words, I see the problem as being at least three times as big as any one observer is willing to admit.

The over-arching problem actually got much worse when clearing and settlement (in the form of NSCC and DTC) were connected under DTCC. Think blue suited brokers at NSCC and grey suited bankers at DTC. NSCC was run by the trading side where net settlement minimized the number of cash and share deliveries to one per day (basically). DTC on the other hand was like a bank for brokers; it's where they keep the shares they need to effect settlement. DTC's status as a quasi-bank provided more regulators and more oversight. Both NSCC and DTC had different Boards, populated from different sides of the houses, with different interests. When they brought them together, it appears that the blue suits won and their Wall Street Cowboy mentality is dominating the organization.

That said, I always believed that they should not have been separated at birth. It is my opinion that there were two dominant personalities at the time and each aggressively sought to have their own area of authority. After those guys retired, the door was open to reunite the two sides. Unfortunately, by then they had grown to be very different. Perhaps because of weak understanding on the part of the Federal Reserve and the SEC about what these two do, the clearing side was allowed to dominate and with that "trust" was no longer the middle name.

(6) **Do you have any opinion as to how large the "ex-clearing" FTD situation is versus the "in-system" FTDs? A ratio?**

The by-the-rules version of market infrastructure dictates that the ex-clearing portion should be very small, maybe 15% of the whole problem. In fact, since the clearing system enables NSS, FTD and stock loan, there's no reason to go ex-clearing with the dirty deeds. However, the entire operation can be accelerated if there is at least one ex-clearing transaction. Therefore, the ex-clearing portion would be about 30% of the problem.

(7) **Any opinion as to how large the total grandfathered position of FTDs was?**

Big enough to give me nightmares.

------START SECOND SERIES OF INTERVIEW QUESTIONS----

(8) **What can we in the U.S. learn from either securities regulation or safeguarding the settlement process from other securities markets in Europe or Asia? Are there routine procedures taken for granted elsewhere (such as providing daily information on short positions) that are somehow ignored or avoided here?**

Fundamentally, Western European capital markets did develop somewhat independently of the US. (An example would be France, which is quite different from the US market because of the different basis in law.) Capital markets in Eastern Europe and Asia, on the other hand, were developed based on the US model. (One notable exception is Malaysia where Islamic capital markets are quite well developed.)

However, when it comes to the processes, procedures and even the computer systems that make up the operational infrastructure of global capital markets, the US is the model — they have what we have. Two factors contributed to this state. First, the sheer size of US capital markets made them so dominant that foreign markets found it necessary to build compatible systems. (We are also notoriously slow to adapt to foreign influence. Can you spell "metric system"?) The other factor is the generous nature of the US taxpayer: we financed, via foreign aid, the development of capital markets in virtually every country beyond the G7 [Group of Seven major industrialized countries]. I worked in Russia and can tell you that we refused to give them shorts or stock lending in 1994 because of the known risk factors.

(9) **Enron went straight down once the bad news broke — and there was likely naked short selling going on. Likewise, WorldCom and Delta Airlines might be other candidates. All had hundreds of millions of shares outstanding--and if naked selling is as rampant in such situations as many think, then there may have been billions of share 'rights' outstanding when they were de-listed. Do you:**
  i. **feel these issues would be good targets for a post hoc forensic examination;**
  ii. **consider that there is any possibility of success in doing a forensic exam, in demonstrating to what degree naked short selling played a role in their demise;**
  iii. **and if so how would you proceed with an in-depth forensic examination, the goal of which would be to lay proof of widespread naked short selling before investors who collectively lost billions, possibly due to the practice?**

The primary difference I see in Enron and WorldCom, compared to the NSS cases I'm aware of, is that those companies were heavily "touted" in the mainstream media before their collapses. Did anyone *not* know what

Ken Lay and Bernie Ebbers looked like before their companies collapsed? On the other hand, I'm a big hockey fan and I did not know that Melnyck owned the Ottawa Senators before I read the Gradient Analytics, Inc. hatchet job.[77] Also, most people are now convinced that criminal activity was taking place at Enron; I don't know that we'll find anything at Biovail that rises to that level.

The forensic accounting for Biovail is pretty straightforward: compare the hatchet job to the financial statements and find the lies. This wouldn't work on Enron or WorldCom because the lies are in the financial statements.

The share "rights", "entitlements" or "phantoms" are another matter altogether. The forensic accounting would look the same for every company because it wouldn't involve their financial statements.

(10) Do you think the DTCC has any valid reason(s) for declining to disclose data and information on the extent of FTDs either as to the market in general, or as to specific companies affected by the FTDs? If so, what is the reason(s)?

From their standpoint, disclosing who failed-to-deliver would be like your bank disclosing details of your bounced checks. Continuing the analogy, your bank is required to disclose certain data that reveals the risks they face (bad debts, for example). In that sense, it would behoove the DTCC to report to someone (whether or not the information is "public") how much they are owed, by whom and for what in order for real risk analysis to take place. The Federal Reserve Bank (fiscal agent for the US government, the government's bank, if you will) does disclose aggregate information about the risk in the banking system so why shouldn't DTCC do this for the capital markets?

As for disclosing FTDs by company, the analogy to banking fails to provide the answer. The Fed (and hence their member banks) all own shares in the same issue: US currency. So whatever fail information is disclosed in banking is disclosed on the same issuer.

The question then becomes: what can be gained by knowing which issues are undelivered? Clearly, as an investor I would like to have this in my information set. The parties who are failing know the identity of the issues; I'm at a disadvantage to them based on information that they not only know but they have in fact caused. That's the worst possible scenario for anyone working with a model of perfect capital markets, which requires that information be free and freely available.

(11) Do you view the DTCC's Stock Borrow Program [SBP] as a tool designed to serve the purpose and motive of naked short selling? Or has it just turned out that way? Note that this presumes that the SBP is a large facilitator – correct me if that is wrong.

SBP (at subsidiary NSCC and SLP, the stock lending program at DTC) was not designed to serve NSS. It was designed to reduce risk in the system by guaranteeing delivery of shares to every buyer in the event a seller could not honor its total obligation. While trade-for-trade settlement would leave only a singer buyer at risk for the actions of a single seller, net settlement spreads this risk to uninvolved parties. Therefore, the centralized system required a method, like SBP/SLP, to accommodate fails that made it all the way to settlement date.

(12) In your opinion, what would be the effects (on shareholders, broker-dealers, hedge funds and others) of an SEC ruling that all FTDs be bought in upon expiration of 10 days after the trade?

I believe that there must be a time limit for FTDs, as well as a time limit for stock loans. As I told the audience at the November 29, 2005 forum held by the North American Securities Administrators, there is no such thing as an innocent fail. There is also no such thing as a strategic fail because failing to settle a trade is not a strategy – it *is* a failure of strategy.

The impact on shareholders would be beneficial – they would get what they actually paid for. Right now, they own phantom shares until the fail is cleared and in the meantime, the broker gets to play with their money for free.

The impact on the broker-dealers would be that they'd have to find a new source for free money, poor things! Seriously, if they've become dependent on this source of cash there would be a shakeout in the industry. There is likely a complete lack of knowledge at the retail level that would have to be corrected in order to maintain customer relations under the new paradigm.

The hedge funds should not have major difficult with this because it is their business to arbitrage risk. Any hedge fund worth its salt would be able to manage under the new system just as well as it does now. How does a hedge fund hedge if the risks are hidden? The best funds should actually flourish under a system where the rules are clearly defined and well-understood.

The impact on others? There will be mass hara-kiri at the SEC and the DTCC before they put a limit on FTDs, so those organizations will need to embark on major recruiting campaigns to replace their fallen leaders.

(13) **Why do you think SEC chairman Donaldson chose to answer Senator Bennett's inquiries regarding naked short selling in closed session rather than in public?**

Because he knows it's a problem and couldn't admit it in public without having his ceremonial knife handy. Because he knows that the problem described by NSS includes the problem of phantom shares, the proxy voting charade and the collapse of corporate governance.

(14) **Please elaborate on the companies that are almost completely destroyed by naked shorting especially on the OTC. I hear rumors of some of these stocks having two to three times the outstanding shares being short. Is this rumor true?**

Why stop at three? No one has yet proved that there is a limit to the multiplication, though there is a theory that some reporting requirements might stall the process after one month.

Keep in mind that it's not just that the shares are shorted. It's also that they are loaned and the loans are not repaid. It's also that shares are not delivered for the settlement of trades, yet the retail brokerage customer accounts reflect the phantom shares. Economics 101: if you increase the supply, you decrease the price.

It's not a rumor, it's a fact. It's a fact that the STA and the Business Roundtable [US association of chief executive officers] have been talking to the NYSE, the DTCC and the SEC about for a decade. Read Drummond's article in the April 2006 issue of Bloomberg Markets (p.96) [See Drummond, 2006]. Important corporate governance issues, including corporate sales and mergers, are already being controlled by criminal elements.

(15) What is the corporate structure of Cede & Co.? Is it a trust? What is the jurisdiction (it doesn't show up on a search for NY companies)? Are securities registered to Cede pledge as security in any way? Why does Cede and its assets not show up in the DTCC annual report?

There is no trust company named Cede, no "company" in fact named Cede. Cede & Co. is a nominee name. It originated in the acronym "CD" which stood for something like "central deposits." It was the name of the department at the NYSE that was the predecessor to the DTC which is now a subsidiary of the DTCC. You should simply look for Depository Trust Company. Shares registered to Cede & Co basically belong to the Participants who have shares on deposit at DTC.

(16) If a US participant buys from the Canadian Depository for Securities [CDS], does the trade always fail? The CDS position size will stay identical on position reports over time (once you net incoming/outgoing certificates into CDS). That seems impossible. Shouldn't some trades go into Canada or out of Canada? It seems that that is where much naked shorting comes from. The US participant goes "where are my shares?" and they say, "don't worry about it, they're in Canada".

CDS is the DTC of Canada, so DTC participants buy from CDS participants (not from CDS). Each depository has an account at the other depository that looks, for all intents and purposes, like another participant account. When I was with the Pacific (see "Part One" of interview), we had an account at DTC which was used for inter-depository settlement. So when CDS participants trade with DTC participants, there is a net settlement position for shares and cash between the two depositories that is settled out each day. The shares are always left in place, physically, for the sake of "immobilization." Periodically, shares are withdrawn from one depository and re-registered for delivery to the other in order to manage the local inventory of share certificates. I remember getting a panicked call from ITT when they say a massive movement of shares from Chicago (Midwest depository) to Cede – they wanted to know who in New York was buying up their shares and were they mounting a takeover attempt. The reality was that DTC was doing a drawdown of inventory from the Midwest, nothing more.

Trades done with CDS participants do not always fail. I've forgotten the specific account names, but there should be a separate CDS account at DTC to reflect inventory (versus the position left behind after settlement). It's when the inventory and the position diverge substantially that certificates are usually moved.

While there are differences in the short selling rules in Canada that can create problems beyond what we already have in the US, it is not necessary to have trades with Canada to generate phantom shares.

(17) **Am I correct that the NSCC obligation to deliver shares to the net long participants is independent from the net short participant's obligation to the NSCC? In other words, if the seller flees, wouldn't the NSCC be on the hook for the shares?**

The NSCC does put itself in the middle, so to speak, of every settlement obligation. In that sense, if any participant walks away from any obligation, the NSCC is on the hook. Their first line of defense is the participant fund, to which each user contributes an amount which is based on their activity.

(18) **I had drinks with a person who is expert in clearing on Friday. He said Patrick should do a rollback (he could always do a forwards split later) and change his CUSIP number. Is my friend right that this would force the system to reconcile all the claims into real shares?**

No, your friend's suggestion could result in the issue being frozen at DTCC.

(19) **How can any stock holder be sure he's holding genuine shares, as opposed to counterfeit? (Certificate holders excepted, of course.)**

Many issuers offer Direct Registration for investors: no certificate, electronic access to the market and you are registered with the issuer. Unfortunately, according to the Securities Transfer Association, the electronic access portion is poorly developed at the broker level; there is little or no training at the retail level; and the costs are borne entirely by the issuer. But if you have direct ownership, on the books of the issuer, there can be no question of your genuine shares.[78]

---------START THIRD SERIES OF INTERVIEW QUESTIONS-----

(20) How can anyone who borrows stock know that his borrow is not counterfeit? Every borrowed share is part of the counterfeit scheme until the loan is repaid with bona fide shares.

Actually, it's the loaned shares that are phony. With the borrowed shares comes the right to vote and the right to receive dividends. These rights are relinquished by the lender, according to industry practice. Unfortunately, industry practice has not included telling you about this. Read on.

(21) What is your opinion on the effect that entitlements have had on the voting of proxies or where shareholders never get to vote their shares because the number of votes far exceeds the outstanding shares?

My opinion is that it sucks for the shareholder! What I know about it is much worse than you may even realize. Here's a link to a document put out by the Securities Industry Association that explains exactly how shareholder's votes are NOT counted and their plans to keep it that way: [NOTE: the link is no longer valid. The document is provided in Chapter 8 of Part IV as an attachment to my comments on SEC proposal S7-12-06].

Here's a sampling of just how bad the situation of over-voting really is in 2006 as reported by the guys counting the votes:

If you don't complain about this, if you don't let out a "mighty yelp" then you will continue to read news articles with lines like this one from the Financial Times, published July 5 2006:

"...More obviously, somewhere along the chain, people would be hurting. For example, brokers, having to make their clients whole, would be kicking up a tremendous fuss. Since this does not seem to be the case, it is hard to believe naked shorting is the bogeyman some claim it to be." (Quote from Securities Transfer Association) [See Chapter 6 in Part III.]

(22) Why does the system not require/verify that a short seller actually has shares available, either owned or borrowed, at the *initiation* of the transaction, and prevent the transaction from proceeding if no shares are available?

The SEC generally believes that broker-dealers may need to facilitate customer orders in a fast moving market and so cannot tolerate the delays associated with actually obtaining shares for sale. In fact, even the "locate" rules as revised under Regulation SHO are full of exceptions to reduce the burden of complying with the locate rule. (The word "exception" appears 88 times in the 24 page final-rulemaking.)

(23) Why does the SEC assist the DTCC in preventing the public from acquiring their own company trading information?

The answer to that question, unfortunately, may be in the political realm. From my own experience, the SEC doesn't know much more about DTCC than you do. They surely know less about it than I do. DTCC simply writes rules that the SEC rubberstamps after a perfunctory comment period. Some people have suggested that because the major banks and brokers sit on the board of the DTCC, and management at the SEC often comes from the same group (or has designs on getting there after their tenure), top-level management does not wants to rock the boat.

(24) What politicians in Congress do you feel are most responsible for holding back NSS reform?

Certainly the Banking Committee is at fault. The Securities Transfer Association and the Business Roundtable have made several attempts to get them to look at the proxy problems caused by short sellers and stock lending. That Committee has consistently rejected their request for help. The same goes for the Financial Services Committee. So take a look at who has served on those committees over the last ten years and you'll have the list.

(25) How involved do you feel the White House is in solving the NSS issue?

I doubt anyone there will get past "naked" without a giggle-fest.

(26) Do you believe Dr. Byrne/Overstock is moving in the best possible direction to resolve his problems with NSS? If not, what would you be doing?

Overstock has problems that go beyond Naked Short Sellers. If the problem were just short sellers, then the dilution of share value and shareholder rights could be corrected when the shorts are covered and the market price moved toward the real value of the firm. But when fails are added to the picture, then the shorts have no incentive to cover. The trade is allowed to remain unsettled indefinitely; there is no margin call because there is no loan. Finally, even where stock lending takes place, the problems are only compounded. Now not only does the original owner of the shares believe they have a right to vote and receive dividends, but the person who received borrowed shares at settlement thinks the same thing. And the SIA admits that they haven't been telling customers that they don't get to vote when their shares are on loan (even though the broker doesn't have to tell the customer when they are lending the shares); and now the customer whose shares are lent is going to get a tax bill from the IRS because "payments in lieu of dividends" are not subject to the dividend exclusion. I tell you as a fact: the Securities Transfer Association and the Business Roundtable have been fighting the proxy side of this for decades. They started at the exchange who told them that proxies are processed through DTCC so it isn't the NYSE's problem; they went through the DTCC who said they were only following rules approved by the SEC; and when they got to the SEC in 2004 they were told: "who cares who votes the shares." The SEC's philosophy is to intercept over-reporting before the issuers sees the over-voting. In other words, they want to hide it away so they can go on denying there's a rhino behind the couch.

A lot of other companies are being awakened to the problem of Naked Short Selling as a result of what they saw during this round of annual meetings. Once they are aware that the proxy problems are only the symptom of the broader issues of shorts, fails and loans, Dr. Byrne should find plenty of company moving in the same direction.

(27) **Do you think hedge funds are properly regulated? If not, what needs to change?**

I have to agree with Marty Fridson (http://www.martinfridson.com), one of the best known financial analysts in New York. He recently wrote: "'Hedge funds to the rescue' is reminiscent of 'Milken is the savior'." Hedge funds have avoided regulation thus far because many academics and politicians believe that they play some pivotal role in the capital markets. Marty declaims the myth that "(t)he default rate will not go as high as in the past cycle because financing from hedge funds will enable many companies to avoid bankruptcy."

(28) **What person or persons have the most control over the DTCC *above* the DTCC BoD?**

The Board of Directors at DTCC is made up of member broker-dealers and banks. So the next higher authority would be the Boards at those banks and brokers.

(29) **Do you own stock in *any* company? If so, do you hold the certificates?**

I have owned some shares of Xerox since about 1989. I do not have a certificate. I am directly registered as an owner with Xerox; that is, I have a book-entry account on the issuer's records. This is commonly known as Direct Registration and thousands of companies offer this form of ownership.

(30) **A broker friend describes the NSS debacle as the "scandal of civilization". How bad do you think the situation is, and what is the worst case scenario if we continue down the track we are on presently?**

The problem is more than naked short selling. The problem is three-fold: shorts, loans and fails. When a stock is sold, regardless of whether the trade is marked "short", if the shares aren't presented at settlement, there are problems created in the customer's accounts when they are given what are called "entitlements". If the fail (or legal short) is covered with borrowed shares, the situation is made worse when a voting or dividend record date passes because no one seems to be able to keep track of who owns what anymore.

If we continue down this path I see two outcomes. One is that companies and investors lose confidence in the capital markets and take their transactions private. We are already seeing a mass exodus of small and medium sized enterprises from public capital markets due to the high cost of Sarbanes-Oxley compliance. This leaves fewer choices in the market place for investors. Also, when investors understand that they are not being treated fairly under the rules of the capital markets, they will seek alternative investments (other assets, or perhaps foreign markets). With the departure of both issues and investors, liquidity will suffer as the markets become narrow and shallow.

The other outcome is that the manipulation allows criminals or others who may have the intention of disrupting the US economy to gain control of US corporations. There was a big fuss in the media and in Washington over foreign ownership of US ports. Yet there is nothing to stop anyone from taking control of a US corporation by generating enough phantom share entitlements that they could vote in changes in ownership and control (mergers, buy-outs, etc.).

(31) **As a simple "commoner", what are the top *three* things I can do to fight the NSS problem, *besides* write my Congressperson and physically hold share certificates?**

1) Inform yourself; read Section 8 of the Uniform Commercial Code[79] or search an online database like ProQuest at your local public library for a good summary of it; read Regulation SHO, including the footnotes and comment letters. 2) Write letters to the editor when you see short sellers and hedge funds being displayed as saviors of the capital markets; or anytime you see the issues being misrepresented. 3) When I worked in Russia, if we had an important meeting that we had to take the Russian team members to, we always gave them one piece of advice: wear dark socks. Nothing looks worse than white socks under a black suit. What I mean is: Be careful of the impression you leave on the people you meet and talk to about the issues. Get to the facts quickly

when you talk to media, politicians, and neighbors. Don't expect them to care about your problem as much as you do. Use the WIIFM approach: everyone you talk to will want to know "What's In It For Me." You have to address it that way to keep anyone's attention.

One more thing: you limit the ability of regulators and politicians to respond to you when you try to sum up the problem as just "naked short selling". It's a nice piece of short-hand when you want to find out if someone has heard about it, but it doesn't do justice to the real problem. Remember: shorts, fails and loans. Although a combination of shorts and fails without loans generates the same result as naked short sales, even one of the three alone can disrupt the financial system.

(32) If the stock borrow program of the DTCC is designed to cover temporary difficulties in obtaining the stock, why is the duration of the borrow not limited to, say, ten days?

This is a question that DTCC and the SEC should be made to answer. Unfortunately, since they can't even seem to get trades to settle in any finite timeframe, it's unlikely they'll consider limiting the duration of stock loans.

(33) We've heard words like "endemic" and "common" to describe FTD issues. Given that, what does that mean? Are there lots of FTD's but concentrated in a few stocks or is it a few FTD's spread all around?

As many of you may already know, Leslie Boni had access to data on fails from DTCC while she was a research fellow at the SEC. Using that report and additional data from the SEC and the stock exchanges, Robert Shapiro found "evidence that as few as ten or less NYSE and NASDAQ threshold securities may account for as many as two-thirds of fails among exchange-listed threshold stocks, and 20 or fewer NYSE and NASDAQ threshold companies may account for as much as 75% of all fails among listed securities." Clearly, some companies have more than their share of fails.

But don't be fooled into thinking that means the problem is limited. What is happening to Overstock today could happen to Xerox tomorrow or Apple on Thursday. There is nothing in the infrastructure or regulation of the capital markets in the US that would prevent it. The only limiting factor being discussed by the experts is the total cash commitment necessary to take down a company (relative to how much cash the company needs to outlast the short sellers). With the trillions of dollars available in the hedge funds, the upper-limit may be quite high.

(34) When these issues have been raised within the DTCC, what has been the reaction? As an SRO, how can they not act?

I was told "You can't balance the world." They trivialize the magnitude of the problem by, for example, comparing the value of failed trades on one day to all trades settled in a year. A Financial Times reporter recently wrote, "The Securities and Exchange Commission, for instance, says that the average daily 'fails to deliver' are down some 34 per cent from January 2005 to May 2006 compared with April to December 2004." Why compare the activity of 17 months to that of eight months? It looks like someone really had to stretch to find a comparison with a decline. So when trivializing doesn't work, they go for obfuscation.

Don't forget that a company like Bank of New York (BoNY) is a transfer agent, a broker and a bank. So the BoNY transfer agent lets out a might yelp about over-voting caused by short selling and stock lending. Meanwhile, the BoNY broker is making a killing on short sales and the BoNY banker is making money hand-over-fist on stock lending. These are the firms whose employees are on the Boards at the SROs. They have no incentive to change anything.

(35) You set up clearing and settling for Russia. If you had carte blanche to reform the US system, what changes would you implement?

First, do not tolerate failure to settle – period. If it's not finished by T+10, buy it in and if you can't buy it, you have to bust the trade. Next there has to be a time limit on stock loans; and under no circumstances should a loan remain open over a record date. Finally, require short sellers to go out and borrow the stock before the sale; with all the electronic interfaces around, I find it hard to believe that the two could not be done nanoseconds apart, thereby avoiding delays in trade execution.

These ideas only address the most urgent needs for reform. However, if we don't fix the big leak, it will be too late to worry about the little cracks.

(36) Many on Wall Street pay lip service to the idea that transparency makes for a more efficient market, though they don't seem to practice that. Would transparency in FTDs make for more efficient markets? What would the outcome be, in the short term, and after a few years of FTD transparency?

Eliminating trade failures as a trading strategy would make for a more efficient market. How long do you think a product market would survive if sellers were permitted to take money from customers and not deliver the goods? The purpose of demanding transparency in FTD data is to be able to combat the acceptance of trade failures as a business practice.

(37) We've been portrayed as a bunch of nutcases. Are we?

I haven't met all of you, so it's hard to say. Jeffrey Dahmer's neighbors thought he was a nice, quite young man…. I will say that this problem is very real, very dangerous and very difficult to fix.

Chapter 12. Publicity Ramps Up

In January 2006, the head of a media company in New Jersey that was victimized by phantom shares asked for my help with a presentation to the New Jersey Senate Judiciary Committee at the confirmation hearing for Bradley Abelow to become State Treasurer. Abelow previously held a position on the Board of Directors at DTCC for four years while he was employed with Goldman Sachs. The press called him a "Manhattan millionaire" and "friend of Governor Corzine" Some reporters noted that New Jersey Governor Jon Corzine was also a Goldman alumnus: co-chief executive officer of Goldman, Sachs & Co with future US Treasury Secretary Henry Paulson Jr. According to the *Wall Street Journal*,[80] when Corzine resigned his post at Goldman it came "against a backdrop of the firm's recent fixed-income trading losses and its controversial plans for an initial public offering."[81] None of that was favorable for Abelow.

Initially, the New Jersey entrepreneur wanted RS to speak at the hearing, again, because of his former Washington D.C. title. However, RS declined to speak because our invitation came from the office of the New Jersey Senate Republicans and RS was a Democratic Operative. I was selected to head up the team, which made sense to me since I was the only one who could speak directly to activity at DTC/DTCC that might be relevant to Abelow's qualifications. We were given five minutes each to present points on "DTCC lax enforcement", "allows for stock manipulation", and "hurts small investors".

Senator John Adler was the head of the committee, but our meetings were mostly with aids from the Senate Republicans Office. I had a chance to talk to Senator Gerald Cardinale (R-NJ29, Demarest) before the meeting began. As I started to explain the impact of phantom shares on corporate governance, Senator Cardinale said to me something that I had heard a thousand times before: "That can't be true. I signed my proxy card; I checked off my choices and I sent it to my broker. Surely, he cast my votes according to my instructions." Here, again, was an educated individual in public service, in a position to make a difference who was not aware that this is taking place. I am coming to realize that if we have to explain this to one person at a time, it will never get fixed.

The hearing was held on February 23, 2006 at the capitol building in Trenton. The details of my testimony are part of the public record. I provided a package of documents to the Committee, including::

- A non-technical summary of Leslie Boni's paper, "Strategic Delivery Failures in U.S. Equity Markets"
- An excerpt on the loss of shareholder voting rights from the transcript of the North American Securities Administrators Association, Inc. public forum held November 30, 2005.
- Excerpts on the role of stock lending in the loss of shareholder voting rights from the Securities Transfer Association, Inc. Newsletter articles and White Paper.
- "Proposal to make DTC stock lender causes participant angst," article from *Operations Management*, April 2002. [82]

The gist of what I offered was to point out the perspective from my experience at DTC:

- By the time of this hearing, it was widely known that there are failures to deliver securities that last for years.
- The New York Stock Exchange (NYSE) publicly admitted that using the DTCC's stock lending program to cover up these failures resulted in the violation of their own "one share/one vote" rule.

- The result of this neglect on the part of the DTCC to close long-term outstanding stock loans has resulted in virtually universal over-voting in matters of corporate governance.

I made it clear to the Committee that DTCC is fully aware that stock lending and fails to deliver are intimately linked and that they create problems for investors who want to vote their shares. While I worked at DTC, I saw an extensive management information system (MIS), where reports on problem items are routinely produced, sorted by age and value. High value items are given first priority for resolution. MIS reports are delivered to a senior clerk for follow up on a regular basis. When stock loan is used to cover a failure at settlement, a telephone call is usually placed to the failing broker if the loan is not paid back in a timely manner. The first calls go something like, "Hi, I need you to close that loan by sending in the stock now." To which the answering senior clerk at the broker/dealer replies, "My customer mailed the certificates to me this morning; I should have it in a couple of weeks." That response puts off the follow up call for a while and the DTC senior clerk moves down the list, which contains hundreds of items every day. In the meantime, anyone with opportunity and motive can manipulate the price of the stock downward so that the second call does not come in two weeks, because the lower value of the item has dropped it lower and lower in priority on the MIS report.

Some of the same companies that provide voting services (known as proxy services) have broker/dealer arms that are themselves members of DTCC and that also hold seats on the Board of Directors. Unfortunately, the DTCC historically has been able to ignore problems brought forward by the STA when they conflict with the desires of the broker/dealer members. And the STA regularly backs down from this fight because DTCC is the largest registered shareholder for the companies the transfer agents service. If the agent does not do things the way DTCC wants them, the DTCC is in the position to make it exceedingly difficult for the transfer agents and registrars by putting into place aggressive demands for expensive automation or restrictive rules and procedures that end up costing the STA members. Transfer agents cannot pass the cost on to their customers because 1) they are usually bound by long term contracts to provides services to companies and 2) the NYSE has rules that prohibit the transfer agents from charging shareholders for their services.

How do you explain year-long failures to settle without pointing to management at DTCC. It hurts small businesses seeking access to capital markets by allowing unsettled trades to be covered with borrowed shares that are then re-sold and re-loaned until the number of phantom shares in circulation surpasses the number allowed by the articles of incorporation filed with the Secretary of State, including the Department of Corporations in New Jersey. Furthermore, it takes away the rights of shareholders to exercise control over companies by voting their shares. In fact, it leaves shareholders with only one option, to vote with their feet, an option that will lead to unwelcome volatility in the stock market. DTCC's failure to enforce the close out of stock lending and their failure to enforce final settlement is being used by stock price manipulators to generate phantom shares which, through the most basic laws of supply and demand, depress the prices of stocks by increasing the supply of shares.

There was not a lot of media coverage on our presentations, but one article posted on NorthJersey.com would draw out DTCC in an unexpected way, which I return to in Chapter 15. DTCC did not dispute anything I said that day in Trenton, but they would take issue with the way my work experience was being represented in the media. They did not dispute what I gave as my title while working at the Depository, but they took issue with the way it was reported in newspapers and on the internet.

Media, mainstream and otherwise

There is not room here to discuss all the media coverage but I will try to cover the most significant. Many of the interviews I did during this period were requested on the subject of "naked short selling." I knew it was the topic that the media believed the public would most easily understand. Even as I was finishing writing this book, when I Googled "Naked, Short and Greedy" the first page of results were all on "naked short selling" – topics related to naked sex did not come up until at least page two. When I agreed to the interviews, I would have them add "systemic capital market problems and settlement failures" to the topic list. The reader can find a lot of material on the Internet by searching my name with any of those phrases.

It seemed like every other member of the pajamahideen was creating (and paying for) websites, writing letters to editors, calling reporters with ideas for stories, even gathering on the streets with posters and sign-boards, handing out flyers. Some of the pajamahideen did not want to be recognized in public. It got to the point where reporters would offer me anonymity when they called for background information. Since DTCC had already outed me with a press release clarifying my employment record (Chapter 15), I had no reason to request to remain anonymous. In fact, I would not spend time with reporters unless they agreed to quote me (and hopefully spell my name right and get my title correct!).

A wave of naked short selling stories appeared in *The New York Times, Fortune, The Financial Times, The New York Post, The Street.com*; and on 60 Minutes and CNBC. Weekly, if not daily articles on "naked short selling" started showing up in *Economist, Euromoney, Forbes, Washington Post,* and *Wall Street Journal*. There were radio interviews, too. For example, I appeared on the *Christian Financial Radio Network* (CFRN) for programs that included open phone lines to take questions from listeners.[83] I was on *Street IQ* and *The Faulking Truth*, among others. I also appeared on Radio Liberty and I even did a webinar for Deal Flow Media on how issuers can protect themselves from aggressive stock trading.

CBS News contacted me to review the financial reports on a company they were planning to talk about on 60 Minutes. The company was badly misunderstood. When the company's attorney told CNBC and *Forbes* reporters that financial analysts had issued negative reports about them to instigate an SEC investigation (which would drive down the stock price), the reporters said things like, "Short sellers do that all the time." They made similar comments about analysts being paid by hedge funds to write negative reviews about companies they wanted to short sell. It was as if the only thing the market learned from the Enron-debacle and the ensuing Sarbanes-Oxley Act of Congress was "how to" rather than "not to."

Patrick Byrnes, then CEO of Overstock.com, had one of his staff give my name to Bloomberg TV Producer Gary Matsumoto, who was working on a story that would focus a good part of the program on Patrick's "self-described Public Relations 'jihad' against Wall Street's looting of Main Street." After several iterations, the final title was *Special Report: Phantom Shares*. The idea was to expose the looting of Main Street that Patrick claimed was being conducted by "an alleged cabal of researchers, hedge fund managers and journalists whom have smeared Overstock in order to profit from its tumbling share prices." Many of the journalists that Patrick attacked had been portraying him "as some half-crazed prophet of Wall Street whose tirades are nothing more than a diversionary gambit to distract from the fact that he is … a marginally competent CEO; or worse, 'a whacko.'" Bloomberg TV aired the Special Report during prime-time on March 13, 2006. In the first day after its release, the program reached Number 5 in the Top Favorites and Number 11 in the Most Views lists on Bloomberg's pay television network, which is distributed worldwide to more than 300 million homes and offices. Matsumoto received a Business Emmy nomination for the report, only the second nomination ever for Bloomberg Television.[84]

Although Matsumoto planned to do an hour long program, it was cut to 30 minutes when released. After submitting to interviews for hours in multiple locations in California and New York, only one tangential quote from me appeared in the final cut: my comparison of DTC to "backstage at Wall Street." I usually explain my work in post-trade clearing and settlement this way: It's like working backstage at the theater. If you are behind the scenes in movie making, for example, there are grips and gaffers; if you are doing lighting backstage at the theater you have kliegs and Fresnel and all sorts of different lights. If you are a theater-goer, you pay for a ticket and watch the show. You do not know what a grip or a gaffer is, and you do not know the difference between a klieg and a Fresnel. This does not affect your ability to get what you paid for which is to enjoy the show. However, if we do not know what is happening backstage at Wall Street, this does affect whether or not we make money on our investment, this does affect, in fact, the safety of our investment. It does affect the rights investors have, if we do not understand what is going on in that black box, what is going on backstage at Wall Street.

A long time friend of mine, Bud Burrell, who sent out emails about the program before and after it aired, let me know a couple of months later that he was going to suggest me to Matsumoto for inclusion in any follow-up pieces – Bud had watched the program and did not even realize that I was in it![85] *Phantom Shares* was very timely: when NSCC released their financial statements shortly after the program aired, it showed that fails to deliver had increased 10% from the previous year to $7.5 billion.

The video clip of me in the *Phantom Shares* program was from my keynote address at the Securities Lending Conference in New York that year. After my presentation, titled "Why Investors and Issuers Hate Short Sellers and Stock Lending," a member of the audience asked the first question rhetorically, "Why don't you tell us what you *really* think!" It was during lunch at this event that staff members from Open Market Operations at the Federal Reserve Bank of New York would tell me that they were seeing a significant number of fails to deliver in bond markets, especially in US Treasury bonds. That comment would provide the impetus to produce a research report on trade settlement failures in bond markets which I would present at an international conference on finance and economics. The paper would also be published in an international financial journal (Trimbath 2011). The Securities Lending Conference was another time that DTCC saw an opportunity to out me as an expert on settlement failures (Chapter 15).

Dan Jamieson, a journalist for *Investment News*, a newspaper/magazine that caters to the financial advisory community, contacted me for a story about the SEC's inaction on "'naked' short selling."[86] Although the focus of the article was short selling, he did quote Dave Patch, who had been following the fails to deliver data, and said that it had been increasing since late 2005, despite an initial drop after Reg SHO was enacted. I seized the opportunity to send in a comment letter to get the focus back on fails to deliver. The *Investment News* carried my letter to the editor on June 25, 2007 under the heading "Naked shorting's crux: BD failure to deliver." I pointed out that Jamieson neglected to describe how the problem was created, which was important because, if investors don't understand the root cause, they would "continue to chase red herrings like the grandfather clause and to blame amorphous entities such as hedge funds until the damage is so far beyond the ability of the broker-dealer community to make restitution that it will take an act of Congress to repair."

As long as the broker-dealers own the central clearing and settlement organization in the US, I continued, they know they won't be required to deliver shares at settlement. I also took exception to a quote in the article from a securities attorney that "Another catastrophic event like 9/11 could induce naked shorters [sic] to take advantage of a panicked market." That is simply wrong. I wrote: "According to the Federal Reserve Bank of New York, we don't have to wait for an event at that level to see a trillion dollars in settlement failures on any given day." While it is true that it happened right after 9/11, it happened again in 2003 and in 2005, without any catastrophic catalyst. "Regardless of any amendments made to SEC Regulation SHO, until something is done to strictly enforce settlement, this problem will persist. Ignoring the source of the problem is no way to find a solution. Worse yet, it holds the danger of lulling investors into inaction. Like a frog in a pot of water on the stove, they won't know they are still in trouble until it is too late."

The FBI calls

My letter in *Investment News* attracted a lot of attention. I recall that it prompted a classmate that I had not heard from since grammar school to seek me out with an email just to say he had read it. Around this time, I received a phone call from a man saying he was an agent with the FBI in New York who would like to talk with me about naked short selling and settlement failures.

I met with the FBI and the US District Attorney in New York; they asked me to keep the content of that meeting confidential. One question they asked me struck me as very odd: they wanted to know if I thought taking peoples' money without delivering their shares would be a crime. So I prepared some handouts with the title: "What's Criminal About Stealin'?" I gave them a binder with seventeen documents, most of which are included in this book.

One thing I wanted to make abundantly clear to them was that the spike in fails to deliver was not related to trading volume, an excuse that the New York Stock Exchange (NYSE) and the DTCC frequently used when confronted with the fails data. That may have been true in the first 25 years of centralized clearing and settlement but things had changed dramatically. Prior to 2002, there was a 76% correlation between market volume and fails to deliver. But, as I said to Wes Christian in 2003, the data shows very clearly that someone began exploiting the lax oversight that allowed fails to occur and to remain open indefinitely. Starting in 2003, the correlation between trade volume and settlement failures dropped to 23%. While trading volume rose by less than one-third in recent years, settlement failures nearly doubled.

	NYSE Volume Traded (Mil)	DTCC Settlement Failures (Thou)
1999-2002	$10,353,482	$3,726,887
2003-2006	$13,338,313	$7,272,155
% Change	28.8%	95.1%

About half way through my presentation, I could see that little dark shadow pass in the space behind their eyes. The question on everyone's mind: What about my savings? What about my retirement money? They knew that ethics would prevent them from using what they just heard to take action for their own personal benefit. But there was nothing to prevent them from asking the question: how can investors protect themselves from this?

Unfortunately, the system of self-regulation in US financial markets leaves the fox guarding the hen house. In 2007, seven companies with 18 employees sitting on the Board of Directors at DTCC (including its subsidiaries), the NYSE and other self-regulatory organizations, had 728 securities rules violations in one year, including 84 violations for rules governing short sales. What hope could there be for the individual investor in search of financial security and the unwary entrepreneur in search of funding in capital markets where the alleged perpetrators are in charge of the organizations that write and enforce the rules?

Company	Regulatory Violations	Violations of Short Sale Rules
Merrill Lynch	242	26
Morgan Stanley	182	22
Goldman Sachs	152	17
JPMorgan Chase	96	7
Edward Jones	41	3
Barclays Capital	8	2
State Street	7	1

Sources: U.S. Securities and Exchange Commission, SEC Action Lookup and Investment Adviser Public Disclosure; National Association of Securities Dealers (now FINRA.org) Broker Check.

Chapter 13. Naked Short and Greedy – the Event

In early 2006, the Chartered Financial Analyst Society of Los Angeles (CFA-LA) cancelled a panel discussion on "concerted failures-to-deliver (FTDs) and naked short selling (NSS)". I and others had agreed to participate and arranged to be in Los Angeles for the June 6 event (see Chapter 14 for more on why the CFA-LA event was cancelled). There were panel discussions and other events on the subject being held in New York and Washington, D.C. but as far as we could tell, there had not been anything on the West Coast. I was based in Santa Monica and, after CFA-LA cancelled, I agreed to arrange for the panel discussion to take place in Los Angeles later that year.[87]

I was able to get the same line-up of speakers, including having Wayne Jett, who originally organized the event for CFA-LA.[88] Wayne, along with CFA-LA Board member Jim Altenbach,[89] was responsible for organizing the event originally planned for June 6. I was joined on the panel by Patrick Byrne and Arne Alsin, the founder and principal of Alsin Capital Management, an Oregon-based investment advisor, and portfolio manager of The Turnaround Fund, a no-load mutual fund.[90] Since neither Patrick nor Arne were based in Southern California we were grateful that they continued to keep their schedules open to us so that we could get the full panel from the original CFA-LA event. We invited representatives from the Depository Trust & Clearing Corporation, the Securities and Exchange Commission and the National Association of Securities Dealers to participate with us. No one from those organizations agreed to come.

After several iterations on the title, including "Short, Naked and Failed: The Damage Done on Wall Street", we settled on the name for the event: "Naked, Short & Greedy: Is Wall Street Abusing the

Practice of Short-Selling Stocks?" Frankly, even if no one in Los Angeles knew what a short sale was or had ever heard of Overstock.com, I figured the title alone would draw a crowd! We filled the event space at the Park Hyatt in Century City with guests from all over California plus five other states, including Nebraska and Virginia. Representatives from the Reason Foundation and the University of California Los Angeles attended along with investors and entrepreneurs – the audience was interesting and interested in the subject.

Press release

2118 Wilshire Blvd. #596, Santa Monica, CA 90403

FOR IMMEDIATE RELEASE

ARE INVESTORS PAYING FOR STOCKS THEY DON'T RECEIVE?

Attend An Eye-Opening Event In Los Angeles on October 19, 2006:

"NAKED, SHORT AND GREEDY: Is Wall Street Abusing Short Sales?"

Los Angeles, CA —What damage is done to investors when the system routinely tolerates stock-delivery failures? Should more be done to stop short-selling abuses?

Two class action lawsuits were filed in April 2006 in Manhattan federal court, by an electronic trading exchange and by a hedge fund, against eleven large prime brokers. The plaintiffs allege the defendants conspired since 2000 to transact short sales without delivering shares to buyers. If true, American investors who paid for tens of millions of corporate shares actually hold nothing but electronic entries.

In 2004, after years of complaints that "naked short sales," *i.e.*, short sales that fail to deliver the shares sold, were systematically attacking and destroying share prices, the Securities & Exchange Commission (SEC) adopted Regulation SHO. But Regulation SHO did not enforce strict requirements to deliver shares in a timely manner. It allowed existing failures to remain undelivered, tacitly permitting lax treatment of stock-delivery failures by brokerages, stock exchanges and clearing organizations.

Important Questions Will be Discussed

Has the SEC's lax enforcement of clearing and settlement procedures created systemic risk in the United States capital markets? Does the failure to provide final delivery for stock trades undercut the rigor of investment analysis and victimize portfolio management? Are billions of dollars in investment value being drained from ordinary investors in the stock market? Does the solution lie in requiring daily reporting on stock-delivery failures and tighter stock borrow requirements? Are pension funds and individual investors already exposed to enormous losses?

These questions and related issues will be discussed by three highly qualified speakers at this enlightening event.

The Panelists

Dr. Patrick Byrne, CEO of NASDAQ-traded Overstock.com, will discuss the effects on a company of high volume trading in "shares" apparently exceeding the number Issued and outstanding, and the unwillingness of Depository Trust & Clearing Corporation to disclose data on stock-delivery failures.

Arne Alsin, portfolio manager and financial writer, will share his insights, reflecting upon how naked short sales generate "phantom" shares, and how this changes the risks and valuations portfolio managers and analysts must consider.

Dr. Susanne Trimbath, a research economist with operations management experience in financial services, will explain how abusive trading practices can exploit loopholes in the stock settlement system, allowing buyers' funds to be cleared for transfer to sellers without actual delivery of shares.

The Panel will be moderated by Wayne Jett, Managing Principal and Chief Economist, Classical Capital LLC, a registered investment advisory firm.

The Specifics

This important event will take place on Thursday, October 19, 2006 from 7:30 a.m. to 11:00 a.m., at the elegant Park Hyatt Los Angeles located at 2151 Avenue of the Stars in the Century

City area of Los Angeles, California. Registration for the event will be $45 in advance (register before October 18), $60 at the door. For further information (and secure online registration) go to: www.STPAdvisors.com/events.html

About the host: STP Advisory Services, LLC, is based in Santa Monica, CA. STP advises clients on capital markets, real estate and the economy.

Press Contact: Irina Somerton

Somerton Public Relations & Public Affairs
Phone: 310 461 1416
Fax: 310 461 1304
Email: IS@SomertonPRPA.com

- END -

STP Advisory Services, LLC
2118 Wilshire Blvd. #596, Santa Monica, CA 90403
Invites You to Attend an Eye-Opening Event Regarding
Unethical Practices **On Wall Street**
Naked, Short & Greedy:
Is Wall Street Short-Changing Investors By Abusing the Practice of Short-Selling Stocks?

Eleven of the largest U.S. broker-dealers stand accused in federal court of conspiring to defraud clients and investors. Are they creating systemic risk and victimizing portfolio management? Are investors already unknowingly exposed to enormous losses? These critical questions and related issues will be discussed in detail at this enlightening event on:

Thursday • October 19, 2006 • 7:30-11 am
Park Hyatt Los Angeles   2151 Avenue of the Stars, Century City, CA 90067
Registration: $45 in advance $60 at the door
Buffet Breakfast & Conference Materials Included in Fee
To register, go to: www.stpadvisors.com/events.html

Wayne Jett kicked it off with a discussion of a lawsuit filed in New York by hedge funds over claims that, by failing to deliver shares for settlement on short sales they initiated, the executing brokers were charging the funds for stock-borrow fees unnecessarily.[91] Patrick was the first panelist; he talked the audience through the path that any company would take when going public before discussing the pitfalls of "Bear Raids," failures to deliver and the regulatory environment.[92] I followed Patrick with a presentation that included most of the material from my comments submitted to the SEC on Reg SHO (Chapter 8). Arne Alsin's presentation probably contained material that most people had not seen before. He told the audience that, as an investment manager he was informed when trades he submitted were on the receiving end of a failure to deliver.[93] Arne made an analogy between the stock market and real estate: imagine that a real estate broker "loaned" your property by renting it out and keeping 100% of the proceeds. This is what brokers do to retail investors. He gave an example of a stock that he owned where he paid the "ordinary tax rates (which are more than double)" rather than the favorable 15% tax rate on dividends because the broker lent his shares to a short seller.[94]

PART VI. ALL SEEMS LOST

Chapter 14. Resistance from Wall Street

Beginning in 2006, some staff at DTCC engaged in a pattern of hostile behavior toward me and attempted to interfere with my ability to carry out my business. Unfortunately for them, most of their efforts backfired. Virtually every person they attempted to intimidate into not working with me actually decided that, if DTCC was that dead set against me, then I must know something they wanted to hide.

It was a scary time for me. DTCC never contacted me directly or told me to stop speaking out. Instead, at every turn, they were behind the scenes attempting to silence me by intimidating others. One name that kept coming up was Joe Trezza, who left DTCC in 2009. I do not remember Joe, though he was at DTC during the same years I was. His LinkedIn profile lists his final title at DTCC as "Senior Product Manager and Operations Vice President." I could not figure out if this was official or if Joe had "gone rogue". One former DTC co-worker speculated that the people making the intimidating calls – and Joe was not the only one – would have been directed by someone in a more senior position, perhaps even someone in the General Counsel's office. Whoever was directing them was careful to maintain plausible deniability. The highest level contact I heard about came from the head of auditing. He had a personal friendship with a conference organizer who laughed off the attempt at getting me thrown out as keynote speaker. It seems absurd, even now, to think of an organization as large and powerful as DTCC stooping to under-handed, back-channel efforts at intimidation to stop me from telling the truth.

I never spoke about DTC or any of the people there with any rancor. I "drank the Kool-Aid" so to speak when I worked in clearing and settlement – I understood the importance of the function and how it could provide a service that is vital to orderly capital markets. But a friend of mine confirmed my fears when she told me, "Two people there, they are almost rabid about the naked short selling. But just to sit there and target you, that is totally asinine but that is the mind-set." Lucky for me, my contacts seemed to enjoy kicking the hornet's nest.

Of course, what probably upset DTC the most about my speaking out is that they knew that I knew about the role of clearing and settlement in Phantom Shares because I brought it to their attention in 1993. I may have been the earliest employee to bring it to the attention of senior management, but I was not the last.

Everyone knew by 2003

My former manager at DTC told me that another employee had come to him in 2002 with the same issue I brought forward in 1993. A then-manager in compliance called attention to the problem of the impact on market prices from stock loans that are left outstanding at DTC. Her perspective was that allowing stock loans to remain open had an adverse impact on the price of the stock because of the inflation in the number of shares that it creates. She was frustrated that she could not get senior management to take corrective action. When the DTC/NSCC merger occurred, the Compliance function was deemed no longer necessary. A woman who worked for the compliance manager confirmed to me that she had seen files relating to "market prices." While I was initially speaking out about Phantom Shares, the then-manger was assigned to work in DTCC's Legal Department, reporting directly to the General Counsel. She could not discuss the issue with me until some years later, after she left that employer. In April 2009, we met and talked on the phone at which time she "spilled the beans" to me.

Prior to January 2002, the Compliance Department at DTC had a staff of 8 or 9 plus two administrative assistants. That department was split up and moved to NSCC after the merger. NSCC had a different way of doing things which prevailed in the post-DTCC world. At NSCC, the former manager had no staff and reported to an NSCC Managing Director where she worked on "special assignments." This is exactly what it sounds like: it was definitely not a promotion. In addition, the head of Compliance would have reported directly to General Counsel so even the line of reporting was cut down. The former head of Compliance stayed at NSCC three months, and then was moved to a customer service position. According to her, "DTCC could see and saw what was going on but took the attitude 'it's not our job.' ... DTCC is not going to do anything unless it is forced to by the SEC."

DTCC clarifies my work experience
Prior to the New Jersey Senate Judiciary Committee confirmation hearing for State Treasurer Bradley Abelow, a former Board member (Chapter 12), I was contacted by Jeff Pillets, a reporter covering New Jersey state government for the Bergen Record. He was writing an article on "the DTCC's role in naked shorting and the effect of failed transactions on the trading settlement system" in advance of the confirmation hearing of "former Goldman Sachs executive" Abelow. Jeff and I talked again at the hearing and by phone after the event. In a February 24, 2006 article on NorthJersey.com, Jeff quoted my comments about the hearing. In addition to misspelling my name, the article mis-stated my title: "Susan Trimbath of Santa Monica, Calif., a former DTCC official." During the hearing I was careful to make the distinction between DTCC and Depository Trust Company (DTC), though it is not always easy and many people confuse the two. I was careful to

make the distinction in the comments that I submitted to the Senate confirmation committee and the press.

In response to Jeff's article, DTCC issued a media statement on March 14, 2006 titled "DTCC Clarifies Work Experience of Former DTC Employee" (see Box below). In it, they made the statement "She never held a position in any operations area that dealt directly with electronic clearance and settlement or the Stock Borrow Program." This was the first time DTCC had publicly acknowledged me. There were press releases, articles and interviews that resulted in a series of Letters to the Editor between DTCC's General Counsel Larry Thompson and Rob Shapiro, who worked for Wes Christian as an expert witness. Although I reviewed and provided input for Rob's responses to Larry, they did not mention me by name.

DTCC press release:

DTCC Clarifies Work Experience of Former DTC Employee

New York, March 14, 2006 – The Depository Trust & Clearing Corporation (DTCC) issued a statement to correct inaccurate information that has appeared in the press and has been represented on Web sites and in public forums regarding the purported work experience of a former employee at one of DTCC's subsidiaries.

Susanne Trimbath has never been an official of DTCC or any DTCC subsidiary or predecessor company. She has never been an officer of the company or any of its subsidiaries. Our records indicate that Susanne Trimbath was hired by The Depository Trust Company (DTC) in 1987 as a manager of transfer agent services, a corporate middle-management position below officer level. Ms. Trimbath resigned from her DTC employment in 1993 holding the same position.

There have been claims that Ms. Trimbath is an expert on clearance and settlement and the Stock Borrow Program. The Stock Borrow Program is now, and was at the time of Ms. Trimbath's employment at DTC, operated by the National Securities Clearing Corporation (NSCC), a

> separate company from DTC. In fact, Trimbath's employment at DTC pre-dates any corporate affiliation between DTC and NSCC, and predates the formation of DTCC.
>
> At DTC, Ms. Trimbath was responsible for representing DTC's interests with transfer agents for DTC-eligible securities regarding DTC's business interactions with these agents. She never held a position in any operations area that dealt directly with electronic clearance and settlement or the Stock Borrow Program.

Source: DTCC press release (no longer available online)

This press release was very odd in that it did not discuss my comments at the hearing – which were not refutable. Instead it was about a story in a paper published by NorthJersey.com. It was not even about the story, which was not favorable to Abelow. It was about my title at DTC and how it was being reported in the press and represented "on Web sites." While the press release was technically true in regards to my work experience at DTC, by making the statement in a sentence without reference to DTC it wrongfully ignored my work experience at the Pacific Securities Depository Trust Company and the Pacific Clearing Corporation, where I did have operational experience in those areas. While my title and official job description did not include them at DTC, I was frequently called on to assist the broker/dealer or banker side of companies that also had transfer agents. Companies such as Bank of New York and U.S. Trust came to rely on me for straight answers. They did not hesitate to contact me when they had problems in other areas, including settlement. In fact, I wrote and reviewed procedures for those functions for Russia, Poland and other US-AID projects. Those procedures (and the specifications for computer programs that included clearing, settlement and stock lending) were reviewed at DTCC prior to implementation. They never pointed to any errors in my work, even in areas they pointed to in the press release as being outside my area of expertise.

This was the first public attempt by DTCC to lay the ground work to undermine my ability to get work in this area by calling my expertise into question. Years later, while giving a deposition in New York, the opposing attorney would show me which "Web sites" DTCC was referring to in that press release. While I was at the Milken Institute think tank, the marketing department insisted on listing my former employer as "Depository Trust and Clearing Corporation." I asked them to make the correction for exactly the reasons that came up in this press release years later. They refused to change it because, they said, "No one knows what DTC is. Everyone knows what DTCC is." I was unable to get it changed, but I understood their reasoning. Especially because, at that point, DTC was a subsidiary; most people would only recognize the name of the holding company.

Although the press release caused quite a stir among the pajamahideen and my allies in New York, I was aware of only one brief rebuttal in the media. When contacted by Christopher Faille of *HedgeWorld*, I admitted to taking the easy way out and just using the full name of DTCC. He wrote:

"Nothing in her testimony was inconsistent with that characterization [of Trimbath's title at DTC], nor did she quarrel with it Tuesday. She testified that she wanted the committee to consider 'how you can have year-long failures to settle trades,' and that the answer to that question was and is 'lax management at the Depository and a willingness to look the other way when broker members neglect their fiduciary duty to small investors.' She said that she saw the hearing as 'an opportunity to bring to light a failure of management [at the Depository] to address this issue' concerning failures-to-deliver 'a decade ago when it was merely a thorn in somebody's side.' She also said that before she went to work at DTC as a transfer agent liaison, she had been an operations analyst for the Pacific Clearing Corp. She was surprised and flattered to find that she's important enough for DTCC to issue a release making the distinction between Depository officers and employees with special reference to her."[95]

The rest of the article was devoted to what Faille called "the more substantive issues in dispute" which were included in a report from a consulting firm with the catchy headline: "500 Million Shares of Stock Are Missing." That title drew a point-by-point reply from DTCC. Again, DTCC could not dispute the content of my testimony, so they went after something more personal.

CFA-LA event

The next attempt by DTCC was successful in getting an event cancelled after they asked me to participate as a speaker. On March 1, 2006 I received an email from attorney, author and securities industry expert Wayne Jett on behalf of the Chartered Financial Analysts Society of Los Angeles (CFA-LA) asking for my participation in a panel discussion. CFA-LA Board members Jim Altenbach and Cynthia Harrington[96] were instrumental in getting the event approved to move forward. The event was scheduled for June 6 with the title "Exposing Systematic Fraud in the Stock Market." Over the course of the next three months, I worked with Wayne on getting speakers, including Patrick Byrne of Overstock.com, to participate in the event. I sent announcements to my personal mailing list. The CFA-LA press release went out on May 26 (see Box).

CFA-LA press release

CFA SOCIETY OF LOS ANGELES

PRESS RELEASE

FOR IMMEDIATE RELEASE   May 26, 2006

To: From: Laura Carney

                             CFALA Press Contact

                             213-247-7186

Following is our press release. Please notify me when any article appears, and let me know if I can assist in any way. – LC

Re: June 6 Event: Exposing Systematic Fraud In The Stock Market

Are giant hedge funds and major banker/brokers conspiring to swindle billions from ordinary investors in the stock market? Are self-regulatory organizations such as NASD ignoring concerns while industry-wide organizations like Depository Trust & Clearing Corporation (DTCC) aid the illicit activity? Are investors already exposed to such large losses that the SEC is frozen into inaction?

These are questions raised by observers of stock trading practices known as concerted failure-to-deliver (FTDs) and naked short selling (NSS). In either case, brokers assist hedge funds in selling shares of stock they do not own. By law, such "short sellers" are required to borrow and deliver the shares sold short within three days of sale. But reports say naked short selling is widespread. DTCC allows electronic entry of shares in buyers' accounts despite sellers' failure to deliver.

On June 6, CFA Society of Los Angeles will host a rare look into FTDs and NSS by three speakers with special insights. Dr. Patrick Byrne, CEO of NASDAQ-traded Overstock.com, will discuss his firm's buffeting by trading of "shares" that appear to far outnumber those officially issued and outstanding. In March at a New York conference, Byrne named a dozen large brokerages with clients who claim several million more OSTK shares than the number held by the brokerages at DTCC.

Dr. Susanne Trimbath, a Santa Monica research economist with operations management experience in clearing and settlement of trades at DTCC, will illuminate current trading practices. In addition, portfolio manager and financial writer Arne Alsin will reveal insights gained as an investor in large-lot trades in markets systemically flawed by FTDs.

Press and public may attend the June 6 noon luncheon event to be held at the downtown Marriott Hotel, 333 So. Figueroa St., Los Angeles. CFALA serves chartered financial analysts through educational programs that assist the valuation of public and private business investments. Details of the event are at:

http://www.cfala.org/cfmfiles/cal/eventlist2.cfm?id=632&t=g&d=Z

On June 2, 2006, just two days before the event was to set begin, Wayne Jett sent a message to the panelists that "the board of directors of CFALA, due to last minute objections by DTCC, has decided to postpone the June 6 event..." When I received the message, I was already in transit from Europe to return to the US specifically in time to participate in the event. While Wayne made several attempts to re-schedule the event at DTCC's convenience, we were eventually told that the CFA-LA had bowed to pressure from DTCC to cancel the event. The cancellation was the impetus for the event that was eventually organized and presented by STP Advisory Services, LLC in Los Angeles.

STP Advisory Services' event

After we got the "Naked, Short and Greedy" event organized in Los Angeles (Chapter 13), we sent out announcements to our email distribution lists, got it posted to a variety of bulletin boards and other websites, plus did regular press releases. The Securities Transfer Association (STA) agreed to distribute an announcement to their membership. On October 17, 2006, I received an email from my friend and colleague Tom Montrone. At the STA's annual meeting that year he was told that the STA's Executive Director was confronted on the phone by a mid-level manager of

Depository Trust & Clearing Corporation (DTCC). That DTCC manager told the STA that DTCC was going to sue the STA for promoting my Los Angeles event "Naked, Short and Greedy." The STA's response to the accusation that they were somehow legally prohibited from promoting events that were "outside the scope of their own business" was that they routinely notify their membership about non-STA events that they believe would be useful or of interest to the members.

When the DTCC manager realized that the STA would not back down, apparently he tried to threaten the STA by saying that DTCC would sue Susanne Trimbath personally. In an email, Tom told me that he "Heard that DTC is going to sue you for misrepresenting your job function." He explained that he was giving me this information so that I might use it to protect myself. He needed to keep this confidential, at the time, because he had to interact with DTCC on a daily basis and DTCC has been known to take retaliatory action against transfer agents.[97]

In any event, the STA Board decided that it was in their best interest to support my work. They even invited me to be the keynote speaker at the STA's quarterly meeting in New York on December 6, 2006. Although the same mid-level manager from DTCC was the first to register for the meeting, no one from DTCC attended.

Securities Lending Conference

DTCC's next attempt to silence me came when they raised questions about my expertise with a conference organizer and its sponsors. I was approached by Josh Galper, Managing Principal of Vodia Group[98] about participating in his firm's Securities Lending Conference in New York to be held on September 18, 2006. After some discussion, Josh asked me to make the morning keynote speech and I accepted. On August 29, 2006 I sent a notice to my personal distribution list. Two weeks later, Josh told me that DTCC called him and Scott Porter, CEO of FMW Media Holdings Inc. (the conference production company). Josh said that DTCC called because they were "very concerned about Susanne Trimbath being on the agenda." When I talked with Scott, he said that he received two calls from DTCC. The first to express concern about me being on the agenda, questioning my knowledge of securities lending. The second call was from Stu Goldstein, who has a long-term personal relationship with Scott. On the pretext of scheduling a lunch later in the week, Stu expressed concern about Susanne Trimbath being on the agenda of the conference. DTCC signed up one of their directors to attend the event, which Josh and Scott suggested might be with the intention of drawing me into an argument or in an attempt to embarrass me. Again, DTCC did not show up for the event. They were unable to confront my knowledge directly, despite, as one reporter told me, trying to label me a "flunky, paper pusher."

Olde Monmouth transfer agent

Sometime late in 2006, I met a lawyer at a social party in Los Angeles. After the conversation came around to "what do you do for a living," he realized that I may be able to help him with a case he is working on for a transfer agent, Olde Monmouth, in New Jersey. Chris Troster, the head of Olde Monmouth, was having some trouble getting into a particular program at DTCC. It turns out that it was a program I worked on while I was at DTC. The lawyers for the transfer agent engage me to assist making contacts with some of my former colleagues in the hope of finding an amicable way to resolve the issue without resorting to litigation. DTCC was none-too-happy to hear from me, but my intervention helped bring the matter to a head. My client told me "you have served to really 'piss them off'" and that was OK with them; they also enjoyed kicking that particular hornet's nest.

The transfer agent initiated litigation against DTCC and asked me to prepare a declaration disputing certain assertions made in responses submitted by DTCC.[99] After Olde Monmouth filed my affidavit in the case, Tom Montrone wrote to me again: "Just reviewed your statement in the Olde Monmouth response. Check your back to see if DTCC has drawn a bulls-eye on it! Have someone else start your car in the morning.... Etc." Although I never felt physically threatened I was nonetheless feeling upset and discouraged at the time by the constant interference with my attempts to get new clients, to earn a spot on the podium and generally to speak out against trade clearing and settlement practices that support abusive stock price manipulation.

Chapter 15. Corporate Governance Fails at Overstock

In a press release on April 21, 2006 Overstock.com announced that a significant number of shareholders had not received their voting materials for the upcoming annual meeting. In it, Patrick Byrne wrote:

"I know a group of folks holding OSTK in 19 accounts at three brokerages, and not a single one of these people has received a proxy in any account. It will come as no surprise that I believe this is a symptom of the failure of our stock settlement system. According to an article in the current issue of Bloomberg Magazine, overvoting (sometimes 2-3 x overvoting) has become routine in corporate America as a result of phantom shares: in such cases, back offices simply throw out excess votes (which means that corporate governance in America is now a hoax, incidentally). In our case, I think there are so many phantom shares of various flavors, and certain parties expect (or should expect) to come under a spotlight, that they are making an effort to avoid sending out proxies where they can. That would explain why we could be in this odd position of having had 75% of the vote already come in, yet 0 out of 19 accounts across three brokerages having received proxies."

In the days and weeks leading up to the annual meeting, I was contacted directly by some of Patrick's family members who were struggling to understand why they were unable to vote their shares. Patrick would have to admit that the 19 accounts mentioned in his press release that were not receiving proxies were, in fact, his cousins. He even joked that he should put a question to the shareholders at the annual meeting about whether or not he should be waging Byrne's War, saying he thought that 65% would vote "against" and the other 400% would vote "for".

I advised Patrick that this is the evidence he needs finally to prove his accusations of the naked short selling by recognizing that the fails to deliver are impacting his shareholders in significant ways. His own family has been stuck with the resulting fails to receive, just as he was when he tried to buy his own stock barely six months earlier. As he said in the press release, Overstock.com was facing exactly the scenario described in the *Bloomberg Markets* magazine article (Drummond 2006a). There are more shares in circulation than there are shares outstanding – and the real culprits are going to turn in votes without getting proxy instructions from actual shareholders. He now has the perfect opportunity to prove what he has been saying – that shorts, fails and loans are damaging Overstock.com. I advise him to adjourn the meeting without accepting the vote. I put him in contact with Carl Hagberg, my best proxy election specialist. Carl agreed to guide Patrick through the process to confirm the number of real votes and to distinguish them from the phantom votes. Most of the cousins agreed that stopping the meeting was the best idea.

Patrick speculated that the phantom votes would try to unseat him from the Board of Directors. When the meeting is called to order, Patrick realizes that not only was he not unseated from the Board but he is re-elected. He accepts this hollow "victory" and is named Chairman of the Board. I stand up and walk out of the meeting.

On May 3, 2006, some of his family members finally begin receiving their proxy materials – more than a week after the meeting and weeks after the deadline for returning votes to brokers in time to be submitted to the company and be counted for the elections at the annual meeting. Patrick either does not count those votes, or at least never acknowledges or releases the information publicly. I am crushed that Patrick would not take this opportunity to win a battle in the war he claimed to be waging.

Although Patrick offered some financial support to cover expenses for the STP Naked Short and Greedy event in the fall, and participated in the panel discussion, within weeks Overstock terminated my consulting agreement. There was a dispute over a service provider that Overstock asked me to work with to help them look more deeply at the available records available from their transfer agent and DTC. When I met with the head of the service provider, at the insistence of Overstock's lawyers, the company CEO offered me compensation to recommend his services! The service purports to be finding evidence of naked short selling; my review found "nothing to convince me that there is value in the service."

Overstock also suggested me to the application service provider because Patrick thought highly of the owner. He thought I might be a valuable addition as a potential member for the firm's advisory board.[100] The service purported to provide intelligence on the shareholders of a public company: who they are, demographics, when share positions change, etc. I was skeptical because I know from my years in the industry that there are three service providers that most public companies already pay for who have the same information:

(1) a registrar to assure the validity of the shareholder records;

(2) a transfer agent to re-register shares when they change hands (e.g. through stock market trades); and

(3) a proxy solicitor who works to get all the shareholder votes turned in on time (e.g. to ensure a majority of shares are voted, to achieve a quorum at annual meetings or to vote for important matters like mergers, etc.).

When I again made contact with the company's founder, instead of discussing ways my knowledge and experience could bring value to the advisory board, he offered me a job in sales!

After looking at the product they were offering, I warned Overstock (and a few other companies) that the service had no value (because the information is freely available elsewhere). Overstock insisted that they wanted me to review all their reports and provide Overstock with an opinion of the value in that work. My meeting with the CEO and a few subsequent phone calls with his staff only confirmed what I already knew: not only was there no value in this service but it also was giving him incorrect information about his shareholders and the potential phantom shares in circulation. Overstock hired them anyway. After this, I had little contact with Patrick. I would not see him again until we were all interviewed for a couple of documentaries or when we attended showings of the films to take part in panel discussions.

Some consultants employed by Overstock and even some "experts" working full-time at Overstock frequently contacted me with questions, asking for written answers, feeding questions to me from other sources to get answers they could give out, maybe even as their own work. It was not until Overstock terminated my consulting contract in 2006 that I learned they would refuse to pay me for time spent with their employees and outside consultants. We resolved the matter amicably, but not without doing permanent damage to the relationship. Patrick's lawyers in San Francisco agreed to pay me to work with one of their consultants, a former Commerce Department official, to help prepare him for a deposition. While they continued to acknowledge my expertise, it was only for me to correct the errors made by the consultants they used on their lawsuits. I was under no consulting contract for this work, had no private documents or other correspondence directly relevant to any of the lawsuits.

In the end, Patrick's efforts were directed to "naked short selling" as the only source of fails to deliver. He published a letter to the editor in the *Wall Street Journal* in April 2006 that began to show some cracks from this version of things relying strictly on naked short selling as the explanation. But it was too little too late. He also pursued litigation where he believed that fund managers and investment research firms were disseminating false and damaging reports on his company. While the activities he fought against are illegal, they are only one part of the problem. Chasing individual crimes only solves the problem for individual companies. The systemic problem, the regulatory crisis, remained unsolved as the Great Recession loomed ever darker in the background.

Last summer (August 2018) Patrick lost his appeal of a lawsuit filed by a Vancouver businessman who was awarded over $1 million for libel and defamation plus other damages. Patrick's Deep Capture website had accused the businessman of funding terrorism through abusive stock trading practices, including naked short selling. Mark Mitchell, who was writing for the *Columbia Journalism Review* when I first met him, but was later employed by Patrick, was also found by the courts to have damaged the businessman's reputation. Visitors to the Deep Capture website today are greeted with this disclaimer:

"At the time much of the content on DeepCapture.com was written, the Great Financial Crisis of 2008 was either on the verge of happening or had just occurred. In those days, emotions among this publication's contributors were raw and, in an effort to get their warnings noticed and appropriate blame placed, occasionally hyperbolic language and shocking imagery were employed. Were we to write these entries today, a different tone would most certainly prevail. Yet, being a record of a pivotal time in our global economic history, we've decided to leave the rawness unedited, with the proviso that readers take the context of the creation of certain posts into account, and that those easily offended reconsider the decision to read them. Agree/Disagree" [Accessed October 5, 2019]

If you click on "Disagree" you are redirected to the SEC's website.

Chapter 16. Senate Inaction

As I was finishing this book, former Special Prosecutor Robert Mueller was testifying before the Senate Judiciary Committee. The back and forth questioning between the two US political parties reminded me of the landmark narrative described by now-retired Professor of Sociology Lawrence Nichols. In 2002, I invited Dr. Nichols to participate in a Roundtable on the Savings and Loan Crisis co-hosted by the Anderson School of Management (University of Southern California, Los Angeles) and the Milken Institute.[101] His research focused on corporate values and white collar crime. Dr. Nichols was invited to apply his analytic framework to the Congressional investigation of Lincoln Savings and Loan. Congress used the hearings to create a narrative making Lincoln "a special symbol of the savings and loan crisis, despite the facts that it was not the largest savings and loan to have failed nor the most costly bailout" (Nichols and Nolan, 2004, p. 166). Similarly in the Mueller hearings, the Senators used more of their five minutes to make statements than to ask questions, thereby driving the narrative, the story, of events in a particular direction. Just like in the case of the Lincoln hearings, there are good guys and bad guys and a repetition of events that played out in newspaper and television reporting. In the saga of "naked short selling," we can also add the internet to the list of sources.

Finance seems complicated to most people; it is understandable that a simple narrative with easily recognizable landmarks would be used to make sense of the interaction of public, press and government. It is a shorthand version, though, fraught with distractions that limit our view. Worse yet, landmarks like "naked short selling" become indelibly imbedded in the narrative. In 2008, the narrative was marked by "the behavior of irresponsible home buyers who got in over their heads and could not pay their mortgages" (Trimbath 2015, p. 128). The role of banks was not clear until after crisis fatigue set in and the media lost its appetite for stories about predatory borrowers. In 2012, five of the largest mortgage loan servicing banks paid to settle charges brought by the federal government and the states. No politician can resist a good narrative and Congress did not behave differently this time.

In July 2007 Patrick Byrne asked me as a favor to prepare some notes for an upcoming speech by U.S. Senator Bennett (R-Utah). Bennett used fifteen minutes in the morning business period on July 20 to call the Senate's attention to "Naked Short Selling." A few paragraphs of what I wrote were read into the Congressional Record, but without crediting my input. Bennett was able to get an article from the *Wall Street Journal* inserted into the record outlining the role of failures to deliver at DTCC in the multiplication of shares in circulation.[102] There was also a memorandum from the SEC fulfilling a request from Bennett to outline initiatives taken by the SEC "regarding various short sale-related items" discussed at a June 20 meeting with the Associate Director and Special Counsel from the SEC's Division of Market Regulation. The SEC memorandum suggested that $7 billion of failed equity trades are all due to exemptions offered to market specialists, one of the issues Patrick was adamant about having changed in Reg SHO.

Despite his best efforts to get action from the SEC and the Senate, Senator Bennett made some serious errors that seemed to disclose a lack of clear understanding of the issues. He made a recommendation that DTCC cannot lend out more stock shares than they have on deposit – but they were already doing that and only re-lending borrowed shares unwittingly (e.g. when members neglected to segregate shares into accounts from which stock was not to be lent). He suggested that "there ought to be a rule which says a broker cannot be paid a commission on a short sale until the shares are delivered." This would not prevent most fails to deliver since many of those trades are not marked as being "short sales" in the first place. Even if something along this line could be managed, the commission is unlikely to be sufficient incentive to discourage the brokers from failing to deliver; they are able to take and use the full value of the shares from the customer's account, exactly as they did to Patrick Bryne when he purchased shares of Overstock.com after the NASAA forum in 2005 (Chapter 10). Even a 2.5% commission is tiny compared to the $1.8 million purchase price paid by an investor. Senator Bennett made up some hypothetical examples of brokers calling DTCC to arrange to borrow stock to cover a short sale (DTCC is a lender of last resort who only arranges stock loans to cover fails to deliver, not stock loans in advance of short sales). Bennett's statement has so many errors that DTCC could easily refute the remainder of his comments, even if they contained a few valid points. From that perspective, I thought it did more harm than good.

Back in 2005, when Senator Shelby (R-Alabama) and a few other Banking Committee members were interested in holding hearings, they were unable to get the idea off the ground. When asked about it in a documentary interview, CA State Senator Harmer said that he believed DTCC was sabotaging their efforts. He said that he knew the CEOs of the large brokers simply did not want "to know what the guys in the back room are doing" (*The Wall Street Conspiracy*, 2012).

Harmer believed that the SEC, under Chairman William Donaldson, echoed DTCC's sentiment about Congressional hearings and that they worked behind the scenes to derail the hearings. Harmer said: "Essentially he was contemptuous about the whole idea. 'You people meddle in this, you don't really know what you're getting into. Leave it to us' – the members of the Black Priesthood, if you will! – 'to take care of it.'" According to Harmer, the SEC worked behind the scenes to derail any possible hearings on the subject. Again Harmer said that Donaldson told him, "Major brokers are running this and you guys in DC shouldn't meddle in it because you are going to upset the apple cart."

A story in the *Washington Post* in 2012 helped explain why there was so much resistant in Congress to reforming the inefficient financial institutions and the processes that supported the creation of the phantom shares that are so damaging to investors and the entrepreneurs who rely on them for capital formation: "In 2008, for instance, 17 lawmakers reported investing hundreds of thousands of dollars in short-selling funds," including bets against US Treasury bonds, the DJIA and the S&P 500.[103]

Treasury Secretary Paulson, according to Harmer, opposed hearings "on the premise that these hearings could have a very negative effect on the stock market if you are not careful in the way they go forward." The Senate Banking Committee caved under pressure from the SEC, Wall Street, DTCC and Treasury. According to Harmer, they "got to" Shelby, who told Bennett, "We were simply the victims of a very effectively executed strategy to make sure that there were no hearings on this." Congress had an opportunity to force the SEC, but sold out to Wall Street. Harmer warned anyone working to uncover the fraud, "As a proponent you would probably be at great risk personally if you had the data, which we don't, and then tried to expose it."

Sadly, I did have the data to at least force the brokers to come forward with the trading records on who was failing to settle. In fact, the NYSE members are required to report fails to deliver and fails to receive in their quarterly and annual balance sheets. The difference is that when DTCC and Wall Street came after me, I did not cave. Their opposition only reinforced my commitment to expose the problem.

PART VII. WHEN THE MUSIC STOPS

As 2006 turns into 2007 there were rumblings beginning to be heard in global credit markets. The Metropolitan Museum of Art in New York is unable to renew overnight loans. The full-blown market collapse comes in September 2008 and by October Congress has passed a bailout and every broker becomes a bank to enjoy the largess. In November, there are $2.5 trillion in Treasury bond trades that fail to be delivered for six weeks. A reporter calls me with this news. When I confirm the numbers, I burst into tears – ready to recommit to moving forward without Patrick Byrne, without the US Senate and without the FBI.

I frequently compared fails to deliver to a game of musical chairs, or as I called it "musical shares." As long as the music keeps playing, everyone keeps walking around the chairs. When the music stops, someone ends up without a seat. In "musical shares," as long as the money keeps flowing in, everyone continues trading stocks. Once the money stops – and this is where fails transactions are like a Ponzi scheme – someone has to end up without their shares. When the global financial markets collapsed, lots of people found out that they did not have a seat.

On September 19, the SEC issues an emergency order prohibiting "short selling any publicly traded securities of any Included Financial Firm." The list includes every bank, insurance company and securities firm they could identify by industry codes. Eight of those companies end up on the Reg SHO Threshold list at the New York Stock Exchange a week later, indicating that the fails to deliver surpassed the regulatory limit of 10,000 shares or 0.5% of shares outstanding:

Bank of America (BAC), Downey Financial Corp. (DSL), Fortress Investment Group, LLC (FIG), KeyCorp (KEY), Reinsurance

Group of America, Inc. (RGA), U.S. Bancorp (USB), W Holding Company, Inc. (WHI) and Washington Mutual Inc. (WM).

Despite the ban on short selling, the fails to deliver continued to accumulate. On the last trading day before the order, September 17, none of those companies were on the Threshold List. I wrote to Chairman Cox at the SEC, begging him to enforce finality of settlement: "This has been my point all along. Why short sell when you can simply fail to deliver? You achieve the same purpose and save the time and cost of borrowing."

Chapter 17. Media Interest after the Financial Crisis

As the financial markets crumbled around us at the end of 2008, suddenly everyone was interested in shorts, loans and fails and how the shortcomings in post-trade processing in the US exacerbated the crisis in global financial markets. Throughout the coming years, I would be contacted by investors, companies and even retail stock brokers who were just beginning to see the connection between those shortcomings and the 2008 financial crisis.

I was again doing radio and podcast interviews every month. In September, Matt Taibbi from *Rolling Stone* magazine interviewed me for "The Great American Bubble Machine" – in which he called Goldman Sachs a "great vampire squid wrapped around the face of humanity, relentlessly jamming its blood funnel into anything that smells like money." The imagery was so vivid that *Forbes* was still referencing that article in 2013.

I lost track of how many times I was asked the questions: "Why does my broker give me a statement that I have shares when the trade never settled?" Legally they can say you have an "entitlement" even if you do not have shares. The brokers have been flying on a wing and a prayer for years, because they can usually get the shares if you ever want them, if you ever request to have them registered in your name. They've been using their own cash to pay you the dividends and allocating your shareholder votes by fractions for a long time.

If asked about the ultimate solution, I would have said in 2003 that forcing the buy-in of unsettled trades could solve the problem. By now, I was not the only one who recognized that the phantom shares problem is far worse than originally thought. The ultimate resolution will be to do the one thing everyone in the system has been dreading since the beginning: start reversing trades until we reach full settlement for every trade in every company's shares. Unfortunately, the only way for investors to protect their shares would amount to suggesting a run on the bank.

The best alternative is to get your shares registered in your name with the company's transfer agent. Even the Depository says that transfer agents are "the key guardian of the amount of stock outstanding and the final recorder of share ownership." But be warned: in the April 2005 article in *Euromoney*, a Depository spokesperson was asked if every shareholder could request and receive their shares from the system. The Depository says "the answer is probably not. There can be shortages." The only way you know for sure is to have the shares registered in your name. And now you can do that without holding a certificate through Direct Purchase and Direct Registration programs offered by many issuers. (See links in Chapter 11, in the Sanity Check interview.)

The Depository is not staffed with bad guys, all just helping to cheat small investors. I understand that admitting that they have been supporting this process for decades would bring great shame on everyone. They would have to admit that the rules and programs they have sent to the SEC for decades have created a system with a big hole in it that enables the creation of phantom shares to the point that transfer agents are seeing not just more shares voted than are registered for the Depository but more shares voted than legitimately exist.

Gary Matsumoto, the Bloomberg TV producer of the *Phantom Shares* program, began working on an article for print on the fate of Lehman Brothers and Bear Stearns.[104] I examined the fails to deliver reported to the SEC, the short selling reports from the stock exchanges, and the closing prices for both firms. I calculated that the fails to deliver explained between 30% and 70% of the variation in closing prices. I had a similar result analyzing the data of a dozen other firms.

The senior managers at both Lehman and Bear Stearns publicly blamed "naked short selling" for much of their problems. This was the gist of the statement from Lehman's former Chief Executive Officer Richard Fuld to the members of the House Committee on Government Oversight and Reform in the weeks after Lehman went into bankruptcy. When they filed for bankruptcy, Lehman listed $163 billion in debt. As of December 31, 2016, according to the notes to the annual financial statements, DTCC had paid out $5,345,809,000 in cash and securities to the Trustee in charge of winding down Lehman's accounts "including the close out of pending transactions" (meaning fails to deliver).[105]

Late Night television, or at least cable television, got onto the story when it became clear that the banks were more responsible than homeowners for the financial crisis. Samantha Bee did a segment on The Daily Show with Jon Stewart that aired on March 16, 2009.[106] Stewart introduced the segment: "As you may have heard over these past few months, the economy is in turmoil. So how can you make the turmoil work for you? Samantha Bee has the answer."

Samanatha Bee interviewed MarketWatch financial analyst David Weidner who said that "Really, the only people who are doing well are short sellers." Weidner played straight man to the comedienne. The most telling part of her report came in the interview segments with Money manager Andrew Horowitz. Horowitz told the story of short selling a particular "hypothetical" company where the stock price "went down $50 a share within days." When Bee gets him to admit that the employees lost their jobs when the company failed, she also has him acknowledge that he made a lot of money. He replies, "It was very nice" as he reaches over to give her a high-five.

Like so many brokers and regulators had been saying all along, Horowitz smirks at the idea: "If this is the law and this is the rule … I mean someone should profit on it." Bee has the last laugh when she says, with a wink and a nod: "Just because you robbed the grave, doesn't mean you killed the guy, right?"

The *New York Times*, Huffington Post, *Reason Magazine* and others ran articles about the show, with headlines like "'The Daily Show' Takes on Short-Selling" and lead-ins like "… short-selling, a practice that bets on the failure of American institutions."

The next night, Jon Stewart had CNBC buffoon-commentator Jim Cramer ("Mad Money")[107] on the show as his interview guest. Jim had famously aped throwing a federal subpoena on the floor, when an SEC regulatory investigation into allegations of collusion between short-sellers and stock research firms demanded copies of communications between the journalist and his sources. Stewart said, "Look, we are both snake oil salesmen to a certain extent, but we do label the show as snake oil here. Isn't there a problem with selling snake oil and labeling it as vitamin tonic?" When Cramer countered that there is a market for his show, Stewart countered with, "There's a market for cocaine and hookers." The next day, CBSnews.com reported that a question about the Cramer interview was received by White House Press Secretary Robert Gibbs during the daily briefing.

Chapter 18. CMKM and the UnShareholders

The story of CMKM Diamonds, Inc. (CMKM) and the UnShareholders starts at the end, well, at least near the end. The story is not really over yet for the CMKM shareholders. Before I can explain what went before the end of the story, it is important for the reader to understand what is happening in the final stages. I hate movies where the story jumps back and forth in time; I just do not know any other way to tell this one. What I need to make clear is that, despite the shortcomings of the CMKM management and their transfer agent, despite any and all criminal activity in and around CMKM, people who invested their money in CMKM were cheated by the system of financial regulation in the US. Before and after everything that happened to them – and it is a lot! – they were cheated by the system.

In the end...

The story for the CMKM investors is not over. There are cases pending, class action suits, criminal complaints, civil lawsuits, etc. Just Google "CMKM" and you will find more than you could ever want to know (e.g. see Selected Resources at the end of this chapter).[108] The truth of the matter seems to be that there never was any value in the company. There are diamonds being mined and to be mined in Canada. But whatever mineral rights claim the founders of CMKM had was only ever owned by the founders – the assets never belonged to the company.

In an attempt to create some value for the shareholders, the remaining management changed the company name to New Horizons Holdings, Inc. (NHHI) with the plan to raise capital for the purchase of oil or gas assets. If successful, they would be able to return the shares to trading status with the hope of restoring some value to the shareholders.[109]

I'm telling this up front, because the allegations of fraud and corporate abuse are the reason why no one heard the rest of the story, the one where brokers were allowed to cheat investors by taking their money and never giving them any shares of CMKM. To understand how serious that problem is I need to explain why no one ever heard about it. Although I will tell the story using CMKM as the example, they are not the only company where investors were cheated. It is not just small companies or Blue Sky companies that never had any value but went public anyway, or even just penny stocks that trade over-the-counter. This happens to every company with publicly-traded shares.

Two years after Reg SHO was implemented, failures to deliver were still affecting 20% of NYSE and NASDAQ listed firms and about half of the firms trading over-the-counter. The stocks of the following well-known companies had fails to deliver reported in their shares *every trading day during December 2007*: Virgin Mobile, PNC Financial, Netflix, JP Morgan Chase, Krispy Kreme, HSBC Finance, Icahn Enterprises (with Carl Icahn as Chairman of the Board), Wells Fargo, E-Trade, Morgan Stanley, Deutsch Bank, CIT Group (Citibank), Bank of Nova Scotia, and Bear Stearns. Not even IBM (13 of 20 trading days with fails) and Microsoft (13 days) escaped the creation of phantom shares. Three years after the SEC attempted to regulate them out of existence, the SEC reported that over $6 billion worth of equity shares failed settlement delivery at DTCC every day.[110]

Number of companies with fails-to-deliver reported at least 25% of trading days in December 2007:

Days with Fails	Number of Companies
20	677
19	150
18	153
17	159
16	192
15	196
14	217
13	217
12	231
11	240
10	257
9	274
8	317
7	328
6	384
5	456

Source: United States Securities and Exchange Commission

The difference between all those companies and CMKM is that I got to look inside the shareholder records, to communicate directly with shareholders and to interview some of the investors who lost everything. What you are about to learn will shock you, but only if you are able to put aside everything that happened "in the end" about CMKM.

Start at the beginning

By the time I met my first CMKM investor at the NASAA Public Forum in Washington DC in 2005, I was already coming up against a trait I found very common among people who were in the fight against what they labeled "naked short selling" or NSS:

they expected to get rich quick. Not rich in a hurry, or even rich on their investments. Someone had convinced them that the naked short sellers could be forced to cover the short sales, which meant those sellers would all rush to the market at the same time to buy shares to cover the settlement shortages. In doing so, they would drive up the prices of the shares. CMKM investors were unique for one particular reason – while most companies have millions even, perhaps, hundreds of millions of shares outstanding, CMKM had authorized and issued *hundreds of billions* of shares. That meant that an ordinary CMKM shareholder might have a million or more shares in their personal trading account! Many held tens of millions of shares and some, when the price dropped to a fraction of a penny, even bought billions of shares. With that many shares, just a small increase in the market price of CMKM's stock would make them rich.

I heard similar claims from the founders, investors, and CEOs of other companies. I witnessed one CEO making plans to book private jets to fly everyone who helped him to the Bahamas for the big victory celebration. This CEO and all the CMKM shareholders suffered from the same delusion – they thought naked short selling was their only problem. I could not make them understand that the system was going to cheat them with or without short sellers, naked or otherwise. When one broker can sell shares to your broker and simply fail to deliver at settlement, they do not have to bear the expense of short selling with stock borrowing for settlement or bear the cost of monitoring and reporting naked short sales. They simply do not deliver any shares on settlement date and the system lets them. In the meantime, your broker is not required to tell you that he took your money and did not get your shares. There will be no record of any short sale.

This could happen to virtually every buyer in virtually every stock and bond investment in the US since the time that the centralized clearing and settlement system was developed in the early 1970s. If a trade failed before that system was developed, at a time when settlement was trade-for-trade and broker-to-broker, if one broker sold shares and did not deliver them to the buying broker, the seller would not get paid and the brokers would "bust the trade" – each party went back to their position as if the trade had never happened. As I explained earlier, we do not do that with centralized clearing and settlement. Unless you skipped reading the rest of the book to see this chapter on CMKM, you understand the problem so I will not belabor it here.[111]

When I first met a CMKM shareholder, this is what impressed me most about them. For many of them, of course, this was not the only stock they invested in. But CMKM was the one where they felt they had something to hang their hats on; where they felt the payoff was certain. The reason was: The Cert Pull.

The CMKM cert pull

On November 4, 2005, CMKM issued a press release announcing a distribution that would require investors to get their shares registered in their own names, i.e. out of DTC:

"In order to be considered a bona fide stockholder of CMKM, a physical stock certificate issued in his/her/its name will need to be presented to the distribution Task Force for confirmation on or before Dec. 31, 2005, or as extended at the sole discretion of the Task Force. Electronic and/or other forms of ownership (i.e. -- brokerage statements) will not be accepted by the Task Force as evidence of ownership. Therefore, CMKM stockholders who hold their shares in 'street name' will need to demand physical certificates from their broker in order to be considered a bona fide CMKM stockholder and be entitled to their proportionate share of the Entourage common stock and any other assets of CMKM to be distributed to its bona fide stockholders."

As a result, on November 17, 2005, DTC issued an Important Notice telling its members to start the withdrawal process. When the Task Force extended the deadline to May 15, 2006, DTC announced that all withdrawals by transfer from DTC would be halted on April 14, a month before the deadline set by the Task Force "in order to ensure sufficient turnaround time for WTs [withdrawals-by-transfer] submitted to the transfer agent." After April 14, 2006, DTC said, they would have certificates issued in the members' name whether they requested them or not in order to complete the process of exiting any remaining shares of CMKM still on deposit with them.

Although, certainly, other companies had used similar tactics to get their stock shares out of DTC, after CMKM's success in exiting the central depository, DTC stonewalled any future attempts by other companies. They got the SEC to grant approval for a rule change that prohibited requests for withdrawal of certificates that could be instigated by issuers. On June 4, 2003 the Securities and Exchange Commission argued that no issuer could refuse to have shares of its stock held by DTC:

"In accordance with its rules, DTC accepts deposits of securities from its participants (i.e. broker-dealers and banks), credits those securities to the depositing participants' accounts, and effects book-entry movements of those securities. The securities deposited with DTC are registered in DTC's nominee name, Cede & Co. (making DTC's nominee the registered owner of the securities) and are held in fungible bulk. Each participant or pledgee having an interest in securities of a given issue credited to its account has a pro rata interest in the securities of that issue held by DTC. Among other services it provides, DTC provides facilities for payment by participants to other participants in connection with book-entry deliveries of securities, collects and pays dividends and interest to participants for securities, and provides facilities for the settlement of institutional trades. By centralizing and automating securities settlement, by reducing the movement of publicly traded securities in the U.S. markets, and by facilitating the prompt and accurate settlement of securities transactions, DTC serves a critical function in the National Clearance and Settlement System."

Source: SEC Release No. 34-47978; File No. SR-DTC-2003-02.

With certificates in hand, the CMKM shareholders triumphantly awaited the promised distribution of assets that would never come. Little more than one year later, in July 2007, the Task Force issued the following statement:

"To date, the Task Force records show that the Company has the following numbers:

Total Received Fax's:	42,723
Total Fax's Filed:	42,723
Number of Certs:	55,495
Total Shares:	634,983,934,884
Number of Shareholders:	39,863

The Task Force has accounted for 634,983,934,884 shares out of a total 703,518,875,000 shares outstanding. Brokerage houses and clearing firms are still on the master shareholder list representing tens of billions of shares being held in street name even though the stock is no longer trading. The DTCC is normally in charge of holding bulk certificates to back up each share being held in street name by each brokerage and/or clearing firm. However, since this stock is no longer trading, the DTCC completely emptied their vaults in April 06 and sent all bulk certs back to the Company's stock transfer agent to re-issue into the names of the brokers/clearing firms with an accompanying list to specify exactly how many shares are to go to each broker and/or clearing firm."

There is another reality that lies near the heart of the problem. DTC did not exit all the shares. As of June 2007, DTC still had three certificates totaling 7,682,648 shares that were issued in their name after their self-imposed deadline for exiting all shares from their system. The Task Force could not account for more than 68.5 billion shares outstanding. This is the point where criminal investigations were opened against the company founders, transfer agent and others. The Department of Justice and others would eventually bring charges for the issuance of unregistered shares. In other words, instead of pursuing the over-arching problem of phantom shares created in the clearing and settlement system, the authorities were only able to pursue criminal violations against a handful of actors in the shares of one unique company. Steve Kirkpatrick, who took over running CMKM in 2011, wrote this on December 5, 2014 in a message confirming the death of former CMKM CEO and insider Urban Casavant:

"Frankly, even after three years of working as CEO of CMKM/NHHI [New Horizons Holdings, Inc.], I do not understand the motives of a few select individuals that specialize in misinformation and controversy. I also do not understand how myths such as bogus trusts, payouts, conglomerates, 'sting operations', and other unverified stories continue to be circulated by some and even accepted by numerous well-meaning and innocent Shareholders. Regardless of your position on these controversial topics, time will prove that all we have left is a severely-damaged company struggling to survive and to recover the needed capital to build a legitimate business for our longsuffering Shareholders. The work will continue daily to accomplish that worthy goal. Thank you and God bless. /s/Steve Kirkpatrick"

Mr. Kirkpatrick's statement also confirmed that the US Department of Justice dismissed all criminal charges against Casavant after his death.

I have never been a shareholder or investor for CMKM nor New Horizons Holdings, Inc. or any other associated company. I was also never hired directly by CMKM to perform any analysis nor did I take any payments from CMKM for any work; I rarely contract directly with companies or individuals.[112] I was hired and paid directly by attorneys and legal firms who were sometimes working directly for the companies. Most of what comes in the final section of this chapter is material I researched while under contract to two law firms. In every case, I received written permission to discuss what I learned in that research.

In the past, the lawyers readily gave me permission to release redacted documents (i.e. with no information that could identify individual shareholders or their account numbers) to media outlets. As I explained above, none of the journalists that contacted me would run the story because of the allegations of fraud and criminal activity against CMKM, its founders/managers and/or transfer agents. One reporter even called CMKM "fraud city." In 2008 and 2009, I provided redacted documents to Bloomberg, Rolling Stone Magazine and Reuters, to name a few. Some of the stories of the struggle by investors to get the shares they paid for are heartbreaking. (See "Examples of Messages from Unshareholders" below.) Each of them told a story that was backed-up with documentation either from their brokerage account statements, letters from the brokers or records from the CMKM register of shareholders. None of the reporters would print the story or even make reference to the plight of active-duty military, hard-working families and American veterans who were cheated.

The part of the CMKM story that I was most involved in is that of the investors who never got shares – those investors which were left holding the phantom shares that they paid for but where shares were never received for them in settlement. I call them the Un-Shareholders.[113] Their story is not unique to CMKM but the story of the CMKM UnShareholders presents evidence of the reality that is the heart of the wider problem.

The UnShareholders

Publicly-traded companies were increasingly concerned about the impact of stock market manipulation on share prices. Corporate executives were correctly focused on taking care of their shareholders. Short selling and stock lending always leave some investor without real share ownership, even when it is not done to manipulate stock prices. Companies were worried about these "extra" or "phantom" shares diluting their market value, and rightly so.

In some ways, the shareholders have it worse: By accepting a retail broker account enrollment agreement, investors unwittingly allow the broker to lend their shares to other investors, including short sellers who are betting that the stock price will fall, which is the opposite of what ordinary investors are hoping. (For more on this, see "Stock Lending" section in Chapter 1.) Even when the investor does not condone stock lending, it can happen as a result of poor record keeping practices at the broker's operations department. When your shares are lent, you own a phantom share until the loan is repaid because, as I explained earlier, the "real" shares go to the borrower, including the right to vote, receive dividends, etc. Furthermore, when settlement failures happen, even the shares you bought may not be in your broker account regardless of what your statement says. These are the most common ways that phantom shares are created.

For every phantom share created there is a "phantom share holder." For simplicity, you can think of them as being on the receiving end of a fail to deliver. If their broker gets a fail to receive, they pick some retail investor to assign the phantom. But no one took an interest in the harm being done to the investors who were left holding the phantom shares. If an investor requested a stock certificate in the CMKM cert pull but did not get one, as happened to so many of the investors who wanted to purchase shares of CMKM, I labeled them "UnShareholders." In fact, almost anyone who receives a 1099 with "unqualified dividends" when they believe they owned regular shares, are probably UnShareholders, too.

The CMKM document review

In June of 2007, two lawyers and members of the CMKM Task Force asked me to review documents submitted to the Task Force along with various shareholder records from the transfer agent and DTC. I was particularly interested in those investors who reported that their share positions were deleted by their brokers and/or where brokers refused to provide them with share certificates registered in the investors' names so they could meet the requirements of a "bona fide shareholder" as described in the CMKM press release.

Although we did not have access to broker trade records, the documents I saw suggested three brokerage firms probably took payments from investors for shares that were never received from the selling broker in settlement: Charles Schwab, Chase Bank and RBC Dain. Investors submitted documentation showing that each of these brokers deleted their CMKM share positions at a time when we can demonstrate that the firms had no shares either in the depository or on the books of the issuer.

The Task Force received documents from investors for 10,499,992 shares that were evidenced by customer account records at Charles Schwab. Schwab did not take any shares in the DTC exit and they had no shares registered to them on the issuer's records. This would indicate that they did not have any shares for at least some of the investors who contacted the Task Force. Schwab also told investors very early, six months before the DTC exit, that they could not get certificates. Schwab's name (or its nominee name) did not show up on the April 14, 2006 Security Position Listing of members' shares at DTC. Schwab ordered certificates for a lot of trustee accounts directly from the transfer agent a month before the exit notice was released by DTC. The last certificate issued to Schwab was on March 13, 2006; that certificate was transferred out of their name on April 28, 2006. Schwab did not appear on any shareholder list after that date. This would seem to demonstrate that Schwab deleted the investor positions at a time when they simply did not have any shares left to deliver. They could not satisfy the withdrawals requested by investors who still showed CMKM shares on their customer account statements.

RBC Dain also had no shares registered in their name. RBC Dain did not appear on the April 14, 2006 DTC Security Position Report, the last day for withdrawals-by-transfer. The final transfers from RBC Dain's certificated shares were done by the transfer agent on April 13, 2006. The CMKM Task Force received evidence from investors showing 11,500,000 shares in customer accounts at RBC. RBC either deleted CMKM from the customer accounts or told the investor that there were no share certificates available, again, on dates *before* RBC received certificates from the transfer agent for themselves and other customers.

The Task Force received documents from investors for 3,760,000 shares that were evidenced by customer account records at Chase under similar circumstances. They had a significant number of shares registered in their own name at the time, so it was possible, though not likely that they could have made delivery to those account holders. The information investors sent to the CMKM Task Force, however, was that CMKM shares were being deleted from their accounts. If Chase could have sent shares, the evidence is that they did not provide share certificates to some investors. Likewise, TD Ameritrade deleted a high number of investor positions. However, the records indicate that TD Ameritrade had shares they could potentially have certificated and sent to investors at a later date, although I have not seen any evidence that they did so.

Finding the phantom shares

Where a shareholder could not get certificated shares from their broker accounts, there is a high probability that these investors were sold "Phantom Shares." To be the owner of phantom shares means that the investor was allocated a fail to receive by the broker after the money was taken from their cash accounts. These investors were obviously never notified of the situation since they continued to receive account statements showing share positions for CMKM.

Shareholders reported to the CMKM Task Force that the brokers in the following table told them they could not get certificates in 2005 and 2006. Each of these brokers had certificates issued *to their company* on the dates listed in the table. That is, they got certificates for themselves *after* they told investors that they could not get certificates.

Broker	Last certificate issued to firm	No. of Investors
Ameritrade	March 23, 2007	10
eTrade Financial	April 5, 2007	6

Royal Bank Canada	January 31, 2006	3
UBS Financial	April 4, 2007	2
Chase	May 17, 2006	2
Charles Schwab	March 13, 2006	2
QTrade	February 26, 2007	1
Piper Jaffray	August 7, 2006	1
Bank Leumi (Israel)	May 4, 2006	1
Bank of America	March 8, 2006	1
Bank One	March 8, 2006	1

Investors at a few other brokers also reported not being able to get certificates. There were no shares registered to those firms either in any of the documents and records I reviewed. This could be because:

(1) the shares are held at the Canadian depository (CDS received shares in the DTC exit);

(2) the shares are held by a correspondent broker; or

(3) the broker may have been the recipient of phantom shares (i.e. hit with the fail to receive) without being notified.

Evidence of phantom shares

Many of the investors reported to the Task Force that the broker deleted CMKM shares from their accounts. This would be in violation of NASDAQ rules.[114] The SEC allows DTC to destroy share certificates of "worthless" securities only if "the securities certificates in question must have been held by DTC in non-transferable status for at least six years."[115] Some of the investors told the Task Force that their shares were "sold" (evidenced in at least one case by the charge of a transaction fee) without any payment to the investor. This would be a breach of fiduciary duty by the broker who took action on an investor's stock position without their consent or authorization. At a minimum, each of those investors should have filed complaints with the SEC and NASD about the shares being deleted.

Of the documents I reviewed, there were 30 investors who presented clear evidence that either the CMKM shares were deleted from their accounts without their approval or that the broker incorrectly told them certificates were not being issued. Twenty-four of them had addresses in the US, and 6 in Canada. The following table lists the brokers' name, the location of the CMKM investor, the number of shares the investor evidenced in their broker account, and the reason the broker gave them for not complying with their request for a withdrawal (certificate). The names of the individual investors are redacted to protect their privacy. Unlike the SEC's Reg SHO fails-to-deliver list, we provide the name of the offending parties (the brokers) and not the names of the victims (investors left holding Phantom Shares).

Broker identified by Investor	Investor Location	Reason Given by Broker
Bank of America	Maryland	position deleted
Bank One	Indiana	position deleted
Charles Schwab	Alabama	position deleted
Charles Schwab	Colorado	no certificates available
Chase Bank	Canada	position deleted
Chase Bank	Michigan	stock declared worthless
eNorthern Brokerage	Canada	no certificates available
eTrade Financial	Alabama	shares "sold"
eTrade Financial	Iceland	position deleted
eTrade Financial	North Carolina	position deleted
eTrade Financial	North Carolina	position deleted
eTrade Financial	Tennessee	shares "sold"
eTrade Financial	Tennessee	shares "sold"
Fidelity	Kansas	no certificates available
Fortis Bank Bruxelles/BBH New York	Belgium	no certificates available
LeumiTrade	Israel	no certificates available
Piper Jaffray	Iowa	no certificates available
Qtrade	Canada	no certificates available, stock declared worthless

Royal Bank of Canada	Canada	position deleted
Royal Bank of Canada	Canada	no certificates available
Royal Bank of Canada	Canada	stock declared worthless
TD Ameritrade	California	position deleted
TD Ameritrade	Military	position deleted
TD Ameritrade	Minnesota	position deleted
TD Ameritrade	Missouri	shares "liquidated" (sold)
TD Ameritrade	New York	"invalid"
TD Ameritrade	New York	position deleted
TD Ameritrade	Texas	position deleted
TD Ameritrade	Utah	position deleted
TD Ameritrade	Wyoming	position deleted
TD Ameritrade	Minnesota	position deleted
UBS Financial Services, Inc.	New Jersey	no certificates available, no TA
UBS Financial Services, Inc.	New Jersey	no certificates available

NOTE: the broker names in the table were reported by the investors.

The claim at the heart of the matter is hardest to show without the kind of discovery one might obtain in a civil or criminal lawsuit. That claim is that the broker never took delivery of the shares for which the investors paid. Proof of this would be in the trading records and the records of the settlement department at the broker. The DTCC settlement position reports would show that the brokers were "long" shares at settlement, meaning they have a "failed to receive" position. Those investors were never shareholders or even "entitlement holders" which is the term the SEC uses for investors who leave their shares with brokers

www.UnShareholders.com

No one tried helping the UnShareholders until Al Hodges opened a website to attempt to identify more than just the CMKM UnShareholders in 2008. I had met Al for the first time when he attended the Naked, Short and Greedy event my company organized in LA a few years earlier. He supported the establishment of the website under the URL UnShareholder.com (now closed) even though he was a certificate-holding shareholder. Al and I worked with knowledgeable and involved members of the legal and financial community who recognized that investors were being damaged but that some of these investors are not shareholders. We collected information from investors who voluntarily identified the name of the company whose stock they paid for and the broker who could not deliver shares to them. What we learned confirmed what we saw in the cert pull data from the CMKM Task Force. Of the 71 investors who identified CMKM as the shares they paid for, 16 did not get shares from e-Trade, 16 from TD Ameritrade and five from Charles Schwab. Bank of America and Royal Bank of Canada were each identified by three CMKM investors. It is no coincidence that the same brokers appeared in this broader search for UnShareholders. The pattern of behavior, once established in a business, can become pervasive. E-Trade and TD Ameritrade were identified as failing to deliver paid-for shares in 25 other companies (in addition to CMKM).

Examples of Messages from CMKM UnShareholders

Military

Iraq

Sent: Saturday, August 12, 2006 1:20 AM

I have 24 Million shares of CMKM stuck in my Fidelity Rollover and Roth IRA accounts and I am being told by Fidelity that I have to open [another] account with $2,500.00, minimum deposit. As you can tell from my e-mail I am in Iraq and I do not have a normal telephone number.

At sea

With permission from the CMKM Task Force and my attorney clients, a screen shot of this May 2, 2006 email from a member of the U.S. Navy on deployment in the Middle East, was provided to Bloomberg, Reuters and Rolling Stone Magazine, among others. In addition to a screen shot of the email, I provided snapshots of the transfer agent's records showing that Ameritrade got certificates issued in their own name 6 days *after* they told this serviceman that CMKM was closed for business and would not be issuing any more certificates. The name of the investor is redacted.

"Hello, I had 2 ½ million shares of CMKX through Ameritrade (now TDAmeritrade) and it reads 0 because they said CMKX had been closed. I am in the US Navy and currently on deployment onboard the USS Abraham Lincoln (CVN-72)."

Canada

Sent: Monday, July 17, 2006 3 27PM

"I ordered [a certificate from our broker] and only today, have called Royal Bank Action Direct on 1 800 769 2660 in Canada who claim it isn't worth obtaining a certificate."

Sent: Saturday, August 12, 2006 12:17 PM

"All shares of CMKM have been deleted from my account at Ameritrade."

Switzerland

Sent: Tuesday, July 25, 2006 7:24 AM

"I got several shares of CMKX in the past and beginning of this year, they were all removed from my account by Ameritrade.... I contacted several times to find out what will they do in order to get my new Entourage shares? The answer was: they do not take any responsibility to reclaim from CMKX management... So I feel trapped....I am living abroad and it is difficult for me to intent any process to get my shares back..."

USA

Hawaii

Sent Sunday, April 30, 2006 9:29 PM

"I have 4,500,000 shares of CMKX that are in a Roth IRA in Ameritrade. I called Ameritrade and it will take longer than the May 15th deadline.

They said it will take 4 to 6 weeks. Also they said I might need to fill out additional paperwork to see if I am even able to get a certificate form."

Texas

Sent: Friday, April 28, 2006 11:33 PM

"I requested a cert for 30 million shares on November 5, 2005. I still do not have the cert. I've emailed Ameritrade several times asking about the delay and I get a different answer from them every time.

Excuse 1 (Jan 19). We have not received the cert from the TA... when we get it we will mail it to you.

Excuse 2 (March 3). We are in the process of separating and addressing the certs. It should be mailed to you the week of March 6.

Excuse 3 (April 7). It was an oversight and the cert was never processed. We will re-request and process as soon as possible. There should be no additional delays and you should easily receive the cert before May 15.

I've been told that I will have the cert by the deadline, but I now have my doubts."

Connecticut

Sent: Friday, April 21, 2006 4:33 PM

"I have not been able to pull [certificates] from Banc of America Investment Services. ... I have tried a 'withdrawal of worthless securities', a 'transfer and ship' ... I just got off the phone with them and they are sending me back a $75.00 check I mailed to them to close out my account because they now are saying that they need a 'withdrawal of worthless securities form' which I sent in Jan. 06."

Georgia

Sent: Friday, April 21, 2006 12:29 PM

"To this date, I still have not gotten my cert from etrade. Since my writing this last message to you, they have given me every excuse and have even gone as far as to tell me on March 14th that my cert was sent and I would have it on the 15th. This was a flat out untruth. Calls after 3/15 have been met with the same apologies for my being inconvenienced, being put on hold while managers are consulted to the close of the call which is always 'we have it, it is being worked on and there is no known date for when you will receive your cert.'"

Florida

Sent: Friday, April 21, 2006 8:48 AM

"I requested my [certificate] on November 11, 2005 from my broker and still have not received it. I was told at that time that it could take three to four months. I have called my local broker several times and believe that the problem is not with his office but with Investacorp where the stock was traded. My broker has called and written Investacorp as well as ADP Clearing demanding my cert but to no avail. He also talked to [the transfer agent's office] and she said their records only show one cert being delivered which I have received and filed with the task force. This cert was from another brokerage account."

Selected resources

- U.S. Securities and Exchange Commission "Information for CMKM Diamonds Investors" https://www.sec.gov/enforce/investor-alerts-bulletins/divisionsenforceclaimscmkmopinion062309htm.html
- CMKX Unofficial Message Board: http://cmkxunofficial.proboards.com/
- Unites States Department of Justice, Offices of the United States Attorneys, District of Nevada, "United States v. Brian Dvorak et al (CMKM), Case number: 2:09-CR-00132-RLH-RJJ.
- Criminal prosecution in the District of Nevada (United States v. John Edwards, et al., 2:09-CR-00132-RLH-RJJ)
- Civil suit out of the Central District of California (David Anderson, et al., v. Christopher Cox, et al., 8:10 –CV-00031-JVS-MLG).

Chapter 19. Two Documentary Films

My friend and colleague Bud Burrell connected me with Sandra Mohr who, with Producer Liz Bolwell, wrote the story for *Stock Shock* (2009, Mohr Productions). Sandra was a fan of satellite radio when she started to hear stories from people who bought shares of Sirius XM. When the stock came under attack it was often listed as one of the most shorted stocks in the market. The documentary film explains "naked short selling" in the context of the experience of Sirius XM investors and the company, using interviews and even cartoon characters to demystify some more technical aspects of market manipulation. I had already moved my office out of Southern California when Sandra contacted me for an interview. CFA-LA Board member Cynthia Harrington graciously loaned us an elegant conference room at her office on Wilshire Boulevard in Los Angeles for the interview. When Sandra asked me to explain the DTC, I described my work in post-trade clearing and settlement as being "a plumber on Wall Street": fixing the pipes and joints that keep after-the-trade processes running smoothly. My comment about the importance of centralized clearing and settlement made it to the final cut: "Nobody cares what the plumber has to say until the sh** backs up in the living room."

The film offerings from several big names in Hollywood would be years behind Sandra Mohr.[116] *Stock Shock* was first out of the gate in telling the real story of market manipulation behind the financial crisis and the impact it had on real investors. Most of the movie versions glamorized the role of the perpetrators. *The Big Short* offered one concession to those on the receiving end: when the character Ben Rickert stops his accomplices from dancing in the casino, he says, "Stop it, stop. Do you have any idea what you just did? You just bet against the American economy. Which means, if we're right, people lose homes, people lose jobs, people lose retirement savings, people lose pensions." *Stock Shock*, on the other hand, is all about all of those people, their losses and their struggles to understand how Wall Street made it all happen. The film was featured at the 2010 Los Angeles Women's International Film Festival held at the Laemmles Sunset 5 Theaters in Hollywood.

Bud was also instrumental in arranging to have me interviewed for *The Wall Street Conspiracy* ("WSC" 2012), a documentary film that took a broader look at the issue with special emphasis on the impact it had on individual investors. Although WSC would not be released until 2012, I was interviewed twice in 2008 for the documentary. As is often the case, only a small part of the interviews ended up in the final edit of the film. The first interview took place on July 31, 2008. Bud asked the questions that day, focusing on my background experience in post-trade processing and on my scholarly research into settlement failures, or what they were calling "naked short selling." Much of that material is covered elsewhere in this book.

After the financial crisis fully manifested in September 2008, the producers invited me back to the New York studios to talk about settlement failures in all forms of securities, including bonds. The second interview took place on November 7, 2008. The producers wanted to focus the interview on making the connection to what was happening in the financial markets over the previous couple of months. They also gave me the opportunity to discuss credit default swaps and how they grew out of control in the months leading up to the financial crisis.

What follows is a transcript of the entire second interview taken from the unedited recordings, which were provided to me by the producer, Kristina Leigh Copeland.[117] Both interviews were recorded at City Stage Studio, 434 West 19th Street in New York City. The director decided in advance that the interviewers' questions would not appear in the film. Instead, they asked me to include the questions in my answers. Therefore, what follows is not in the typical Q-and-A format you would expect to see in a printed interview. The transcript has been edited for grammar and consistency and to remove some repetitive material that is presented elsewhere in this book. Otherwise, we stay as close as possible to the original content.

Transcript of November 7, 2008 interview by producers and directors of The Wall Street Conspiracy (2012)

As I described the last time we met, prior to the implementation of Reg SHO, we were only able to see numbers for settlement failures on the equity side when NSCC released the year-end figure in the notes to their financial statements. That number has been increasing since we started watching it. When I look at the data, I can see a spike in the numbers right around 2001. After that, there's a very steep trajectory of regular increases.

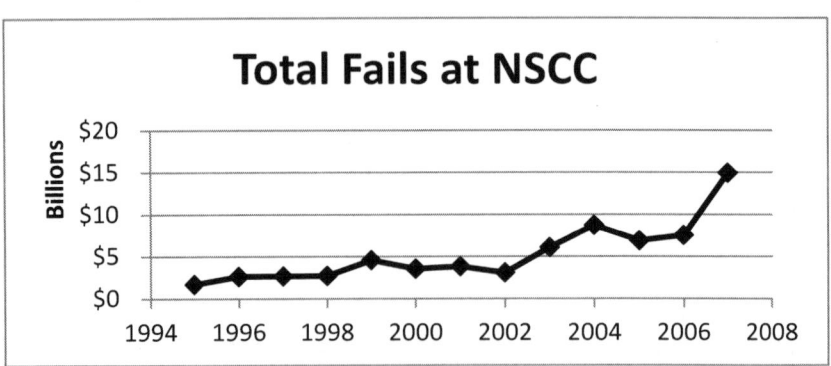

Data Source: NSCC Financial Statements

What is particularly scary about the fact that these settlement failures exist at the DTCC is that they have behind them what they call a clearing fund, and that is like a deposit that each of the participants makes that could be used to cover any obligations they incur at the point where, perhaps, the broker or bank participant goes bankrupt, for example, or the situation that Drexel Burnham or Lehman Brothers found themselves in. When there are unsettled obligations in the system for them, then the DTCC could go into the clearing fund to get money to be able to try to resolve all of these differences. In the case of Lehman Brothers, they claim to have been able to resolve **most** of the outstanding obligations without giving a lot of details.

The concern I have is that the clearing fund is growing more slowly than the settlement failures. The settlement failures are growing about 60% faster than the clearing fund. As unsettled trade obligations build up in the system, there is not enough money in these back-up funds that the DTCC had to be able to fulfill those obligations in the event of additional fails among the participants. That is only on the equity securities (stocks) side; it is probably the low end of the numbers. In addition to what is reported annually, of course, that value of fails to deliver fluctuates day-to-day throughout the year. The peaks are not always at the same time of year. There is no pattern to it, but they do tend to get significantly higher at certain times of the year even though the depository only releases one number. On the equity side, just at NSCC, we know that on December 31, 2007 there were $14 billion of trades unsettled in that system. That was up against a clearing fund, a participant fund, of about $4 billion. They are "underwater" by three fold on that.

On the bond side, I did some research in 2007 which I successfully presented at an international conference on accounting, economics and finance in May of 2008. I subsequently revised the paper and published it (Trimbath 2011). In that paper, I estimated just the settlement failures in the bond markets. There is very little public data about trading in bond markets and therefore very little public data on settlement failures. I extrapolated from data that is available from a variety of sources to put it together. I estimated that at the end of December 2007 there was about $400 billion of unsettled bond trades in the US financial system. I continued to monitor the data on trade settlement failures in bond markets through early 2008. In April 2008 that number actually doubled to $800 billion. In the last four weeks, just among the primary dealers in US Treasury securities, they reported $5 trillion worth of failed trades. And that is not just 1 week of $5 trillion that is 4 consecutive weeks of $5 trillion in fails.

Dan Jamieson, a reporter for Investment News contacted me last month about this data.[118] I explained to him what it was and confirmed that he was reading it correctly. He was just as shocked as I was that it was so high. The numbers have never been this high. Even when they spiked and peaked in the past at $1 trillion or $2 trillion level, settlement failures didn't stay high like they have now.[119] For his article, Jamieson had contacted the FRB-NY to try to get comments from them. He asked me, "Who else can speak to this?" So I told him to contact the two economists at FRB-NY who had written about this in the past (Fleming and Garbade, 2002 and 2005). When Jamieson contacted them, they told the reporter that he could not quote them in the article. When he got back to me with this, I told Dan, "I think this is a story as well: the fact that they won't talk about it." They won't make any comment as to, first of all, why fails to deliver in bond markets are so high, higher than it's ever been, double what it's ever been and, on top of that, why it is sustained at that level for such a long period of time.

Other researchers have looked at this and come to the conclusion that fails in UST and in all the bond markets happen because the failing parties make money at it. Some researchers say that it's an investment strategy, but actually it is a money-making **scheme**. A strategy is something that you think through, it is a profitable situation that if everyone did it you would still be ok – perhaps anyone could engage in. A scheme is something that only benefits the scheming party; if a lot of other people engaged in the same activity the benefit would be diminished; if everyone did it the market would collapse. These are just schemes because they are selling things that they don't have. And, in fact, the markets collapsed in September.

The settlement failures, in the bonds in particular, are tied to very closely to the economic and financial crisis that we find ourselves in. If the regulators were to enforce delivery of the sold bonds, it would force up the prices of bonds as any broker who had an open settlement failure would have to go out to buy the bonds in the open market. As the prices of the bonds went up the interest rates would come down without any artificial interference from the Treasury, from the SEC or from the FRB. At the same time, if we were to enforce the delivery of sold equities, you would see a surge in prices that would help dramatically in the recovery of the stock market right now.

Credit default swaps and mortgage bonds

You also asked me to talk about how the credit default swaps (CDSs) relate to this. A CDS is like a little insurance contract. Let's say I buy some mortgage-backed securities (MBS), and I am concerned about my long term investment. I could lose my investment if, say, the mortgage holder (mortgagee) defaults and they can't make the monthly mortgage payments of principal and interest. To protect my investment, what I do is, in addition to buying the bond, I pay a small premium to another organization. That premium gives me insurance. If the bond issuer defaults on payments because they didn't get mortgage payments or defaults on the principal so that I would otherwise lose my investment, the insurance provider pays off. It's like having insurance on your house; you pay a small premium, you hope nothing happens, but if it does, the insurance company will have to replace it. A CDS is basically that. The credit is the bond, the default is the risk that you don't get paid on the bond, and the swap is that you give the default risk to someone else.

Unfortunately, in the mortgage markets, there was such a rush and demand for MBS because of the fees the banks and brokers were earning that there were more MBS sold than there were mortgages. This was the first mistake that happened in the market. There was such a demand for them that money from the mortgage bonds was put back into the mortgage market and loaned in very inconsistent ways and in improper ways. Bad mortgages were written, this is true; but there is also evidence that more bonds were issued than there were mortgages. We have cases in Florida and Ohio where the bondholder attempted to foreclose on the underlying property and the courts told them "you can't because you don't have a lien, you don't have the documentation in place to say that you, the bondholder, actually have some interest in this property." The homeowners have walked away from court with ownership of the house. The bondholder got nothing.

On top of that, you now have CDS: again, multiples of these insurance contracts were written on any one mortgage bond. The academics that I talk to who watch these issues and research them say the multiple is between 9 and 15. So, for every $1 worth of underlying mortgage bond there were $9 worth of insurance written. Well, if someone said to you, "You have a million dollar house, I'll give you $9 million worth of insurance on your house," how tempting is it to let something happen to your house? Because your house is only worth $1 million if you sell it, but the insurance is worth $9 million! This is what happened in the mortgage markets. Bear Stearns began to report problems in their sub-prime mortgage funds three to six months **before** there was a spike in the sub-prime defaults. Why? Because for every $1 in mortgage payment that didn't come in, Bear Stearns (and firms like them) were on the hook for $9 worth of payments. It was **that** pressure that pushed them to the brink and over; not, strictly speaking, an excess in the actual default rate. The default rate in the sub-primes at the beginning of 2007 was no different than it had been in 2003.

If you look at this data, look at this information you have to ask why were New Century and Bear Stearns and these other funds who got involved in these MBS, especially the sub-prime mortgages, in trouble so much earlier than the sub-prime mortgages. And the answer is two-fold:

(1) they simply misapplied the practical application of financial innovations having to do with issuing mortgage-backed securities; and
(2) they sold more bonds than existed.

The trade settlement failure rate in MBS in 2004 averaged 40%. Every other mortgage bond trade failed to settle. The average daily fail rate for trades in MBS between 2000 and 2008 was 15%. There were that many more bonds sold than ever existed. Well, of course, this is going to collapse. This is what people like Wes Christian have been talking about on the equity side. What you are seeing on the bond side is simply that the numbers are so much bigger. If you had $6 billion worth of problem in equities, you have $6 **hundred** billion worth of a problem in bonds. When a $600 billion problem falls on your head – then you have serious problems. Then you are going to see markets collapse and the sort of financial turmoil that we have right now.

Beyond the US

We don't know a lot about what's happening as far as statistics coming out of overseas and the European markets for failures to deliver. We know a couple of things. We know that the system they have is the same as the system we have. DTC and the NSCC were the model upon which most other systems were designed. The U.S. system was the first and, therefore, became the most widely known and recognized; and it was also extremely efficient. All of the models in many of the other countries, not just in Europe, but also in Asia and in Africa and India, have the same system in place. They have the same problems we are seeing here it, but it is not visible. One of the reasons it is not visible, according to the Bank for International Settlements (BIS), is that in many countries, they don't require the reporting of fails to deliver and fails to receive. Their brokers and banks are not required to report trade settlement failures. In the US, we have reporting so that we are able to see more of it. The BIS study was on about 30 developed economies and most of them just don't collect information on it. The problem is there, we just don't know the extent of it. In 2002, one report estimated that 15% to 20% of all cross-border trades failed to settle; 33% in emerging markets.[120] There was another report that came out of the UK in 2006 that indicated that the fail to deliver rate was eight times higher when an individual investor was on the buy side than when an institution was the buyer.[121] When an individual purchased a security, they were eight times more likely to be on the receiving end of a fail to deliver, in other words, individual investors were frequently getting stuck with the fail to receive.

Phantom shareholders

Another way that what we are talking about in this documentary that relates to the financial problems we are seeing now is that if you understand this idea that more shares are being sold than exist then it's important to recognize that for Fannie Mae and Freddie Mac multiples of outstanding bonds have already been sold, pushing down the price and doing these other sorts of damages to the companies. In the case of Fannie Mae/Freddie Mac the evidence shows that there are phantom shares in circulation. Looking at publicly available data from the NYSE, we've seen that institutional owners alone have 113% of the issued and outstanding shares. Let me repeat that: institutions like banks, brokers, and pension funds own 113% of the outstanding shares of Freddie Mae and Fannie Mac. Individual investors and non-institutional holders also own some of those shares. This is just clear, direct evidence that more shares were sold than ever existed.

I was at a securities lending conference on Monday and I made a presentation on the corporate governance implications of securities lending which is directly what we are talking about here today. An interesting fact that someone brought out was that at their last annual meeting, Bank of America received 130% in votes: they received 30% more votes than they had shares outstanding. That's just the number of people who actually voted their shares![122] You can imagine how many shares were sold beyond what they actually authorized and issued. If you think that you can sell 30% more shares than exist and not have a direct impact, not only on the share price but also directly on the company, then just look at what's happening to banks right now. That's the impact that happens.

Some lawsuits and criminal cases have been successful in making claims that the brokers are selling of unregistered securities when they create Phantom Shares. I don't even say that they are selling securities, unregistered or otherwise! They are selling air, they are selling nothing. I don't say that anyone is selling unregistered securities into the market place because I don't call these securities.

They are selling air. There is nothing there. There is the aspect that this is stealing. They take people's money and they give them nothing – exactly nothing.

CDS are contracts and those contracts are being registered and stored at DTCC in New York. They recently, in fact on November 4, 2008, began releasing data about how many contracts they have registered. They hold about $32 trillion worth of contracts. That's the both the buyer and the seller have registered the contract. The way that these contracts are tracked is that there is a buyer – the person buying protection – there's a seller – basically someone who is insuring a credit – and then there is what they call the "reference party" – whose debt are you guaranteeing against default. You can go in and sort the contracts that they have registered now by whose debt is being protected. Some of the biggest, those with the highest dollar value insured and the highest number of contracts are foreign governments – the debt of Turkey, Brazil, e.g.. Right after that you have the debt of Goldman Sachs and JP Morgan, GMAC (General Motors Acceptance Corporation). That's the credit, the debt, that's being protected by the CDS. The buyer of a CDS wants protection in the event that the debt of those companies goes into default for non-payment of interest and/or principal.

The new things you asked me about for this second interview, I guess, is to try to tie together what's happening in the financial markets now with the problem of phantom shares. I've tried to say this in different ways to make it as clear as possible and I think the best way to look at it is to recognize that the problem that you see and talk about on the equity side, is multiplied 100 times in the bond markets and then another 15 times through the credit default swaps. Basically, for every $1 in real value that any company or country puts into the financial markets, brokers are ramping it up and trading something like 1,875% of it. Another way to look at it is that if a homeowner defaults on a $100,000 mortgage, it can do $187,500,000 worth of damage to global financial markets.

You know, I worked in clearing and settlement for many years. My career in clearing and settlement started in 1985 with the Pacific Clearing Corporation and the Pacific Securities Depository Trust Company in San Francisco which was fairly early on, it was within the first 10 or 15 years before these organizations even existed. Clearing and Settlement as we know it today was really only started in the early 1970s. So I got into it pretty early, and I had been at the FRB before I went to the stock exchange. I was already aware of how payment systems and securities issues worked. The clearing and settlement system that you have in the US, and as I said, this model has been exported around the world, was originally designed only to handle equity securities.

Eventually, it was successful and there was a need, a desire, to process bonds in it as well. But rather than writing a brand new system just to handle bonds, they simply made bonds look more like equities so they could run them through the same computer system. That's the same thing that happened with mutual funds; mutual funds looked like equities in the system, no different than a share of $1 in a mutual fund was like one share in an equity. Just for the way that the system processed everything. The same thing with the bonds, everything that you've heard and you believe and you've come to understand about what happens to equity securities is happening to mutual funds, funds of funds, SPDRs, ETFs, bonds. The difference is that while one share of stock costs on average $35, one bond costs on average $1,000. Where you would have $6 billion or $14 billion worth of fails in equities, you would have $600 billion worth of failed trades in bonds, $800 billion, $1.2 trillion – you just add more zeroes to it.

Now you begin to understand how everything you hear in the complaints and about financial turmoil in credit markets include bond markets. Bonds are credits. They are debt, the debt of a company, the debt of a country. When you come to understand that then when I talk about trade settlement failures in US bond markets, you understand that I'm talking about these credit markets that are, in fact, at the root of the turmoil that we see in the markets today.

Ferreting out the data

In general, there is more information available about settlement failures than just what DTC releases in the clearings system for equities and some UITs. We have data from the primary dealers that are reported to the FRB-NY about bonds: treasury bonds, government agency bonds, mortgage-backed bonds and corporate bonds are the only areas that they report. There is one other place where we are able to get information about the broader magnitude of fails to deliver and fails to receive. Members of the NYSE have to make reports to their self-regulatory organization of their balance sheets and their income statements. They release this on a quarterly basis, and the last figures I looked at were for the 2008Q2. They were reporting about $190 billion worth of settlement failures. Of course that's not all of the bond fails that the primary dealers report to the Fed, but it is significantly more than equity fails that are reported by the NSCC to the SEC. We can at least look at that and come to understand that although there may be some overlap what the NSCC is reporting as a $14 billion fail, the members of the NYSE, the parallel number is easily close to $400 billion.

One of the most difficult issues for someone like myself, an economist, and someone who wants to do research in this area is getting accurate data because it is very piecemeal. For example, these reports that I talked about coming from the NYSE, just from the NYSE members, where we see in the second quarter of this year almost $400 billion worth of settlement failures reported overlaps with the $14 billion reported by NSCC. It includes that and other things, right? But it does not include all of the bond failures that are reported to FRB-NY. Because we don't have access to underlying data, it's very difficult to reconcile them. That's not to say that the data does not exist – just that it is not made public.

In my own research, what I did was to use the transactions and the failures that are reported to the FRB-NY to calculate a failure **rate**. Once the rate is established, it can be applied to transaction data, which is easier to find. So, what is the failure rate where the primary dealers are buyers and sellers and the trade fails to settle? When we have that rate, we can use that as the minimum rate – really, my estimates are very conservative – at which we could say that all trades fail. If the primary dealers themselves are experiencing this rate, and if there are non-primary dealers of which there are hundreds trading, I think it is safe to assume that is at least the same for both. Primary dealers have to meet higher standards to get that designation from FRB-NY; one could assume that they should be less likely to fail to deliver securities than other dealers; and certainly less likely to fail to deliver to each other. I take that fail rate and go to a separate source and find out what are the total trades occurring in these securities and I apply the failure rate to the total market. That's how I'm able to come up with an estimate of what the total fail rate is that is, I assure you, very conservative but rock solid.

Economics = Accounting + Finance

The first time I became aware of the way that some trades could affect the number of shares in circulation goes back to 1993. When I went to the senior managers at DTC and they said that they wouldn't do anything about it because, "You can't balance the world." I remember thinking that wasn't a very good answer. At that point I already had two business degrees: I had a bachelor's and a master's in business. I had studied accounting, I studied corporate finance, and I knew that the number of shares authorized by the company and the number of shares issued and outstanding was a really important figure.

It is important when it comes to accounting statements, when it comes to the balance sheet, even when it comes to the income statements. All of the theories that we have about what are the prices of stocks, all this is based on "per share". The most fundamental pieces of information that you have about a company is how many shares are outstanding. Why? Because the questions that everyone talks about are "what are the earning per share?", "what's the dividend per share?", "what is their operating income per share?" In finance and accounting, you can actually take and do the company's entire balance sheet just on a per share basis and that tells you something about what you should pay for that share. So, for a senior manager at the DTC to say, "You can't balance the world. It's not important how many shares are in circulation" simply says to me, "This individual doesn't understand accounting and finance." In fact, the person I was talking to had a Bachelor's in History and had simply worked his way up in the company to become a senior manager. So, maybe he really didn't understand it.[123] But I was very disappointed that he said that.

An explosion in FTDs

In 1993, the numbers were very small. It was a couple of million dollars' worth of extra shares, a couple of million dollars' worth of failed trades in the system. By 2003, when I met with Wes Christian for the first time, that had become $6 billion. It just was shocking to me. I remember telling Wes that it looks as if somewhere between 1993 and 2003 somebody figured out that there was a hole in the system. Somebody figured out that there was this little loophole, this little crack in the system where you could actually just make money by selling shares that didn't exist. And the system itself would never stop you, there's no punishment for it, there's no fines or fees, there's no one saying "you broke the rules, you can't play anymore." The loophole was beginning to be seriously exploited, making a lot of money for those taking advantage of it.

Since that day in 2003, I've watched the numbers just explode. The degree to which this is being exploited is shameful. To know that for four years I've been writing letters to the SEC, to the FRB, to my representatives in Congress and the Senate, and they have not taken the first step to stop it, the first step being "enforce delivery of what is sold." If you sell me shares and you take my money, someone, someone should be forcing you to give me what I bought. And to this day, no one is doing that.

Almost everyone knows some people that experienced loss as a result of the September 2008 financial crisis: losses in their jobs and their stock market portfolios. I get worried about people. If I spent 4 years trying to explain this to regulators and government officials and writing about it and writing research papers about it, talking to reporters about it, endless hours with reporters about it and somehow it's not getting across, it's frustrating. I firmly believe that if I could accurately communicate to you what is happening you would be up in arms to try to get action to correct this. When I talk to people about this, regulators or reporters or whatever, each time I do this with someone for the first time, as I'm talking to them I can see it begin to happen behind their eyes, it starts to set in. "Where's my 401k?" "What's my pension plan invested in?" "Where's my money?!?" "What should I do?!?" That panic starts to set in on people. At some point I usually congratulate them for not running from the room screaming, which I think would be a really natural reaction to this.

What I usually tell people is that there really are not a lot of other places you can go to. The idea of me explaining this to you and helping you to understand it is not to tell you to take all the money out of your 401k, sell all your stocks, liquidate your pension fund. It's not to tell you to do that because, where else do you go with your money? Where else do you invest? I tell you so that you go to the regulators, your Congressman, and you talk to these people who are in a position to make the changes and **demand** that they enforce settlement. Demand that they take action. When you buy stock, they must give you stock, not an entitlement, not a phantom; that they give you what you pay for. This is the reason that I talk about it and try to make it clear.

How does that make you feel?

There are days where, I feel like I've had my head in the sewer all day long, because in order to do the research that I do I have to look at ho w much is going on, who is doing it, who are they doing it to, which securities are they doing it in, and each time I do, I run up against a roadblock where either the data is so spread out that you can't get it or it is being hidden intentionally. "We only release it once a year." "We only aggregate it. We don't have to give you the breakdown." "We only report it for 22 brokers, not all 322 brokers." Each time I come up against that and I recognize that it's not that difficult to fix because the fix is simply to insist that if I pay for something, you give me what I bought. I'm certainly not one of the people on the planet that **can** fix it because it's not up to me to enforce the rules and to enforce the regulations, to enforce the option that Congress has already given to the depository and clearing corporations which is anyone in that system who fails to deliver money or shares for settlement, they can be thrown out of the system. I think the first time that that happens is when we can really say some success has come about. That's the point where I can say to myself, "After five years of every day thinking about, writing about, talking about this", that's the day when I can say "yes, now something has happened." The first time someone who sells shares that they don't own and can't deliver for settlement is told that they can no longer trade in this system, they are simply not allowed to play anymore, that's when we've made progress.

At this point I feel like we haven't made any progress because no one has been forced to make settlement, no one has been forced to deliver. People have been fined for breaking rules about naked short selling, short selling and stock lending. I'm not saying that short selling, naked short selling and stock lending have nothing to do with it. They have a lot to do with it! Naked short selling and failing to deliver are two sides of the same coin. One path is direct and one path is indirect, but they get you to the same place. You take someone's money and you give them nothing. The difference is in how you get there.

My emphasis from the beginning has been on FTD, that's the first piece to fix. OK, there are other problems with short sales and stock lending which we can deal with later. But if you don't stop this FTD then nothing else matters. Here's a perfect example. August and September 2008, SEC put out some restrictions on 300 or 400 financial firms. They said you can't short sell any of these stocks. OK. So I checked the list against the companies that are on the Reg SHO Threshold List.[124] Reg SHO is a short sale rule but it only measured FTDs. It doesn't actually measure short sales. So there were about two dozen financial companies who were not on the FTD list before the restrictions went in on short selling, but **were** on the list **after** the restrictions went in! What does that say?

If I can't short sale, so what, I can just fail to deliver; it's the same end result. In fact, I save money by not having to process paper work on the short and not having to pay fees to borrow the shares for delivery. They sell something, they take your money, they give you nothing. What did that restriction do? What was the point of that rule? It did nothing because it did not prevent the fails to deliver.

I lay the blame squarely at the feet of the Depository Trust and Clearing Corporation's subsidiaries, DTC and NSCC. The Securities and Exchange Act of 1933 specifically gave them the right to require that shares and securities be delivered for settlement. It goes one step further to allow them to punish those who don't deliver by refusing to have them in the system. They are not doing what they were created to do. Until they do that, this problem doesn't stop.

The DTC is like a cooperative, owned by the users. When I say they are a "self-regulatory organization" (SRO) I am saying that they regulate themselves. The banks and brokers who use all the services there, who process trades there, who borrow and lend securities there, who fail to deliver there, are the same parties that sit on the Board of Directors (BoD). The BoD then does, of course, what BoDs do in all corporations, which is to give direction to the organization, to appoint the senior managers, all those sorts of things. The same parties that are failing to deliver are the same parties who would have to give instructions to enforce delivery. The fox is watching the hen house. The same parties who are failing to deliver are the same ones who are in charge of making sure that no one fails to deliver. In that scenario, how could anyone expect there not to be more of the same.

It is impossible for me to discuss fails to deliver without considering who gets the fail to receive. Every fail to deliver results in a fail to receive – unless the shares are borrowed, but let's put that aside for the moment because it doesn't have to be complicated. If the selling broker fails to deliver shares for settlement that means the buying broker failed to receive shares for settlement. The question is always then who gets the fail to receive? In the clearing and settlement system, there is a random algorithm that they process that each time there is a fail to deliver they then go and assign the fail to receive to one or another of their participants.

Let's say that your broker gets one of these fails to receive. First of all, they don't tell you that they got a fail to receive. If you were an institutional buyer, or a high-value client, they will tell you that they failed to receive and they will give you some monetary compensation for the delay and inconvenience. You and I as individual retail investors, they don't tell us, they don't have to tell us, they don't want to tell us. Because if they did, they would have to share with us the revenue they earn on our money (since brokers don't have to pay for shares they fail to receive), which they don't want to do. The question then becomes, "Well, how did I get assigned dividends in lieu instead of real dividends? How did I get picked out for that?" The problem is, we don't know. We don't know and they won't tell us.

Phantom votes

When it comes to the voting, we have a little more information about it. On the voting side, the NYSE members, each one individually decides how they will allocate the excess shares. They send you your proxy material; you fill in your vote and give it back to the broker. And you think, "Oh, I voted in the corporate election, I have some say in how the company is run. I'm a shareholder, I have clout with the company." But the reality is if you were assigned the fail to receive, then the broker has many options, none of which they have to tell you. They can, in fact, throw out your vote and just not count it. They can randomly assign your vote to some real share that wasn't voted. They can vote what shares they actually do have proportionally based on how many phantom votes come in. But the key thing to understand with all of these little processes and procedures and lotteries and everything else going on: it's all done in secrecy. There is no transparency. They don't have to tell you, they don't have to tell the NYSE, they don't have to tell anyone. They don't have to tell the company whose shares they voted and the SEC isn't interested.

Imagine now that there is a large merger up for vote. Let's say it's the merger of Compaq and Hewlett Packard. Let's say that there are a lot of these extra shares around and they have more votes than shares coming in. And let's say that your broker/dealer is, oh, I don't know, JP Morgan, for example, who was actually one of the advisors on that merger deal. They stood to gain more in fees if the merger went through than if it was voted down. Do you think that they would be so careful about your vote that if you voted against something they were in favor of that they would not be tempted to only turn in the votes that they thought should be counted, those that were most favorable to their position as opposed to trying to make sure that everything was done according to – well, I would say "according to the rules" but, hell, there are no rules! They just make them up as they go along. And they think that this is perfectly fine. I think it's an outrage. I think it's a travesty. There are professional people in the industry that is engaged in proxy voting, who are engaged in counting the votes for corporations, who say it is criminal.

CDS: phantom or real?

There are a number of reasons why the number of credit default swaps available, being written, and being provided in the US economy increased dramatically. One reason is certainly that we had more bonds being written than there were underlying credits (like mortgages). We call these structured securities. A structured security isn't just like a straight bond. On an ordinary bond, ordinary security, you lend the company money and they issue a bond. Just like you could buy a Treasury bond, you could buy savings bonds: you lend the government some money, they give you a bond, they pay you some interest, and when it matures, they return the principal – very vanilla. In a structured security, it's not as cut and dried. What happens is that the assets are separated from the income stream. Now, at this point, it's possible to put all of the, let's say, less risky payments in one pile, in one security, and structure the more risky payments in a separate security. But in order to get a really good credit rating, a really good Standard & Poors or Moody's credit rating, so that you can get a good price when you sell them, you buy a credit default swap. The trustee of the structured security puts that "little insurance contract" – remember a credit default swap is like a little insurance contract: you pay a little premium to a default swap seller, and if your bond fails – so if your bond collapses and the issuer goes bankrupt, the seller of that insurance pays you off. So, as the structured securities became more risky there was more reason to write credit default swaps.

Another reason is that we are leaning more and more towards "Casino Capitalism." I work overseas a lot. I worked in places like Egypt, India; I've done work in Russia; I've had contact with stock exchange people in Poland and Romania. When I go overseas to the emerging markets, the one thing I hear over and over again is, "Well, your American stock market is just like a casino. You're just gambling that the price goes up or the price goes down." I try to explain to people, "No, that's not true. The American stock market is where companies go to get the capital they need to create jobs, jobs that pay wages so that people can have savings that they can then invest, that can be borrowed by companies, to create jobs, etc." But when I come back home and I look at CDS, structured MBS, the way that these things are being written improperly; I see the settlement failures in the securities markets, I see the over-voting and I see the phantom shares… and I begin to think that maybe they are right. We have let our capital markets become what they think it is: a casino. The credit default swap, unfortunately, is like the biggest casino. It is all about betting on whether or not the underlying bond issuer will fail, betting on whether or not a homeowner will be able to make their next mortgage payment. There is no limit to how many can be sold and you do not have to own or have any economic interest in the underlying asset(s) or credit(s).

Another reason that there are more CDS around now is that in the rush to get more mortgages issued (Wall Street needed to do more mortgage bonds) they all just screwed it up. The banks and the brokers messed up the paper work. They were writing bonds without having the proper paperwork for the mortgages. In some cases, the same mortgage was being used in multiple bonds. Not because it was right, not because they should, just because they made a lot of mistakes. There was such a rush to get so much of this stuff done that the mortgages themselves, yes, became more risky because there was more money to be made in the fees if you could keep this chain rolling. The mortgages sell the bonds, the money from the bonds let them write more mortgages, they just keep going, you understand?

There was this huge rush to just keep writing more mortgages which put a lot of money in the housing market where thing like income standards that were accepted by the lenders went by the wayside; they just started writing mortgages for unqualified buyers.

Then there were mistakes in getting the mortgage paperwork associated with the bond: the same mortgages sold into multiple bonds, some mortgage bonds sold without mortgages underneath them or with improper documentation associating the bond with the mortgage. As a result, these securities became increasingly riskier for all of these reasons. As that was recognized, the potential for default also went up. Eventually, that plays into itself: the fact that those mortgages and the mortgage bonds were sold throughout the world, and to all sorts of different organizations, they then put those organizations at risk. The organizations who invested in those badly written bonds themselves became risky. You just had this kind of snowballing, on-going, ever-increasing problem.

For example, AIG became risky because things they invested in became risky. AIG is an insurance company; they were issuing debt, what is called "Commercial Paper" that was being bought by the money market mutual funds (MMMFs). Why? Because MMMFs have to keep a certain amount of their investment in short-term, high-quality investments – like insurance companies! They were buying AIG's paper; they were buying commercial paper and debt that AIG used to finance its business.

Meanwhile, AIG is selling CDS on risky mortgage bonds. When AIG became at risk, they then put all the MMMFs at risk because those MMMFs were required to buy the paper of insurance companies, which were thought to be low risk because they were heavily regulated. So you see the problem with that wasn't just

AIG, but it was what the failure of AIG would have done to all the parties down the road. Global financial markets are more and more interrelated. As we move forward in time, as we automate and as we truly globalize, financial markets become more and more interconnected. What some countries and some organizations don't understand is that CDS are, in the end, legal contracts. A share of stock in the US is **not** like a share of stock in France or in Cairo. There are laws associated with corporate governance, with the payment of dividends, with standing in bankruptcy court for various investors that are different across national lines. Someone in France who buys a share of stock in the US may or may not understand what it is that they are getting into. It is the same way with CDS contracts – the rules that govern CDS written in the US are the laws of the US, not the laws of the country where the buyer lives.

Where is my perp-walk?

In the end, I'll be waiting for the perp-walk. Who are they going to walk in handcuffs to the car? And who is going to do it? Is the Justice Department going to do it? Or is the FBI going to do it? Who are the enforcers here? Part of the problem is that the foxes are watching the henhouse. You have people with vested interests in all these self-regulatory organizations who have been given broad latitude for enforcement who have no motivation whatsoever to enforce anything. The bigger the problem gets and the worse it gets, there is even less motivation for anyone to do anything about it.

I compare it to dealing and an alcoholic. What's the first step to recovery? Admit that you have a problem. In order to admit that they have a problem, the regulators have to admit that they've known about it for a long time and done nothing. This is not going to happen. This is a very difficult thing to do. This, in fact, is part of what pushed Japan into a 10-year recession. Their problem was that the government was supporting inefficient industries. In order to correct it, they had to admit that they had been supporting inefficient industries for many years. The government did not want to make that first admission and, therefore, could not take the next step which was to stop doing it. So that's the problem we have.

US regulators have to admit that they have allowed settlement failures, fails to deliver in this system, in this country for a long, long time. Which regulator has got the courage, the will, to admit that as a first step toward reform? Is there political will among people, investors, voters, to stand up and say, "You've got to fix it now!" Can the people then force the issue so that the regulators admit, whether they want to or not, that they've been ignoring it for years, admit that it has to be fixed, admit that there has to be a change made.

How did naked short selling play into our current financial crisis? The better question is how **didn't** it. If you just look around you, what do you see? Stock prices falling, bond markets collapsing, credit markets falling apart, and there is no liquidity. If you look around you, and you understand everything that you've heard me say in this description of the problems with fails to deliver and naked short selling and stock lending and all these other ideas, the connection should be obvious. No matter how many 700 billions of dollars the government throws at it, if you are giving people money and getting nothing, then all you've done is to make the problem $700 billion bigger! It's not going to fix it until you say, "If I give you $700 billion, you must give me $700 billion worth of whatever the heck it is I bought."

America sneezed

All the markets worldwide are being affected by a financial crisis created in one country. When the US sneezes, the world catches pneumonia. If you look back over the summer of 2008, as the US financial markets became more and more dramatic, there was more and more turmoil. At some point the dollar started to gain against the Euro and the Pound; at some point, other countries started cutting their interest rates and talking about, "Let's all work together to fix this." Sometimes it's hard to understand just the sheer scale of the US. We hear a lot about China and how fast they're growing, but when you start at 10 and you grow one, that's a 10% growth rate! We're already at 300, so if we grow one, that's a one-third of one percent growth rate. Just the sheer scale of the US economy dwarfs everything around us. Consider the economy of the state of California, its GDP, would rank 6th in the world among all nations. It is the 6th largest economy in the world. This gives you some idea of the sheer magnitude of the US economy. This is, in fact, one of the reasons why the European Union was forming: as individual countries, they could not have an impact on the world economy. As a group, they could become larger and as a larger group they could have more influence.

Also, our capital markets are, despite our problems, deep, liquid and broad. There are a lot of choices of what you can invest in. Just look at equities: you have seven or eight different industries, such as basic materials, mining, consumer products, manufacturing, etc. We have a lot of companies, all of which have opportunities to grow and to pay dividends and to be good investments. We have such deep markets (meaning there are a lot of people with a lot of money who invest in stocks and bonds issued in the US) that countries and companies from around the world come here to sell their bonds. We have become such a large part of the world economy from the financial side that all of these other countries are buying not just our goods but, they are buying our investments – they are buying US Treasuries and US corporate securities.

When we have a problem here, the investors we are talking about are not just US citizens, they are citizens from around the world, investors from around the world. They are governments from around the world, they are corporations from around the world, all of whom are having the exact same problem that you and I, who are worried about our 401k's and pension plans, are having. That's a big part of why the turmoil that started here spread around the world.

Another reason why the US is such a large part of the world economy is that we buy their products and they buy our products. Anyone can see it. You go into any store, go into the grocery store, go to a clothing store, and try to find something made in the USA. Just look at how many different countries they're made in. We have products from around the world here. If you go overseas and you look in their stores, they have our products there. I bought Iron City Beer, which is only made in Pittsburgh (Pennsylvania), in Moscow, Russia in 1993. This is the realization of globalization that not just our consumer products but our financial products as well are very much linked and tied together. That's a big part of how this really started to spread around the world. We sneeze and the world gets pneumonia means that when we have an economic problem here where we stop buying goods then that's a problem for other countries because we as consumers buy products from them.

Why small companies are targeted

Smaller companies are easier for naked-short-sellers and those who are interested in manipulating the price of shares to attack. To be an effective manipulator, you need to be able to have a percentage impact on the firm's market capitalization, that's their total value in the market (the number of shares outstanding times share price). If that's small enough, let's say you have a $100 million company and you need to affect it by 30%, you would need $30 million to do that. But if that was a $10 billion company, now you need $3 billion to do that. It's just much harder to raise that kind of money to be able to have enough of an impact on a large company. Now, that's not to say that it doesn't happen. It doesn't always happen in an effort to drive down the share price. Sometimes it happens to take control of corporate assets, say through, mergers and acquisitions which can be approved by the phantom votes, as opposed to just really trying to drive down and change the price of the shares.

You don't have to make a 100% change, or even a 90% change, in the number of shares outstanding to affect the outcome of a corporate vote. If you can affect 30% change in the number of shares, if you can get 30% more votes than you are supposed to have, you can affect the outcome because not everyone votes their shares. In the last corporate election of Bank of America, it received 30% more votes than they had shares issued and outstanding. That can actually change the outcome of corporate governance. That can change the outcome of whether or not they were able to issue preferred stock to take advantage of the Treasury's emergency lending made available to banks to alleviate the stress of the financial crisis. A lot of those banks that want to take advantage of the lending from Treasury have to issue preferred stock to the Treasury to get it which means that they have to take a shareholder vote. The outcome of that shareholder vote could make a difference for whether or not banks merge – that also has to be approved by shareholder vote. As I explained earlier, if the phantom shares and votes are out there, then someone other than a legitimate shareholder could influence the outcome of that activity associated with corporate assets.

I don't know if naked short selling would prevent legitimate lenders and legitimate investors from giving money to companies. I know that it dissuades lenders and discourages small companies from accessing capital through the stock market. What it clearly does is to discourage small businesses from going public. One of the reasons that we talk about the democratization of capital, and one of the reasons that our capital markets are one of the places that a lot of companies want to come to do their issues is because there is so much capital available here, and we have transparency, and all these other ideas. But if small companies come into this capital market, do an IPO and get crushed, then the next small business is going to think twice about coming here. So where else do they go? They have to go to private capital and when they go to private capital they lose all the things that we told them were advantages of coming to US public capital markets: transparency, disclosure, oversight, all of these sorts of safety features. If they are missing, then why would a small company come out?

My company, STP Advisory Services, put on an event in late 2006 in Southern California (see Chapter 13). I told the attendees about the problems with short selling, fails to deliver and stock loans, Patrick Byrne talked about what happened to his company (Overstock.com), and Arne Alsin, a fund manager who also participated in the panel discussion, talked about how shareholders are never told that they didn't get the shares if you are an individual investor. When we opened the microphone to audience questions, one gentleman stood up and asked, "So, why should I, as a small business, issue public securities in the United States?" My answer to him: "I give up. Why would you do that?" He was taken aback! I said, "Seriously, why would you do that? After everything I've just told you, why would you do that?" The possibility of just losing everything, losing your company, losing everything you've put into it, and having someone actually grab the assets from you by driving the market value of the company down to zero and simply snatching up your assets … why would you go out in that? No, it's **very** discouraging. It will discourage investors from coming into the marketplace because they don't know that they are getting what they are paying for. It will discourage small businesses from coming to the capital markets to get the funding to expand their businesses because they don't know that they are going to be treated fairly either.

Can it be fixed?

People often ask me, "So, what's the solution? How do we fix it?" At this point, I'm not sure that it isn't too late. We've gone so far into this and have for so long tolerated the settlement failures that I'm not sure that there exists today the political will to begin to enforce rules that they've ignored for so many years. I'm not sure that it isn't just too late. Remember, earlier I said that, "The brokers must be making a lot of money at this because they are giving you payments in lieu of dividends, and if you sell your stock they pretend like you had it and give you the price difference." People say, "Well, why are they doing this?" They do it because they make money at it. "Well, if they are making money at it, why are we worried? Won't they just pay us in the end?" I say to you, they didn't take your money and put it in a nice little safe savings account at the local thrift and S&L earning 5% interest that they can pay you when you come by. They took the money and it's gone. It's just not there. There is not enough money in some safe place waiting to make everyone whole. This to me is the most frightful part of even attempting a solution is whether or not it **can** be fixed.

It should be clear by now that the self-regulatory structure in the financial markets is what has allowed these things to happen. Therefore I do not expect them to be part of the solution. Where does that solution come from? I thought that it would be the Securities and Exchange Commission; but obviously, they are not interested in fixing this. Then I thought that perhaps we would have to go to Congress, but I know individuals who have been talking to the Senate Banking and Finance Committee, same thing with the House, for 10 years! They have been told, "Who cares? It's not interesting. Why do you think this is a problem?" So, to be honest with you, I'm not sure where the solution will come from.

It is really difficult as a researcher to get specific data about the settlement failures and the fails to deliver. Ideally, we would have data on the fails to deliver in every security type and we would be able to line that up with what the lending has been because, again, this is another way that shares are multiplied through lending. It's really hard to get the data because it is fragmented. There's one place for equities that includes some bonds and mutual funds. There's one place that only has bonds, but that place only has MBS issued by government entities not issued by private organizations. There's another place that does only MBS issued by the private organizations but not by government entities. There's so much overlap that it's really difficult to get the whole picture. Part of the reason is because there actually are different entities in charge, different regulatory agencies.

In fact, the trading platforms are completely separated. You know the NYSE has equity trades, but they didn't have bond trades until 2006. Then in January of 2007 they passed a rule that if your equities are listed on the NYSE, you can list all your bonds, too. They are trying to get bond trades moved to the NYSE. Before that, bond trades were done off-exchange (over-the-counter), and they were settled ex-clearing (outside NSCC). The NYSE is trying to get more trades for all security types, but it is still fragmented. So, part of the reason that it is hard to get the data is because they are reported in separate places. The reporting is not consistent. What they report vary from entity to entity. As I get further and further into this, as the fail to deliver numbers exploded – this year it absolutely exploded! – it seems to me that we are meeting more obstacles in even trying to get the data.

For example, the most transparent location for getting a lot of data about trades and fails was the Federal Reserve Bank of New York. But I went to their website after the FTDs went to $5 trillion. I noticed that they had a graphic right at the front where you get the Treasuries fails data that shows what the total fails are from, say, 1994, I think when they first started releasing it. And I realized that the whole chart still only went to $3 trillion which was the last peak, but the new peak was $5 trillion. I thought they didn't change the scale on the chart on the front to show the new peak of $5 trillion. They wrote back and they said that it was for illustration purposes only and not to be used for… like they never intended to update it. And it ended in 2005, which the last peak that there was and that peak, as I say, was about half of the current value is. It seems as if there are additional efforts being taken to try to, if not hide the information then at least to make it a little harder to find. You really have to dig back behind the numbers and figure out exactly what's happening there. Otherwise, the next time you go to the Fed's website, there will just be a chart with the sign reading "Gone Fishing."

PART VIII. THE TRAGEDY OF A DOWNER ENDING

This is the part where most stories offer you a happy ending. If you skipped to the ending without reading the opening pages, then you missed the part where I warned you that this was not going to have a happy ending. I cannot even offer the reader the "Or Is It...?" ending where the major threat is still out there but maybe what was done so far shined enough light on the problem that the regulations will be corrected. Although the Dodd-Frank Act (DFA) fell short of making actual corrections, it was not even fully implemented before the next Administration started putting through the repeals. Our politicians are too ignorant, too lazy or too corrupt to take the necessary actions – or maybe all three. If they are ignorant about the reality of finance, then they are too lazy to put in the effort to find out how it really works, in which case they take the word of bankers who make political donations to corrupt politicians whose only goal is re-election.

The Tragedy is that so many companies lost the access to capital that is a keystone of US capital markets. Barker Minerals (Chapter 21) is one of the exceptions: they continued to operate, largely using personal funds, by transforming their business model. Barker went from extracting minerals to selling claims to the mineral rights they accumulated. In 2019, I am still getting questions from investors throughout North America and Europe who invested in CMKM. Some are still looking for an imaginary gigantic payoff, other are just searching for ways to make sense out of what happened to them (i.e. were they fooled by the company or were they cheated by the brokers). Most still do not understand that if they left their shares with a broker, they do not have any shares and maybe they never did. Their beef is with the broker, not the company. For them, it does not matter if the company recovers any lost funds or not, or if the SEC gets some restitution for shareholders. The SEC calls them "entitlement holders" who were never "shareholders" because they never had any shares. We call them the UnShareholders. The company does have a list of actual shareholders and they are actually trying to make a go of a business and the people on that list will be entitled to some portion of any monetary recovery the company is able to make.

After the financial crisis hit, it seemed almost as if lawyers and investors and public companies did not know what to do. It seemed to me that there was so much uncertainty about what new rules, laws and regulations would be written, that no one wanted to start any new litigation. There were no more stand-alone brokers. Merrill Lynch was taken over by Bank of America, Lehman Brothers folded, Bear Stearns was absorbed by JPMorgan Chase, and even Goldman Sachs filed to become a bank so they could get in line for money from the Federal Reserve. I had a few cases, including one as expert witness in support of the Enron Creditors. Most of my work in the first few years during and after the Great Recession was doing research into the importance of infrastructure for economic growth (see, for example, Oswald et al. 2011).

Chapter 20. GAO faults SEC and Other Revelations

After the financial crisis manifested in 2008, the Government Accountability Office (GAO), at the request of Congress, reviewed the SEC's handling of the "naked short selling" crisis that came to light more than five years earlier. They would come to the same conclusion that Rod Young, founder of Eagletech Communications, Inc, presented to the SEC in 2006:

"…if you had spent but a fraction of the resources that you have spent on this proceeding [against Eagletech] on investigating just one complaint of manipulation you would have saved some innocent shareholder the loss of his pension savings or his child their education fund."

On September 15, 2008, two assistant directors and two analysts from the GAO interviewed me by phone. They were in the Financial Markets and Community Investment Team that "helps ensure that U.S. financial markets function smoothly and effectively." The interview was part of their process for reports requested by members of Congress to address complaints from constituents by assessing the effectiveness of Regulation SHO.

The GAO subsequently published two reports:

(1) Securities and Exchange Commission: Oversight of U.S. Equities Market Clearing Agencies (February 26, 2009);[125] and

(2) Regulation SHO: Recent Actions Appear to Have Initially Reduced Failures to Deliver, but More Industry Guidance Is Needed (May 12, 2009).[126]

GAO would conclude that the SEC neglected to investigate even one of the thousands of complaints received about "naked short selling" and "fails to deliver" in the years leading up to the financial crisis in 2008. Five years later, in 2013, the SEC would fine the $6 million for "a failure to enforce or even fully comprehend rules to prevent abusive short selling." It was a slap on the wrist for a problem that was there before long before 2008.

The GAO interview was conducted by telephone, with the questions sent to me in advance of the call. I provided several documents to them, many of which are already incorporated into *Naked, Short and Greedy*. The transcript of the interview presented here has been lightly edited for clarity.

1. *What are your views on the effectiveness of Regulation SHO in reducing large and persistent failures to deliver (FTD) and the potential for manipulative naked short selling (NSS)?*

First, let's make clear the relationship between FTD and NSS. The end result is the same: a buyer pays for shares they do not receive. How you get there is very different and it's the how you get there part that is regulated by SHO. Any trade can fail to deliver but only a short sale can be naked. Reg SHO was proposed to only allow a broker to mark a trade "long" if the seller has full control of the shares when the sale is entered (or is "reasonably expected" to have them). The problem is that when a broker fails to deliver, they can retrospectively declare a sale short by reporting that they failed to mark the trade short; or vice versa as it suits their needs. OK, so one of the original requirements in the final rule approved August 6, 2004 was to require that all trades be marked "long" or "short" whereas prior practice was only to mark "short" trades. Since we only know the FTDs and we have no information on which of those trades are marked "short", how do we know that NSS has been reduced?

The SEC is frequently quoted as saying that FTDs are not an indication of NSS; that is until Goldman and 16 other firms needed to be protected. Then, finally, [SEC Chairman] Cox admitted in his

Wall Street Journal piece that there is a link between the two. But you cannot "unring the bell". Obviously, FTDs are rising instead of falling. The straight forward statistics show this.

We would be especially interested in discussing with you any analyses you have conducted relating to FTDs or Regulation SHO.[127]

   a. What are your views on the pervasiveness of manipulative naked short selling?

Why would a broker bother to naked short sell when they can just fail to deliver? If they are prevented from shorting because a stock goes on the threshold list it does not create a problem for the broker: they just fail to deliver the shares for settlement and, if questioned, say it was a long trade where they "reasonably believed" the customer had the shares. You and I are not allowed to trade that way, but the brokers are.

   b. The number of threshold stocks as well as overall failures to deliver (FTD) has returned to pre-Regulation SHO levels or higher. What factors might account for this increase?

The lack of real punishment creates the conditions for moral hazard, where the brokers see there are no consequences for bad behavior. Therefore, they have no incentive to stop the bad behavior. The solution is

(1) Reveal the names of the failing brokers so that investors have complete information when they make the decision to select a service provider;
(2) exit brokers who FTD shares from NSCC; and
(3) have the broker enter a reversal for the trade (i.e. return the cash to the investor).

NSCC and the brokers *must* have records of who sold what and which of those did not deliver. If they do not, then this is a much bigger problem than any of us ever imagined.

2. *Some market participants argue that naked short selling creates "phantom shares" that in effect inflate the outstanding public float of an issuer's securities and can depress its stock price. Can you discuss how phantom shares are created and the role of current clearance and settlement procedures in the process?*

I coined the term "phantom shares" in a meeting in New York with Carl Hagberg, Ray Riley and others. We call shares "counterfeited" when phony certificates are printed. In that case, there is some piece of paper at least attempting to represent the share. The phantom is different in that you do not have to attempt to re-create any official document. Tolerating FTDs directly creates unlimited phantom shares; until the failure is closed, there are shares in circulation that should not exist; the investor who has the phantom share can sell it, lend it, pledge it as collateral for a bank loan, etc.

Stock lending also can create phantom shares even without NSS/FTD because there is no due date for the return of the shares. The central depository system encourages the creation by letting brokers relend phantom shares. Finally, because the short sale/stock loan scenario allows voting rights to be multiplied, the brokers have become "hooked" on FTDs in their corporate governance and other investment strategies. [See, especially, the article "Corporate Voting Charade" in *Bloomberg Markets*, April 2006, discussed in Chapter 6 or Part III.] Their behavior is just like a drug addict's. They've gone through all the stages from experimenting to dependency.

- Experimental: The first time a broker failed to deliver shares for settlement and got away with it, they continued to do it because they found it profitable.
- Recreational: The spike in FTDs after the 2001 recession and terrorist attack that impacted Wall Street indicates a conscious

decision to use failures as an option. A researcher at the SEC even called fails to deliver "strategic."

- Misuse: With greater frequency, the brokers began to experience some negative consequences as 1) issuers started complaining about the excess shares in circulation; 2) Federal Reserve researchers took notice of the bond problem in 2003 publications; 3) the SEC proposed Regulation SHO, etc. At this stage, drug users begin to monitor their consumption. In the case of the brokers failing to deliver, the SEC required reports which meant that they had to monitor themselves. By that point, the brokers have already incorporated FTDs into their business plans. This is a critical juncture in the continuum toward dependence; like a point of no-return.

- Abuse: brokers line up to get various exemptions in the regulations to permit FTDs in their particular situations. "Intoxication" happens more often, or in the case of FTDs, the number of fails rises after initially dropping.

- Dependency: The first step to recovery is to admit that they have a problem. So far, they are still telling regulators that "we can handle it; we can stop anytime we want." Some regulators are buying into that story. They have entered the first stage of co-dependence.

3. *What are your views on the locate and close out requirements of Regulation SHO and SEC's efforts to implement and enforce them?*

This seems like a waste of time as long as failures to deliver are tolerated. It creates one more excuse to blame someone else. The real solution is to require that sold shares be delivered or reverse the trade. Also, while I understand the role of short sales and stock loans in the market place, I think it's quite clear that is the red herring being used to distract us from the real problem.

Since the implementation of the regulation, SEC has taken a number of actions to either modify or propose to modify these requirements. Please discuss any views you have regarding the following:

a. SEC August 2007 amendment eliminating the grandfather exception

The main problem is that Reg SHO has no real teeth for enforcement. It took two years after the original rule was approved for the question of liability to come forward. In other words, the brokers are never called to be responsible for their behavior. As I said, this on-going tolerance for unacceptable behavior is a stage in co-dependency. People ask me all the time: "how can an FTD happen? How can you sell what you don't own?" The answer is, brokers can and they do. And there are no consequences. If someone told you, for example, that you could sell cars all day long, collect the payments and never deliver the cars, a lot of people would do it. It makes them rich and there are no serious consequences. The 2007 Reg SHO amendment only says you cannot short again without borrowing: but only DTCC and SEC know who failed to deliver so how is that functional? Where is the operationalization of even this weak rule?

b. SEC's current proposal to narrow the option market maker exception:

A proposal like this has been opened and re-opened for comments three years in a row (2006, 2007 and 2008). For me, it is a "Who cares?" moment. My view was, is and remains that either the shares are delivered on time or the deal is reversed. Do you really want someone to make a market where they can sell as many shares as they care to, without any limit on the quantity? Do you want them to be able to do that with just a promise to deliver the shares at some indeterminate date in the future without compensating the buyer for the risk, use of funds, etc? Instead of exceptions and exemptions, we should be looking for ways to mandate final delivery of shares for money.

> c. *SEC's July 15, 2008 Emergency Order temporarily requiring all persons to pre-borrow or arrange to borrow the securities of 19 select financial firms prior to effecting a short sale order*

This Order was cronyism, plain and simple. I'm glad it happened because now at least the SEC and the banks/brokers have to admit that NSS/FTD is a real problem that can do serious damage to a company. That is, after all, the first step in recovery! The next one is to admit that the SEC is powerless and have DTCC impose sanctions on its members.

> d. *Recent public comments by the SEC Chairman stating that the Commission is considering eliminating the "reasonable grounds" alternative altogether (for locates) as well as introducing other remedies to prevent "distort and short" and naked short-selling abuses, such as the reporting of substantial short positions*

[NOTE: On September 14, 2008, the day before this interview, Lehman Brothers announced they would file for bankruptcy and the sale of Merrill Lynch to Bank of America was announced.] Given what happened this weekend I'd say this idea comes too late. Now the SEC wants us to stand up and applaud because they are "considering" doing the right thing? I want to know who is failing to deliver, I want to know the names of the brokers who victimized public companies so I can avoid doing business with them.

> e. *SEC's proposed "Naked Short Selling Anti-Fraud Rule"*

This is good and bad. Good because it establishes liability but bad because it lets DTCC push responsibility back to the broker who can push it back to an "unknown seller." As long as I worked in financial services, brokers followed an unwritten rule called "know your customer." They did not take business from parties they did not know because they did not want to risk aiding and abetting criminals, even unwittingly. Brokers were liable for what they executed. These sellers [that fail to deliver shares] are insiders, either directly inside the broker or someone well known to them; otherwise, they would not take the order. Further, novation makes NSCC liable; and Congress gave them the authority to throw out any broker that does not deliver securities. If the brokers are held to their liability, then DTCC will have the incentive to take appropriate action. If they can pass responsibility off to some unknown (and unreachable) party, then the moral hazard continues to grow. In economics, an efficient law is one where liability accrues to the party in the best position to take action to correct the situation. The efficient law is already in place. This "Anti-Fraud" rule introduces inefficiencies. Of course, why does NSCC not throw out the members who fail to deliver shares for settlement? Easy: the same banks and brokers who fail to deliver have seats on the Board of Directors. NSCC also does not have the money to make good on the fails. At year end 2007, they reported about $13.2 billion in unsettled trades but only $4.9 billion in the clearing fund they could use to pay for shares to close them out. That's about 60 cents on the dollar. Probably less, because the fails are stated at the current market price; but the fails themselves serve to drive down the market price by increasing the supply of shares in circulation. The trade date value, i.e. the amount of money taken from investors who received no shares, is undoubtedly higher.

4. *Some market participants have recommended that the SEC could take one or more additional steps to reduce failures to deliver and manipulative naked short selling. What are your thoughts on these suggestions? Do you have any other recommendations?*

a. *Allowing the NSCC or DTC to buy-in member positions or impose stiffer fines for FTD.*

Buy-ins [allowing the party that did not receive shares to purchase them on the open market and charge the cost back to the party that failed to deliver] have not worked. For stocks where there are already a high number of fails, the buy-in trade usually fails to settle, too. The bottom line is this: the broker have sold shares that never existed. Where do they think they will get them? The holders of phantom shares, if they are aware of their situation, will be willing to hold out for huge profits. The more efficient solution is to reverse the trades and give back the original money with some use-of-funds compensation. By the way, the compensation should be set at a real-risk level. For the investor who bought shares they did not received, it is as if they loaned money to the broker. They may have been willing to take on the risk of investing in, for example, IBM, but instead they are taking on the risk of some firm like Bear Stearns or Lehman Brothers. The required rate of return for that investment could be significantly higher. This is also the problem with fines. The fines are based on the current market value of the shares; the goal of abusive NSS is to drive down the share price; as the price falls so do the fines.

b. *Revising regulations governing margin and cash accounts (i.e. Regulation T and SEC Rule 15c3-3.b.3) to make it easier to borrow stock, especially OTC stocks. (This suggestion comes from individuals who believe that improving the supply of lendable stocks will reduce the instances of FTD)*

I cannot comment on the broker regulations; my expertise is in clearing and settlement. However, I will say that increasing lending is not the answer. It is, in fact, part of the problem. Stock lending is done as a loan with no due date. By increasing the number of shares in circulation, you can drive the price of the stock to $0. Even [SEC] Chairman Cox admits that NSS/FTD drives share prices down. If you can do that, then there is $0 cost to the scheme. Every share you can sell becomes pure profit. I have letters, faxes and emails from individual investors which, when compared to the stock transfer records of a company, prove that brokers were getting shares registered in their own names on the same day they were telling investors that the shares were worthless and no certificates were available. Contrary to regulations, these brokerage firms (big ones like Ameritrade, Royal Bank of Scotland, etc.) were deleting investors' positions in a security while they were getting shares for themselves. These were straight cash accounts, too, not marginable, and some were IRAs.[128] When I add up the numbers, it is painfully clear that these brokers had many more shares recorded in the investor accounts than they ever owned. This will come to light as Lehman is unwound.

Furthermore, there is no real evidence that increasing the lendable supply will resolve FTDs. In fact, the very idea is illogical. For example, a 2006 article in *the Journal of Banking and Finance* said this:

> "Yet, contrary to payment systems, a disruption in securities settlement cannot be fully accommodated by providing liquidity. ... because ... participants may not only be short in cash, but also in securities. ...[I]t is precisely during crisis periods that uncertainty about repayment is greatest and holders of securities will be the least willing to lend. ...[C]entral banks may be able to take some measures to help resolve the shortage of securities; however, these policies have their limits, especially in the case of SSSs that settle non-treasury securities." (Devriese and Mitchell, 2006)

I've written about this in the bond fails paper (Trimbath 2011). I'm gathering similar information now on the equity side. Owen Lamont at Yale has been a major advocate of the position that the

FTD problem can be solved by increased lending. Lehman Bros is a major donor to his research budget! The implication of bias is that obvious. Stock loan is already being used to dupe institutional investors out of their voting rights. Until the stock lending process is better monitored with required payback dates, it will continue to be a cause of the problem and not a solution.

In his 2011 report on the financial crisis, Chairman Phil Angelides of the Financial Crisis Inquiry Commission (FCIC), wrote: "In many respects our financial system is unchanged from the eve of this crisis. We believe much more needs to be done. There were warning signs, the tragedy is, they were ignored. The crisis was avoidable, the crisis was a result of human action and inaction, and it could happen again if we do not learn from history." It was true in 2011 and some market observers, myself included, believe it is true today.[129]

Chapter 21. Barker Minerals' Unique Approach

It was painful to watch so many self-serving false-protagonists through the years leading up to the financial collapse. Maybe all of that was exactly what I needed to push past my fear of the 800-pound gorilla that chased me relentlessly in the form of DTCC. I had to give up all dependence on support, both moral and financial, from Wes Christian and Patrick Byrne and simply move forward on my own. I committed to go my own way. So when Barker Minerals called me asking for help, I said "yes" even though I rarely worked directly for companies or investors.

Barker Minerals Ltd. first contacted me for help in mid-2010. We had some preliminary discussions, including a conference call with founder and President/CEO Louis Doyle, and VP Communications Robert Kuhl. As they explained to me the data they had accumulated and the process they used to analyze it, it became clear that this was a company that had put a lot of effort into understanding and documenting what happened to them in the capital markets. I met them in Vancouver, and had a chance to learn more about their business.

Barker Minerals has more than 20 projects on its 100% owned exploration properties. Eight of the projects are drill-ready for mining gold or other minerals with commercial value. I recognized that they were putting the same level of effort into running their business as they were into chasing down the source of the fails to deliver. Barker scored high on both counts with me; I had seen too many CEOs become so obsessed with suspected market manipulation that not only could they not see straight enough to ferret out the underlying sources but they lost sight of the business objectives as well.

Barker and I came to an agreement whereby I would review the data they had collected and analyzed then produce a report describing the evidence in context. With what they gave me, I was able to examine real evidence about fails to deliver in their stock, including records that identified the failing brokers. Barker insisted that none of the brokers identified with having excessive short sales, naked short sales or failures to deliver shares for settlement would be named in the first report, which was finalized in October 2010. It started from the premise that the low market price of Barker's stock was unreasonable in the face of the company's substantiated claims to minerals on the properties it owned.

After reviewing the data, I was able to align trade data with settlement failures. The first thing that stands out in the data is that on the trading days with the highest volume, there are twice as many with price declines as there are with price increases. Statistically, you would expect them to be about half each.

The data alone did not point to any particular broker that was engaging in "naked short selling" but it suggested a failure to deliver rate of 17.5% of shares traded, which is realistic based on other company's I had analyzed. After looking at additional data sources, it became clear that the brokers who sell shares they neither own nor can borrow before settlement, subsequently borrow from other brokers at the Canadian depository. Unlike the fails reports NSCC is required to make to the SEC, the Canadian depository did not release the numbers. Even without it, Barker collected trading, depository position and transfer agent records that indicated long-term fails to deliver in shares of the company.

In the 2010 report (see **Appendix 1**, page 290) I recommended some additional analysis to further strengthen their claims, including a methodologically rigorous event study that could be used to prove the impact of fails to deliver on the market value of the stock. Louis and Robert completed that additional analysis, refining their charts over the year and keeping a running total of the trading and settlement activity. They contacted me in late-2011 about doing an updated report with the new data. The event study was based on actual shareholder records; the 2012 report (see **Appendix 2**, page 311) would include only their initials to protect the privacy of the individuals. Although the data was collected on a daily basis, Barker reported intermittent evidence of market manipulation to the Canadian securities regulators and documented the investors who were assigned the failures to receive (i.e. the buying investor in a trade where the seller fails to deliver). Evidence of the manipulation was also sent to the Royal Canadian Mounted Police (RCMP). Taken as a whole the facts and documented events painted a picture of widespread manipulation This time, however, we included the names of the brokerage firms that were selling stock in trades where they could not deliver shares for settlement.

At the conclusion of the first report in 2010, I urged Barker to begin making detailed reports to the Canadian securities regulators each time they detected specific instances of market manipulation in any form. Barker used the information system they developed to document and file complaints with the Investment Industry Regulatory Organization of Canada (IIROC). Before they would meet with Barker, the regulators asked for confidentiality to protect "a very real possibility that a current active investigation is underway." Eventually, the securities regulators requested that Barker suspend publishing this information in Company new releases.

The Canadian government invested in excess of $2 million to validate the economic potential of the areas surveyed under the

Barker project and the surrounding area. Unfortunately, the situation in Canada was not especially different than the US experience with financial regulators. There is evidence that the regulators shared Barker's documented cases with the specific brokers who engaged in the manipulative activities – but without sanction.

Louis Doyle, with help from Robert Kuhl, refined the data tracking methodology and began offering it commercially under the product name "Pro Long Strategy." The analytical tool can be used to link specific trades with settlement failures. To date, Barker Minerals has accumulated over ten years of daily data including buys, sells and settlements. No other company has implemented the program.

In 2019, Barker Minerals Ltd. continues to explore the 100% owned Tasse Diamond project in the Cariboo region of British Columbia. Research published in the scientific journal *Tectonophysics* (Polat et al. 2018) identified rocks present in the project site as favorable for the formation of diamonds.[130]

PART IX. UNRESOLVED REGULATORY CRISIS

"It's about being tough on the outside, while you try not to lose yourself. It's about what we hold on to if anything is to have meaning ... And the life that we are leaving for our children."

Miles describing his next movie, *Get Shorty*, Season 2

The term "crisis" proliferates in media and academic journals each time there is some turmoil in financial markets as well as in politics. In finance, a "regulatory crisis" can mean the sudden appearance of a regulator at the firm's offices or a major enforcement case against the firm. The body of literature surrounding this meaning is in the context of "crisis management." It has little to do with problems created for the economy by the entire system of financial regulation.[131]

This broader sense is closer in meaning to the description of a "constitutional crisis." Like most financial regulations, the US Constitution "was written against the background of a perceived crisis" (Levinson and Balkin 2009, p. 708). Similar to American politics, the topic of "crisis" comes up regularly in talk about American capital markets. In finance, as with the Constitution, "the language of crisis is ubiquitous, applied to controversies great and small" (ibid. p. 709). There is nothing new about applying the term "crisis" to turmoil in financial markets.[132]

To clarify what constitutes an actual constitutional crisis, Levinson and Balkin (2009) direct us to think not of episodes of turmoil but of fundamental design; in our case, the design of the system of financial regulations. They define three types of constitutional crises which I will apply to the regulatory crisis at hand. I follow them closely, in some places only substituting "regulatory" for "constitutional." Looked at in this context, it seems clear that the events leading up to and following from the 2008 "financial crisis" meet the definition of a "regulatory crisis." Since the three types were defined by Levinson and Balkin, the initials LB are added to the title of each type.

An LB Type One Crisis would arise when the leaders believe that circumstances require violation of the regulations. Several events in the summer and fall of 2008 meet this definition. First, despite at least five years of regulations designed to permit short selling on an on-going basis, the SEC put out an emergency order to prohibit short sales in bank stocks. Next, Congress gave approval of extraordinary powers to the U.S. Treasury to provide over $700 billion to revive failing banks. Finally, the Federal Reserve bought up the bad assets of the failing banks, increasing its balance sheet from $900 billion to $4 trillion.[133]

An LB Type Two Crisis occurs when the regulators prefer to support the status quo over making real reforms. What Levinson and Balkin call excessive "fidelity" eventually leads to ruin or disaster. The status quo in capital markets is self-regulation. By allowing the banks and brokers to continue to regulate their own activities in bond and equity markets, the SEC continues to rubber-stamp rules and regulations that not only do not stop but in some cases even promote the creation of phantom shares. Fails to deliver not only harmed entrepreneurs in search of capital for job creation but they were also directly responsible for the collapse of global credit markets.

Finally, an LB Type Three Crisis creates the conditions where public disagreements about the regulations lead to extraordinary forms of protest. LB write that these protests go "beyond mere legal disagreements and political protests; for example, people take to the streets, armies mobilize, and brute force is used or threatened in order to prevail" (p. 714). The vocal pajamahideen and their ilk picketed in front of the NYSE, NASDAQ and DTCC years before Occupy Wall Street took up residence in lower Manhattan. After the collapse of global credit markets and the full onset of the Great Recession, protests spread throughout the world. For example, in France, hundreds of factory workers took executives hostage over threatened cutbacks. Occupy Wall Street in the US became the subject of a special report by the Department of Homeland Security; a dozen FBI field offices plus other federal agencies monitored their activities. In Oakland (California), the Occupy protests were met with "an overwhelming military-type response" according to a report from a court-ordered external monitor of the Oakland Police Department.

If a central purpose of capital market regulations is to make financial activity possible, then regulatory crises mark moments when regulations fail at this task. For example, the regulations did not adequately address the situation where fails to deliver endure; Congressional law specifically tells the central clearing organization that they can refuse membership to brokers that fail to deliver for settlement.[134] It is apparently not politically feasible; and regulators justify avoiding dealing with a serious problem based on narrow interpretations of the laws governing the self-regulated clearing organizations. The conditions for a regulatory crisis are met.

The latest numbers

When you look at the available data on settlement failures in the system today, keep three things in mind. First, that the very system of centralized clearing and settlement in the US was built to stop settlement failures. Second, the current system of using sell orders to offset buy orders ("netting") reduces the end-of-day settlement obligations by about 97%. That means you need to divide the values of fails to deliver by 0.03 to find the value of the trades that failed to settle. When you read that the fails reported to the SEC are about $1 billion per day, that is equivalent to over $33 billion worth of trades. Finally, Wall Street benefits from a service that automatically resubmits settlement failures, what DTCC calls "fail transactions." When this happens, the records show that the fail transactions were no longer outstanding. In other words, the next day begins with zero fails. This service is called "Reconfirmation and Pricing Service" ("RECAPS"). In 2011, RECAPS was enhanced and renamed "Obligation Warehouse" ("OW" or "OW Service"). The OW Service expanded the resubmit service to track, store and maintain all the fails from NSCC/DTC settlement plus fails transactions from outside DTCC ("ex-clearing").

The following is a sampling of the most recent data available. As described elsewhere, it is not possible to get a complete picture of the magnitude of the problem of fail transactions in the US, let alone globally. We offer the following simply to make the point that the problem continues today, despite decades of efforts to achieve regulatory reform:

- Securities and Exchange Commission: 914,261,864 shares valued at over $17 billion failed to deliver in the first two weeks of July 2019, an average of about $1.9 billion every settlement day at NSCC.
- NASDAQ: Short interest rose 1.3% in the second half of June 2019 (Reuters report, July 11) to 9.031 billion shares on trading volume of about 2.8 billion shares per day.[135]
- NYSE: As of July 15, 2019 reported 16.076 billion shares short on about 3.6 billion shares traded daily.
- Federal Reserve Bank of New York: Primary Dealers failed to deliver $163.5 billion bonds (US Government, federal agency and other mortgage-backed bonds plus corporate bonds) as of July 17, 2019. That's a fail rate of 17.7%, greater than the fail

rate in mortgage bonds in the years leading up to the 2008 collapse of global credit markets (Chapter 19). The Fixed Income Clearing Corporation (a subsidiary of DTCC) reported an additional $50 billion fails to deliver in US Treasury and federal agency bonds on the same date.

- European Central Securities Depositories Association (ECSDA)[136]: Although data is not readily released on the value of fails in Europe, the ECSDA estimated in November 2014 that fails to deliver averaged €10.7 billion per day (about 2% of value traded).[137] On August 1, 2019, the Deutsche Börse tweeted about a new service (Buy-in Agent Service) to help close out fails to deliver.

How do you solve a problem

Rod Young, founder of Eagletech Communications, Inc., laid responsibility for the damage done to his company by the lax enforcement of capital market oversight squarely at the feet of the regulators and Congress. If a fraction of the effort put into writing and approving rules for storing fails at DTCC was put into forcing delivery of stocks for settlement, maybe the new OW Service would be unnecessary. California Senator Harmer made it clear that his view was that without a grassroots mandate from the people, Congress never would take action (WSC, 2012). Congress had an opportunity to force the SEC to take corrective action long before the collapse of credit markets in 2008. Instead, they sold out to protect the "Black Priesthood" of Wall Street.

If you got to this point in the reading and you still are not angry enough to take action, to march in the streets, storm the gates of the barbarians, then you are typically American. We have a tendency to sit back and think "oh, the government will fix it." When the government fixes it, the citizens end up paying for it. And so do their children. And so do their children's children. If you want to put a stop to it, be prepared to storm the bastions after you read this book. The final chapter in *Lessons Not Learned* (Trimbath 2015) describes other steps you can and should take immediately to protect yourself and your family.

It is difficult to explain to people how it is that what they believe to be true, what they have even seen in writing on every monthly statement from their broker, simply is not true. The first sign that they are "getting it" comes as a slight shadow passing over the back of their eyes. It is there, that idea that their 401k or IRA is not safe. The nest egg for retirement or the savings for the kids' education may be nothing more than numbers on paper and not real shares of corporate stock or real government bonds. At some point, they go into denial. I often heard, "If what you are saying were true, the federal government would fix it." That, of course, is our most dangerous moment, when we wish it was not true, when we wish it was all a mistake and our stocks and bonds were safely stored in some strong American bank. Denial makes us vulnerable to the next financial collapse because the regulatory crisis continues unresolved.

Epilogue

There will always be criminal elements in financial markets. What we do not have to accept is the failure of self-regulatory organizations. For decades, investors have settled for a small rate of return in their investment accounts, while the companies holding their money have earned trillions of dollars in income. Investors settle for an account statement while the brokerage firm pretends the shares are there.

At a time when the financial sector has lost its moral compass"[138] a Presidential Memorandum signed by Donald J. Trump (February 3, 2017) looked toward "rescinding or revising" the Fiduciary Duty Rule. The rule was designed to force all financial intermediaries to protect the interests of investors from actions taken by brokers and advisors that would promote their own financial interests over their clients. Trump put high priority on allowing "Americans to make their own financial decisions" and he claimed the Fiduciary Duty Rule was standing in the way. As of October 7, 2019, the Department of Labor still will not pursue claims against investment advisors for violating impartial conduct standards. DTCC has argued in various places (e.g., SEC rule change filings) that not only do they not have any duty to individual investors but also that the companies whose shares they hold on deposit have "no legal or beneficial interest in the securities they are requesting to be withdrawn from DTC."

Carl Hagberg and I take a different perspective. In all our years in financial services, from insurance to banking to stock exchanges and central depositories, every professional we came into contact with considered it their duty to always act in the best interest of their clients. Carl made it clear that much of the activity described in this book presented examples of DTCC's breach of fiduciary duty to the issuers whose securities are deposited there. Our position is that the companies that issue shares in the nominee name "Cede & Co" do so with the understanding that the rights of ownership – and voting is among those rights – would be properly safeguarded.

The question of "fiduciary duty" is a complicated one from the perspective of the law. Even more complicated is whether the organization where an investor places their buy and sell orders is a fiduciary: investment advisors are but brokers are not. In reality, most "brokers" are also advisors but every individual investor would be wise to find out exactly who they are dealing with. In the same way that I advocate for investors reading the account agreement forms, it is important to look at the other disclosures.[139]

All of this means that investors and entrepreneurs are on their own when they venture into US capital markets. You have to protect yourself and the wealth you hope to accumulate to protect your future and that of your children. Investors need to remain alert to the impact of stock market manipulation on share prices. Short selling and stock lending always leave some investor without real share ownership, even if it is not done with the intention of manipulating stock prices. Companies need to watch for the "extra" or "phantom" shares not only because they dilute market value but also because they can deprive real shareholders of voting rights.

By accepting a retail brokerage or other stock-trading account enrollment agreement, most investors allow the broker to lend their shares. Even when the investor does not allow stock lending, it often happens as a result of poor record keeping practices at the broker-dealer level. When the shares you leave at the broker have been lent, you own a phantom share until the loan is repaid. Furthermore, when settlement failures happen, even the shares you buy may not be in your brokerage account regardless of what your broker statement says. These are the two most common ways that phantom shares are created.

For every phantom share there is a "phantom-share holder." Corporate executives are correctly focused on taking care of their shareholders. But no one has taken an interest in the harm being done to those investors who are left holding the phantom shares – those investors who have not received delivery of shares they paid for or whose shares have been lent out without compensation. Those UnShareholders especially need to take action to protect themselves. If you find that you are an UnShareholder, please start by filing a complaint. The North American Securities Administrators Association (www.NASAA.org) has links to securities regulators in all US states, the Canadian provinces and Mexico. Under "Investor Education" they also have instructions on how to check out a broker/advisor before you begin investing. If you decide to get out of the financial system completely, the final chapter in *Lessons Not Learned* (Trimbath 2015) has some resources for alternative investment options available to individuals.

Although I chose to write from my personal experience, this book really has two other stories: one about the investors and one about the entrepreneurs. The message from all three perspectives is clear: do not settle for less perfect, less competitive, less honest capital markets. America deserves the healthy, robust, deep and liquid capital markets that built the railroads, steel mills and auto plants that moved her into a leadership role in the industrialized world; the capital markets that funded a boom in electronic communication so far-reaching that it has been transforming the way we live every day for nearly 20 years. American capital markets are needed to fund the coming boom in technology that will deliver on the promises of the last century: a future with long, healthy lives, and an end to conflicts driven by scarcity in energy, food and water.

Achieving the full potential will require regulatory reform. Otherwise, the financial sector may not survive the next crisis.

References

Barth, J.R., S. Trimbath and G. Yago (eds., 2004). *The Savings and Loan Crisis: Lessons from a Regulatory Failure*, The Milken Institute Series on Financial Innovation and Economic Growth, Kluwer Academic Press, Boston.

Dateline: *Broken Dreams*, Producer Sharon Isaak Hoffman, Editor Andrew Finkelstein, Television newscast, NBC network, original air date July 31, 2005. Unable to confirm episode number.]

Devriese, Johan and Janet Mitchell (2006). Liquidity risk in securities settlement, *Journal of Banking & Finance* 30 (2006), pp. 1807–1834.

Drummond, Bob (2006a). "Corporate Voting Charade," *Bloomberg Markets*, April, pp. 96-104, Bloomberg News, New York.

Drummond, Bob (2006b) "Games Short Sellers Play," by Bob Drummond, *Bloomberg Markets*, September, pp. 120-128, Bloomberg News, New York.

Depository Trust and Clearing Corporation ("DTCC", 1999. *Annual Report*, the Depository Trust & Clearing Corporation, New York.

Depository Trust and Clearing Corporation ("DTCC", 2004. *Annual Report*, the Depository Trust & Clearing Corporation, New York.

Depository Trust and Clearing Corporation ("DTCC", 2005. *Consolidated Financial Statements*, the Depository Trust & Clearing Corporation.

Fleming, Michael J. and Kenneth D. Garbade (2002). "When the Back Office Moved to the Front Burner: Settlement Fails in the Treasury Market after 9/11," *FRBNY Economic Policy Review*, November, p35-57.

Fleming, Michael J. and Kenneth D. Garbade (2005). "Explaining Settlement Fails", *Current Issues in Economics and Finance*, 11(9), September 2005, Federal Reserve Bank of New York.

Levinson, Sanford and Jack M. Balkin (2009). Constitutional Crises, *University of Pennsylvania Law Review* 157(3) February, pp 707 - 753

Montrone, Thomas L. (2006). "Beneficial Shareholder Voting Rights: "A Mockery of Shareholder Democracy," *Registrar and Transfer Company Newsletter*, vol. 2006 (52, Spring) (pp. 6 and 9). Also available in STA 2006.

Montrone, Thomas L. (2006). "The Saga Continues: Short Selling and Over-Voting," *The Corporate Governance Advisor* 14(6), pp 13-15.

National Securities Clearing Corporation ("NSCC", 2005), *Annual Financial Statements*, National Securities Clearing Corporation, New York.

Nichols, L. T. (1997). 'Social Problems as Landmark Narratives: Bank of Boston, Mass Media and "Money Laundering"', *Social Problems*, 44 (3).

Nichols, L. T. and J. J. Nolan III (2004), 'The Lesson of Lincoln: Regulation as Narrative in the Savings and Loan Crisis', chapter 9 in Barth, Trimbath and Yago (eds, 2004).

Oswald, M., Li, Q. McNeil, S. and Trimbath, S. (2011). "Measuring Infrastructure Performance: Development of a National Infrastructure Index" Public Works Management and Policy, 16(4), pp. 373-394.

Reinhart, C.M. and Rogoff, K.S. (2009), *This time is different: eight centuries of financial folly*, Princeton University Press, Princeton.

Securities and Exchange Commission ("SEC", 1968). *34th Annual Report 1968 For the Fiscal Year Ended June 30th*, U.S. Government Printing Office, Washington, D.C.

Securities and Exchange Commission ("SEC", 1973). *39th Annual Report of the U.S. Securities and Exchange Commission For the Fiscal Year Ended June 30th*, U.S. Government Printing Office, Washington, D.C.

Securities Transfer Association ("STA", 2004). *Treating Shareholders Equally: Alternatives for Street Proxy Distributions*, White Paper & Concept Release, December, Securities Transfer Association, Hazlet, NJ. (Note: Executive summary and quote from page 4 on impact of shorts, fails and loans on voting rights included in Chapter 8 as attachment to Trimbath's Reg SHO comments.)

Securities Transfer Association ("STA", 2005). "Street Proxy Tabulation Results: Over-Voting Still Pervasive." *STA Newsletter*, Issue 4. (pp. 1 and 4) Securities Transfer Association, Hazlet, NJ. (Note: Excerpt included in Chapter 8 as attachment to Trimbath's Reg SHO comments.)

Securities Transfer Association ("STA", 2006). "Beneficial Shareholder Voting Rights: "A Mockery of Shareholder Democracy," *STA Newsletter*, Issue 2 (pp. 1 and 8-9). Securities Transfer Association, Hazlet, NJ.

Securities Transfer Association ("STA", 2007a). "Corporate Secretaries Call for Complete Overhaul of Street Proxy Process" prepared by Tom Montrone. *STA Newsletter*, July (pp. 1 and 5). Securities Transfer Association, Hazlet, NJ.

Securities Transfer Association ("STA", 2007b). "2007 Proxy Committee Report: Street Positions Reported to have Large Variances", *STA Newsletter*, July (p. 4) Securities Transfer Association, Hazlet, NJ.

Stock Shock (2009). *Stock Shock* (DVD). Directed by Sandra Mohr. Los Angeles: Mohr Productions.

Trimbath, Susanne (2000). *High Yield Financing and Efficiency-Enhancing Takeovers*, Policy Briefs (22), Milken Institute: Santa Monica, CA.

Trimbath, Susanne (2008). "Trade Settlement Failures in U.S. Equity Markets: The Schematic for a Capital Market WMD," Unpublished Working Paper, STP Advisory Services, LLC, Omaha.

Trimbath, Susanne (2009). "No Accounting for Corporate Governance," *Journal of Accounting and Organizational Change*, 5 (3), p. 417-424 (2009).

Trimbath, Susanne (2011). "Trade Settlement Failures in U.S. Bond Markets," *IUP Journal of Financial Economics* 9(1), pp. 53-78. Working Paper version presented May 2008, Academic Session on Credit Risk & Credit Derivatives, International Economics and Finance Association's 6th NTU International Conference on Economics, Finance and Accounting, Financial Engineering and Financial Intermediation, National Taiwan University, Taipei May 2008.

Trimbath, Susanne (2015). *Lessons Not Learned: 10 Steps to Financial Stability*, Spiramus Press, Ltd., London.

Wall Street Conspiracy, The ("WSC", 2012) *The Wall Street Conspiracy* (DVD). Directed by Kristina Leigh Copeland. New York: Brown Saddle Films and Hop On Films.

Appendix 1: Report for Barker Minerals, Review of Data and Documents, October 14, 2010

[corrected December 3, 2010]

The following report presents a review of data and documents provided to STP Advisory Services, LLC (STP) by Barker Minerals Ltd. (Barker) regarding evidence they perceive to be in support of the conclusion that the company's stock is the subject of a range of manipulative market activity.

Clarification of terminology

STP is engaged to review specifically for evidence of "naked short selling." We believe this term is a misnomer, although the underlying market manipulation is the same. It is virtually impossible to separate naked short selling from settlement failures without examining individual trading tickets. Even then, when dealers are caught selling shares that they can't deliver at settlement they often claim that the sale was not short – but intended to be a long sale – to avoid the accusation of naked short selling. Other times, when regulatory focus is on settlement failures, they claim these were short sales but that the tickets were not marked short; and then lay the blame on the failure of the lender to deliver borrowed shares in time for normal settlement. The failure to properly mark trade tickets could result in what Barker refers to as "unreported" short selling. Naked short selling has only ever been legitimate in very limited circumstances.

In any case, it is impossible to know the intention of the seller just from the data. The evidence, which is the same in either case, is quite visible – no shares are delivered at the required settlement date. The result is that the broker/dealer has sold shares that were not authorized and issued by the company. Therefore, we prefer the terms "settlement failure" and "failure to deliver" as more descriptive of what can be identified by an examination of the available data and records.

Prior research on settlement failures

In early 2007, we published an academic review of trade settlement failures in US bond markets – a subject that had not been addressed publically before although industry insiders were aware of the problem for at least a decade. This study was accepted for presentation at the academic session on Credit Risk & Credit Derivatives in the International Economics and Finance Association's International Conference on Economics, Finance and Accounting, Financial Engineering and Financial Intermediation (held at National Taiwan University, Taipei, May 2008). The paper was revised based on comments from attendees and others and finally published by Capital Markets World, Inc. ("Trade Settlement Failures in U.S. Bond Markets," *Journal of Securities Operations and Processing* (November 2009), New York).

Although some of the procedures and settlement processing organizations vary slightly from bonds to stocks, the underlying issues are the same: securities are being sold by broker/dealers who do not own them (and do not borrow them) so that true investors fail to receive securities at settlement despite having their cash accounts debited for the proceeds. A companion paper, focusing on trade settlement failures in U.S. equity markets, is in the working paper stage.

Just as there are some differences between bond and equity trade settlement, there are some differences in securities settlement operations and procedures between the U.S. and Canada. Many of these differences have disappeared over the last 20 years with the implementation of the recommendations on clearing and settlement from the Group of Thirty (G30) working group and subsequent efforts from the Bank for International Settlement (BIS), the International Monetary Fund (IMF) and other multi-national organizations to standardize trade, clearing and settlement processes globally. The remaining differences are not especially relevant for the purpose of this report, which is to review data on equity market trade activity and records of share ownership. In this particular case, the transfer agent/record keeper for Barker Minerals is Computershare, Inc. – which I am already familiar with for their share recordkeeping services provided to companies in both the US and in Canada.

While employed by the Depository Trust Company (DTC) in New York, my role was liaison to the corporate trust departments. This included interacting with transfer agents, registrars and industry groups in Canada (e.g., Canadian Transfer Agents Association). Prior to that, I worked in operations at the Pacific Securities Clearing Corporation and the Pacific Depository Trust Company. Both the Pacific organizations and the DTC had relationships for inter-depository settlement with the Canadian Depository for Securities, Ltd. (CDS). DTC is now a subsidiary of the Depository Trust and Clearing Corporation (DTCC).

The problem of "phantom shares" – when investors pay for shares that are not delivered to their accounts – is well documented. The harm done to investors and companies was documented throughout the public comment period leading up to the approval and revisions to the regulations on short selling (Regulation SHO) by the United States Securities and Exchange Commission (SEC). A subsequent study by the U.S. Government Accountability Office (GAO) found that, despite more an initial decline in fails to deliver, after more than five years of regulatory action it was "not clear whether this trend can be sustained." (*Regulation SHO*, GAO Report to Congressional Requesters, GAO-09-483, Washington, D.C. 2009). Although regulation in the US resulted in the DTCC releasing fails data to the public (via the SEC), no such data is available from the CDS.

In summary, the primary harm done by settlement failures is that 1) it damages asset values through the increase in supply of shares in circulation, 2) it impairs the issuer's on-going ability to access capital, and 3) it violates the voting rights of shareholders (reduces effective corporate governance). Furthermore, investors lose the use of their funds between settlement date and the date when securities are eventually delivered (the close-out date). This results in 4) investors being exposed to undefined risks for which they are not compensated, and 5) missed opportunities for alternate investments.

Background
Public equity
Barker Mineral's initial public offering was in November 2001 for 3,321,962 shares which began trading in 2002. As of August 31, 2010, there were 119,679,183 shares outstanding. In addition, there are unexpired warrants and options outstanding for 50,670,000 shares and 20,412,000 shares, respectively. There are 501 registered shareholders including only one registered nominee – the Canadian Depository for Securities, Ltd. (CDS) – with 39,870,424 registered shares. Approximately 80 million shares are held in certificated form by individual registered owners. Barker has about 500 additional shareholders who are known to be non-objecting beneficial owners of shares registered at CDS. Based on private placement investors' requirements for documentation plus insiders themselves Barker estimates that up to 25% of shares held at CDS

are in registered retirement savings plans (which would not be available for lending to cover short sales).

Purpose of study

On the surface, the low market price of the company's common stock does not align with the fact that the company has substantiated claims to mineral properties. Our review begins with a description of how settlement works and why it fails. Then we present a review of the data on changes in Barker's stock price and volume to identify anomalies. Next, we attempt to identify settlement failures with trade and settlement data.

Settlement process

The following is a generalized description of an ordinary stock trade transaction for purposes of illustrating examples of how settlement failures occur. While several variations exist, this is the most common process. The investor submits a buy order to a retail broker who submits it to an executing broker/dealer who trades on an exchange (or in the over-the-counter marketplace). Most trades, regardless of where they are executed, will be submitted to a central clearing and settlement organization – like CDS. CDS will have access to securities on deposit and procedures in place for the cash side so that settlement can be effected regardless of distances between the parties, varying time zones, differing currencies, etc. There were 228.2 million equity trades executed on exchanges in Canada in 2008 (according to the BIS). CDS processed 203.6 million equity delivery instructions, though these are not necessarily associated with exchange trades. Neither BIS nor CDS provides any statistics as to the percentage of all trades taking place in Canada that are cleared and settled through a central counterparty (i.e., CDS, DTCC, etc.), though the percentage is generally believed to be in the range of over 50% for total trades to nearly over 90% for exchanged-based trades.

One important difference between the US and Canada is that NSCC is the central counterparty associated with the New York Stock Exchange, NASDAQ and the American Stock Exchange. In Canada, only the Toronto Stock Exchange is associated with CDS. Trades at the Montréal Exchange and the Intercontinental Exchange (ICE) over-the-counter (OTC) markets are not necessarily included in the CDS reports that Barker Minerals relies on for their analysis. As a result, Barker's data on settlement failures may be incomplete with the implication that their data may tend to understate the problem. It is worth noting that CDS helps its participants comply with the US Securities and Exchange Commission Regulation SHO (for reporting fails to deliver) on cross-border trades but does not report settlement failures within its own system. Therefore, it is left to companies like Barker to do their own estimates.

Why settlement fails

Four reasons are generally offered as to why trades fail to settle on time: operations (paperwork or certificates); lack of securities for lending (to satisfy delivery requirements from short sales); investment strategies (related to interest rates charged for lending); and market manipulation.

Operations: There is little reason to blame settlement failures on paperwork and certificates for stock transactions. By 1999, 88% of all securities transactions in the US were settled through electronic movements, an indication that the drive to eliminate problems associated with paper certificates continued to make progress in the more than 20 years since the central securities depositories were formed. According to a research study by the Securities Industry Association (SIA), certificates are involved in "just over one-tenth of 1% of all trade transactions processed daily" (DTCC's 2004 annual report, p. 23).

Lending: There is very little reported short selling activity in Barker stock. Reported open short positions peaked in March 2007 and have been reported as zero since early 2008. Stock loan data is not available. Contrary to suggestions presented by Owen Lamont (Yale University professor who testified in the Regulation SHO hearings in the U.S.) and others, STP demonstrated in the 2009 journal article mentioned above that increasing the supply of securities available for lending does not lead to a reduction in settlement failures.

Investment Strategies: Leslie Boni (SEC economics researcher, now with a hedge fund in Southern California) attributed the extraordinary increase in settlement failures to investment decisions knows as "strategic failures." The SEC backed away from this view during the Regulation SHO hearings before Congress after the market collapse of 2008.

Manipulation: FRB economists Fleming and Garbade, (in 2005) explained settlement failures in bond markets as the result of the lack of clear incentives to avoid failing, such as the fees and penalties suggested in their earlier report which were not implemented. Prior to 2008, only Regulation SHO in the US made any attempt to stop the practice and even that had little teeth for enforcement despite four years of studies, hearings and publications on the matter.

In the course of laying out the guidelines to prevent settlement failures in US Treasury markets, the Federal Reserve Bank of New York's Treasury Markets Practices Group (TMPG) describes by name several intentionally abusive practices such as "slamming the wire" (holding back deliveries until immediately before the close with the intention of causing settlement fails) and requests from traders for settlement operations to "hold the box" (a demand to delay settlement of an executed trade). The fact that these practices are colloquially named and described in such detail seems to us to be, in and of itself, an indication that they are common causes of settlement failures.

Analysis

Descriptive statistics

Barker Minerals requested that we review data for a 16-week sample period from March 2, 2007 to June 21, 2007. In this time frame, they have identified multiple instances where Stockwatch reported stock sales at the Toronto Stock Exchange (TSX) that far exceeded the net delivery of shares for settlement through CDS. The Stockwatch reports are limited to trading activity on TSX-Venture where the stock is listed, but Barker has not seen any other trading activity in the stock.

The sample period selected has a relatively low variation in price and trading range compared to the annual statistics shown below. Of the 20 days with the highest volume since 2006, there are twice as many days with price declines as there are with price increases. We looked at the trading range as a percentage of the opening price and found that, although there was a spike in this activity around the sample period, the volatility continued to increase after that point, with peak volatility appearing in 2008. A graph of the trading range as a percentage of daily opening price is available in

Dates	Price Variance[1]	Trading Range Variance[2]
2006	0.0038	0.0060
2007	0.0016	0.0104
2008	0.0034	0.0257
2009	0.0036	0.0192
3/2-6/21/07[3]	0.0008	0.0085

Appendix: Trading range as percentage of opening price.

Notes: 1. The variance of the closing price; 2. The variance of the daily trading range expressed as a percentage of the opening price; 3. This is the sample period Barker selected for the review.

Identifying settlement failures
Trading records versus CDS positions

Barker provided spreadsheets aligning trade data from Stockwatch with settlement data (securities position changes) from CDS ("Broker Trading Activity Charts"). We note in the Broker Trading Activity Charts that none of the broker accounts at CDS display a negative (short) position despite net sales versus zero-balance holdings. Although I have seen the specific records, Barker requested that no broker names appear in this report. As a result, I will refer to them only by initials. For example, Broker N begins the week April 6-12 with a balance of zero (0) shares, is a net seller of 1,000 shares at TSX, has no change in their CDS holdings and records an ending balance of zero (0) shares. Likewise, Broker S has a net debit of 20,000 shares for the week April 13-19 but also records a balance of zero (0) shares. (See *Appendix: Excerpt of Broker Trading Activity Chart* for details.)

According to CDS Rule 6.2.14, CDS does not create a negative balance in a participant's account as the result of trade settlement. The data combined with the CDS Rule could support the conclusion that these shares were debited for trade settlement – which explains why they do not result in net negative (short) positions on the records of CDS. At DTCC, many trades that fail to settle are required to be re-submitted, where they receive new settlement dates (in essence, erasing the fail to deliver by creating a new record). I could not find a specific rule at CDS regarding this issue. Further investigation would be required to clarify the CDS rules and procedures under these circumstances.

There are several other brokers who have high levels of stock sales while showing zero holdings at CDS. I reviewed Transfer Agent records to confirm that these brokers have no registered share holdings (either in firm name or firm nominee name) outside of CDS. We note that some brokers who are net buyers of shares also have no net change in position at CDS. It is possible that these trades are settled through a clearing broker. Although the data presented in the spreadsheet is insufficient alone to point to any one broker as engaging in "naked short selling", we note that the net sales of 3,134,287 shares in the period March 2 to April 26 exceeds the net settlement at CDS by 1,147,257 shares. Total sales for this period as reported by the TSX were 6,422,621 shares – suggesting a fail rate of 17.5%. Based on our prior research, this is a realistic estimate of the turnover represented by fails to deliver in equity securities.

To complete the review I requested that Barker Minerals provide evidence from the same time period of direct holdings (either in firm name, in firm nominee name, or at a custodian bank) of shares alongside trade and settlement activity for specific brokers. Although TSX trades can be submitted to CDS, if the Stockwatch trades take place elsewhere, it is possible that they were designated to settle outside CDS. Some trade activity might be settled broker-to-broker or through in-house accounts. However, there are no shares registered with any nominee or custodian other than CDS. The share register indicates that there were no other shares attributable to these brokers, clarifying the point. Barker was able to provide STP with several more examples.

As a result of their subsequent additional research, Barker indicated that some selling activity against zero balance positions may in fact have be reflected in the reduction of shares from another CDS participant – which is unusual. We can think of very few reasons why one international institution with its own trading, clearing and settlement operations would rely on another party for settlement in this manner. One possibility is – exactly as Barker initially suspected – that the selling participant failed to deliver the shares for settlement and CDS "borrowed" the shares on their behalf from another Participant, resulting in the reduction of shares in the CDS account of a participant was who not party to the trade.

Here is another example for which I have seen the records:

> Broker D, CDS Participant #M.... March 2 through June 7, 2007. Broker D entered the period with holdings of 8,500 shares at CDS and no shares directly registered with the transfer agent. Broker D sold 73,500 shares, purchased 42,000 shares and delivered net 8,500 shares for settlement through CDS. Broker D ended the period with 0 shares at CDS and no shares directly registered with the transfer agent. There is no evidence of shares purchased to cover these long sales through the end of the two-month period or of shares being made available by another CDS participant to cover the difference.

The details are provided in *Appendix: Excerpt 2 of Broker Trading Activity Chart*.

Conclusions

Although CDS does not release or report settlement failures, the situations seen in the trading, depository positions and transfer agent records indicate that long-term fails to deliver may exist in shares of Barker Minerals.

Barker has made significant progress in documenting the problem. Looking over the larger set of data provided during this review, I am concerned about the 2008 and 2009 activity. The variability in stock prices and volume is much higher than the sample period which is the focus of Barker's own review. Trading in 2008, in particular, appears to follow patterns seen in other cases I have reviewed (e.g., some financial firms before the September 2008 market failure).

I cannot over-emphasize the importance of acting quickly. According to their 2009 annual report, CDS has applied for regulatory approval to destroy company share certificates if they are non-transferrable for 7 years (i.e., CDS is unable to re-register shares). DTCC received regulatory approval for a similar rule, which basically lets them destroy all background records on fails to deliver after 2 years of non-transferrable status. The sooner Barker can get this information organized, presented and disseminated, more public companies will be able to protect themselves. As more companies begin to take action, pressure can be brought to bear on regulators to remedy this situation. My recommendation is to report each incident of suspected abuse and manipulation to regulators and government entities. The Canadian government has invested in excess of $2 million to validate the economic potential of the areas surveyed under the Barker project and the surrounding area. If Barker does not receive some support and protection in the public capital markets, the Canadian government will potentially not see the full benefit of their investment.

Suggestions for further analysis
Event analysis
The low market price of the company's common stock does not align with the fact that the company has substantiated claims to mineral properties in areas of interest to the Canadian government. Events like shareholder rights plans and private placements have been known to precede negative market reactions in most industries. However, in mining and exploration, private placements are usually perceived as positive events. In order to make the argument that the price is being manipulated around the announcement dates, there needs to be an independent source of

the news. Working only with internally generated press releases makes this difficult unless Barker can document that they were widely disseminated. For example, Barker has data on hits to their website that suggest that the information is widely read.

Another reason to initiate an event study is to examine other possibilities like "wash trades", "churning" for volume, etc. Initially, it will be necessary to eliminate known reactions. The nature of the market for junior company exploration stocks is unique enough that much of the existing research on the behavior of stock prices around public events does not apply. We would also need a more rigorous statistical study to confirm the possibility of pre-shorting price increases in order to differentiate that from the appearance of other price behavior.

I recommend that Barker consider doing a technical event study – where the data on press releases is added to a database with stock prices and volume to determine if the observed changes are statistically significant. This would include an in-depth review of press releases to be designated positive, negative and neutral. Such a study generally compares the stock price behavior (relative to some norm) for a range of dates before the event to the behavior during and after the event.

Document failure to receive

The information provided for review on investors' failure to receive shares at settlement is of significant interest, although it is not documented sufficiently to provide any conclusions in this report. The dollar value of shares purchased but not received is tantamount to a loan from the investor to the broker for the period from settlement to receipt. The investor may be entitled to a claim for compensation from the broker for the use of funds during the period. Even if the dollar value is small, the claim could present an opportunity for access to more detailed information about the parties involved in the settlement failure. I offer some suggestions in the *Appendix: One Clear Example* for improving the documentation of these events. Some key facts that need to be brought out are: was there a difference in the share price from when the money was debited from the investor's account to when the trade was settled for shares that were delivered to the investor? What is the broker's credit rating compared to the variability (a measure of risk) in the stock price? This information would be useful for compiling a claim for compensation for the investor from the broker.

Other considerations
One thing that is particularly useful is to try to get information from the brokers about their account holders (identify the non-objecting beneficial owners) underlying their position held in the central depository's nominee name (e.g., CDS or DTC). If you can get accurate information, aligning it with the depository position listings might reveal where the "fail to receive" is hiding in the data – revealing one partner to the trade – by knowing where brokers report more shares in client accounts than they are holding at the depository. Companies and transfer agents I've worked with have reported that some brokers disclose three or more times as many shares in investor accounts as they have holdings. In the US, unfortunately, brokers can subscribe to a "service" provided by Automatic Data Processing (ADP, the industry utility that processes the data for presentation to companies) that reports back discrepancies to the broker first so they can adjust their reports before the company sees it. This has cut down – though not eliminated – records of over-reporting.

The data that Barker is collecting and presenting, needs a clear data dictionary, descriptions of databases used, etc. This will serve two purposes. It will keep the terminology and abbreviations consistent across documents; and it makes the data and results accessible to a broader audience. Some of the terminology, e.g., "Stockwatch," won't be easily understood by anyone who hasn't worked in the financial services industry or been a direct investor in equity securities. A suggested presentation is included in *Appendix: Glossary – presentation suggestions*.

Appendix: Trading range as percentage of opening price

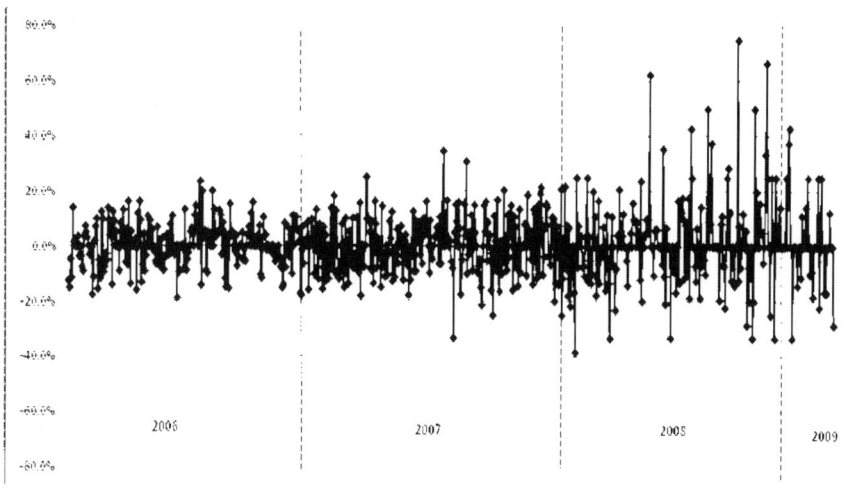

Appendix: Excerpt of Broker Trading Activity Chart

Barker Minerals Ltd.
Broker Trading Activity Chart
March 2 - April 26, 2007

Date:	March 2 - 8 2007	March 9 - 15 2007	March 16 - 22 2007	March 23 - 29 2007	March 30 - April 5 2007	April 6 - 12 2007	April 13 - 19 2007	April 20 - 26 2007	CDS Net (-)	CDS Net (+)	SW Net (-)	SW Net (+)	SW Sell	SW Buy
Share Price	.24-.24	.31-.29	.29-.28	.31-.29	.32-.40	.40-.40	.44-.39	.44-.40						
Broker N														
CDS Net	0	0	0	0	0	0	0	0	0					
SW Net	0	0	0	0	0	-1,000	0	0			-1,000			
SW Buy	0	0	0	0	0	0	0	0						0
SW Sell	0	0	0	0	0	-1,000	0	0					-1,000	
Holdings	0	0	0	0	0	0	0	0						

Broker S														
CDS Net	0	0	0	0	0	0	0	0	0					
SW Net	0	0	0	0	0	0	-20,000	0			-20,000			
SW Buy	0	0	0	0	0	0	0	0						0
SW Sell	0	0	0	0	0	0	-20,000	0					-20,000	
Holdings	0	0	0	0	0	0	0	0						

Appendix: Excerpt 2 of Broker Trading Activity Chart

Barker Minerals Ltd.
Broker D Trading Activity Chart

Date:	March 2 - 8, 2007	March 9 - 15, 2007	March 16 - 22, 2007	March 23 - 29, 2007	March 30 - April 5, 2007	April 6 - 12, 2007	April 13 - 19, 2007	April 20 - 26, 2007	CDS Net (-)	CDS Net (+)	SW Net (-)	SW Net (+)	SW Sell	SW Buy
Share Price	.24-.24	.31-.29	.29-.28	.31-.29	.32-.40	.40-.40	.44-.39	.44-.40						
Broker D														
CDS Net	0	-8,500					0	-8,500						
SW Net	0	-20,000	-8,500	-5,000		2,000	0				-31,500			
SW Buy	40,000					2,000	0							42,000
SW Sell	-40,000	-20,000	-8,500	-5,000	0	0	0						-73,500	
Holdings	8,500	0	0	0	0	0	0	0						

Date:	April 27 - May 3, 2007	May 4 - 10, 2007	Mary 11 - 17, 2007	May 18 - 24, 2007	May 25 - 31, 2007	June 1 - 7, 2007	June 8 - 14, 2007	June 15 - 21, 2007	CDS Net (-)	CDS Net (+)	SW Net (-)	SW Net (+)	SW Sell	SW Buy
Share Price	.38-.37	.32-.35	.36-.34	.34-.33	.30-.27	.29-.24	.27-.29	.33-.30						
Broker D														
CDS Net	0	0	0	0	0	0	0	0						
SW Net	0	0	0	0	0	0	12,000	0				12,000		
SW Buy	0	0	0	0	0	0	12,000	0						12,000
SW Sell	0	0	0	0	0	0	0	0						
Holdings	0	0	0	0	0	0	0	0						

Appendix: One Clear Example – documentation suggestion

When investors purchase shares on the open market and request delivery of the certificates, they may encounter delays and/or resistance from the retail broker. The following summarizes the events that could be documented to provide evidence that the trade failed to settle.

Date/Time: Investor placed "buy" order, number of shares, name and location of brokerage.

Date/Time: Investor received confirmation statement indicating that trade executed, including price and settlement date.

Date/Time: Investor's cash account is debited and investor's securities account is credited with shares (entitlements reflected in periodic brokerage statements).

Date/Time: Investor requests share certificate, method of request and who received the request at the brokerage. Date/Time of Broker's response. Investor should repeat request or inquire on status at least once per week until the certificate is received. Each contact should be documented.

Date/Time: Transfer agent receives request to issue the certificate to the Investor; whose name the shares come out of (probably CDS); When the Investor finally receives the certificate.

At all critical dates: Transfer agent and CDS records showing the number of shares registered or held at CDS on behalf of the broker/dealer.

Appendix: Glossary – presentation suggestions

CDS – Canadian Depository for Securities: Central counterparty for trade clearing and settlement in Canada, central securities depository for securities immobilization. "CDS Net" indicates a net change in member (broker/dealer) position in shares of Barker Minerals during a given period (day or week).

Minus TA – used in summary Broker Trading Activity Charts to indicate an adjustment for shares transferred into or out of CDS.

SW – Stockwatch: Trade data source which provides list of buying and selling broker/dealers with number of shares in each trade.

TA – Transfer Agent: Agent engaged by Barker Minerals to maintain records of ownership, distribute dividend payments, monitor voting rights, etc. Computershare is the current TA; prior TA was Pacific Corporate Trust.

Appendix: Limitations and Disclaimers

We take as given the data provided to us by Barker Minerals. Our efforts did not include confirming or expanding data except as noted below.

We were given copies of transfer agent records, Stockwatch reports, Canadian Depository for Securities, Ltd. (CDS) position listings, etc. We saw no evidence that any of these may have been altered in any way from their original sources. I reviewed the list of registered holders and found no indication of shares held by custodians or nominees other than CDS.

The present analysis takes as given the validity of the mineral properties. Our expertise is in economics and finance, specifically trade settlement; we claim no expertise in minerals or mining. Purely as background, we found mention of Barker Minerals' exploration projects in the 2001 and 2002 report *Overview of Trends in Canadian Mineral Exploration* by the Canadian Intergovernmental

Working Group on the Mineral Industry (*Survol Des Tendances Observées Dans L'exploration Minérale Canadienne*, Groupe de Travail Intergouvernemental Canadien sur L'Industrie Minérale) which is available from the Natural Resources Canada (Resources Naturelles Canada) website.

It may also be noted that after the 2000 passage of the Investment Tax Credit for Exploration (ITCE) and the Mineral Exploration Tax Credit (METC), significantly larger percentages of exploration and deposit appraisal expenditures in Canada were done by companies and prospectors such as Barker Minerals. Junior company spending rose to 44% of total in 2003 and 53% in 2004, "the first time since 1987 (and only the second time in the history of Canadian mineral exploration statistics) that junior spending exceeded that of senior companies" (from *Overview of Trends in Canadian Mineral Exploration* 2009, Part 6. Historical Exploration and Deposit Appraisal Statistics by Louis Arseneau and Ginette Bouchard, Natural Resources Canada). Barker Mineral's activity is within the same general timeframes. During the course of our discussion and meetings, Barker made available more references and resources than I could check in the timeframe of this report.

Appendix 2: Report for Barker Minerals – Updated Review of Data and Documents (July 16, 2012)

Executive summary

This updated review and expanded statistical analysis on the share price and trading activity in the common stock of Barker Minerals Ltd. shows serious evidence of fails-to-deliver (FTD) or naked-short-selling (NSS) in the publically-traded common stock shares (TSX.V:BML). The evidence specifically identifies broker-dealers who are passing the fails-to-deliver and fails-to-receive back and forth among themselves to avoid detection, regulatory reporting and potential tax consequences. Through Barker's open communication with shareholders, no individual investor has been denied access to registered shares.

Barker executives developed and refined a straight-forward data capture and analysis that can be used to discover which brokers and how many shares on what dates are involved in manipulative activity. Using trade data in combination with settlement reports they are able to methodically cross-reference activity to get to a net position – which reveals where shares are sold but not delivered (NSS) and subsequently delivered (without matching sell-trades) to disguise the underlying activity. Many of the transactions caught by their reports are similar to the "wash trades" recently revealed in the case of Overstock.com. Two example event analyses are presented in an Appendix.

The mining industry continues to be important to economic growth in Canada (PWC 2011). Representatives from several Asian governments have visited Barker to discuss their 100%-owned, approximately 400,000-acre highly mineralized claim block in East-Central British Columbia, Canada. The closer Barker comes to proving the mineral content of their claims and reaching an accord with a buyer for their discoveries, the more at risk the BML shares become to manipulative stock market activity designed to "grab" these assets from the exploration Company. Barker Minerals Ltd. has passed the stage where more and further research is necessary. The latest developments and improved methodology and reporting which they are calling the "Pro Long Strategy" provide solid evidence upon which they can take legal action.

Background and the 2010 report

The report submitted at the end of 2010, "Report for Barker Minerals: Review of Data and Documents" ("the 2010 Report", Trimbath 2010) contains a complete description of the normal process for the settlement of stock trades and a discussion of how settlement failures or naked short sales (NSS) occur. The statistical analysis in the 2010 Report indicated that there was abusive NSS resulting in phantom shares of Barker Minerals Ltd. common stock (BML) in circulation.

One important fact confirmed in that report bears repeating here: the broker-dealers with the heaviest trading activity (and correspondingly low settlement activity) have no shares outside of the Canadian Depository for Securities Ltd. (CDS). Because there is no record of legitimate shares for these broker-dealers outside of CDS, phantom shares are the only remaining explanation for the extraordinary volume of activity. CDS is the only nominee with registered shares – no other nominees and no other companies are registered as shareholders in BML. Once the CDS shares and ownership changes at the transfer agent are accounted for in the settlement of buy/sell market trades, the remaining activity is attributable to phantom shares.

Of the 151 million BML shares currently issued and outstanding, 103 million are registered to individuals and the remaining 49 million are held at CDS. The beneficial owners of 34 million[1] of the shares held at CDS have been identified as individual investors (based on regulatory reports and Barker's internal tracking methods). A significant number of those are known to be in registered retirement savings plans. Therefore, Barker estimates the natural, market-based limit on short interest (covered by stock borrow) to be approximately 15 million shares. Yet in March 2011, trades for more than 3 million shares failed to settle. This should only happen if the entire 15 million shares are already "on loan," making BML shares "hard to borrow." Alternatively, trades are intentionally allowed to fail at settlement in order to manipulate the supply (and price) of shares in circulation. When shares are hard to borrow the cost of borrowing is very high. Under these circumstances, the stock price has to drop by a greater amount for a short selling strategy to become profitable (see Cirangle 2012). Since November 2010, monthly fails-to-deliver in BML have been as high as 69% of trade volume, with cumulative aged fails (potentially 1 year or older) of 1.8 million shares or nearly 12% of float.

The underlying problem being addressed by Barker Minerals is that securities are being sold by broker/dealers who do not have them (and do not borrow them) so the number of shares in circulation exceeds the official supply. Trade settlement failures disrupt capital markets by:

(1) damaging asset values by artificially increasing the supply of shares in circulation,

---

[1] Numbers may not sum due to rounding. Figures in this paragraph are approximate. The last shareholder list, including identification of the non-objecting beneficial owners of shares held at CDS, was as of December 16, 2011.

(2) impairing the issuer's on-going access to capital,
(3) reducing effective corporate governance by violating the voting rights of shareholders, and
(4) denying investors access to the use of funds between settlement date and the date when securities are eventually delivered.

This final point – that the broker holds the investors' cash without delivering stocks, is especially risky because it:
a) exposes investors to excess risk for which they are not compensated, and
b) causes investors to miss opportunities for alternate investments.

The potential danger in this final point became reality with the loss of customer cash through losing investments made by MF Global (October 2011) and Peregrine/PFGBest (July 2012) (Associated Press, 2012).

> *Classic Asset Grab: The Story of Eagletech*
> The primary perpetrators in the Eagletech cases were Tonino Labella and John Serubo. Labella owned 75% of Valley Forge Securities, Inc. and acted as its Chairman and CEO. He also controlled a number of domestic and offshore securities and investment entities that he used to manipulate Eagletech's stock. Serubo provided office space for Valley Forge in Florida. Labella and Serubo solicited investors to buy shares even before they approached Eagletech. They pretended to sell shares to investors for US$1.00 to US$2.50 each for a total of US$1.4 million – before they had any actual shares to sell. Subsequently, they approached Eagletech and got them to issue a large block of shares (10 million) in exchange for an infusion of US$1.2 million cash. The stock was then transferred to a brokerage account at Valley Forge and sold into the public market, including Valley Forge's own retail customers. Fifteen other brokers, in exchange for generous kickbacks of up to 50% of the value of the trade, generated US$12.7 million of sales on the initial block of shares for which they paid Eagletech only US$1.2 million). To close out their profits, the

> brokers told the original investors that their shares had been sold for between US$4.00 to US$8.00, resulting in a positive return. In fact, the soliciting brokers had sold the shares they did have (which were fewer than they led the original investors to believe) in the open market for higher prices, providing kickbacks to their circle of selling brokers and realizing a significant profit while maintaining the fascade that the original investors ever owned shares. These activities took place between August 1999 and December 2000; the SEC litigation was filed in February 2005 with the stock selling at 6 cents a share. (SEC v. Labella, Serubo, et. al., 2005). In addition, the U.S. Attorney for the District of New Jersey obtained indictments against four individuals for criminal securities manipulation activities in Eagletech stock (see United States v. Labella, No. 05-CR-87 (D.N.J.)).
>
> After Labella and Serubo took their profits from the transactions, there remained a significant number of retail investors who were on the buying end of the $12.7 million of sales – sales of phantom shares of Eagletech stock. The SEC failed to pursue the matter further and eventually forced the deregistration of Eagletech's stock over a technicality (failure to timely file paperwork). Due to the downward pressure put on the price of shares of Eagletech by the excessive number of open market sales orders (which could not be fulfilled because no shares existed), Eagletech no longer had access to capital and was unable to afford to bring their communication patent to fruition. John Serubo died in 2009, shortly after appearing in a documentary (Wall Street Conspiracy, 2012) where he confessed his role in the manipulation of Eagletech's stock. Based on information provided by Serubo, it appears that Serubo and others helped make the technology developed by Eagletech available for commercial use in Europe without attribution to the inventor, Eagletech's founder, Rodney Young.

Introduction to 2012 report

In mid-May 2012, documents in a U.S. court case were publically revealed, exposing broker-dealer internal emails in which the type of trading activity evidenced in the 2010 Report on Barker's tracking methodology is discussed as commonplace despite various U.S. rules and regulations to the contrary (Cirangle 2012).

Those emails show that broker-to-broker settlement failures (FTDs and NSS) are used for the purpose of manipulating stock prices. In light of these revelations, the evidence discovered and organized by Barker should be taken even more seriously by regulators and the judiciary in Canada. Broker-dealers purposely and intentionally "create supply and perpetuate selling in stocks" like BML (Cirangle 2012, p. 18). In one email, the Merrill Lynch Professional Clearing Corporation President admits, they are "failing when we have over a million shares of stock available." If this is the case for BML, it means the entire turnover – as high as 30 million shares in April 2011 – could be phantoms. Our analysis around the events of March 30, 2011 (see the first example in the Appendix) show that TD Waterhouse had 12 million share of BML in their CDS account, yet failed to deliver 1.3 million shares for settlement.

The purpose of this report is to review progress on the suggestions from the 2010 Report, update the statistical analysis, and outline Barker's strategic moves to fight against manipulative trading in BML shares. The next section updates the actions taken by Barker on the suggestions for further analysis described in the 2010 Report. These have all been completed. The updated statistical analysis has been expanded to include new data sources. Barker's strategic action plan is described in the penultimate section, followed by a concluding section with suggested "next step" actions for consideration.

Update on recommendations

The 2010 Report included suggestions for further analysis. The recommendations included ways to improve the methodology used to identify "naked short selling" activity and Barker's documentation produced in preparation for taking action.

The 2010 Report also included a minor recommendation to add a data dictionary. This has been completed and is very helpful for making the reports accessible to a broader audience. The following sections update the steps taken by Barker on the major recommendations.

Report each incident of suspected abuse and manipulation to regulators

Summary: The Canadian government invested more than $2 million to validate the economic potential of the areas surveyed under the Barker project and the surrounding area. That investment is put at risk when exploration companies are unable to access public capital markets for early stage financing. STP recommended that Barker document as many instances of suspected market manipulation as possible. Barker needs this documentation to press for support and protection for the public capital markets from the Canadian regulatory agencies.

Barker did this. They began sending detailed letters to the Investment Industry Regulatory Organization of Canada (IIROC). In a May 2011 letter to IIROC, Barker very clearly describes a scenario whereby failing to deliver securities for settlement can be combined with a depository stock borrow program for profit at the brokerage. This profit comes at the expense of the Company and its (genuine) investors.

Barker's letter outlines an argument that has not been made clear before: using the stock borrow program enables brokerages to short sale securities without having to report a short sale as required by regulatory authorities. The recognition of a "fail to deliver" at settlement is the first line of defense against "naked short selling." Otherwise, much of this activity can only came to light after a financial institution collapses or when a whistleblower comes forward (see, for example, *Wall Street & Technology* 2009).

Many manipulative trades are not marked as short sales and simply allowed to fail delivery at settlement. For example, in 2011 UBS was fined in the U.S. and Europe for "mismarked" short sale trades (i.e., short trades that were marked as "long") and short sale trades executed without "reasonable grounds" for being able to borrow and deliver shares for settlement. UBS failed to properly supervise traders in the U.S. (where BML shares also trade) throughout 2009 and 2010. Millions of short-sale orders were placed without locates (*Technology Business Journal*, 2011). According to the chief enforcement officer for the Financial Industry Regulatory Authority (FINRA), "If there were failures to deliver, short selling would have the ability to affect the market, especially in hard-to-borrow, thinly traded stocks," (*Reuters Hedgeworld*, 2011). By early 2011, UBS accumulated 77,000 FTD shares in BML or more than 80% of shares sold.

The problems at UBS were not brought to light until UBS began to review their internal procedures in response to a FINRA investigation. If UBS had used the stock borrow program available at most central securities depositories (including CDS), these trades would never have been discovered by FINRA or any government regulatory agency. The failure to deliver at settlement is the event that will alert most regulators to possible manipulative and/or illegal market activity. Barker has developed an excellent process for tracking the settlement failures (and more, as outlined below under "Barker's Strategy") independent of support from either the central clearing and settlement organization or any regulatory authority.

In a follow-up letter of July 2011, Barker named specific parties (major brokerage firms) that approached them in an attempt to draw Barker into financing arrangements that would subject Barker to additional risk (see the boxed-text above on Eagletech).

One party that contacted Barker said they were looking for shares for a "panicked broker" who told him *"help me now, I'll help you later."* In other words, if the broker that called Barker could get them to issue some shares of BML (to use for settlement by another broker under pressure to deliver shares), he would receive favorable treatment in future transactions. In my research on settlement failures, I came across a similar situation in bond markets. A large insurance company investor was told that if they did not force the buy-in for some bonds they purchased but failed to receive, the failing broker would assure the insurance company could buy bonds in an upcoming auction to which they did not normally have access. These activities undermine market efficiency.

In a specific example, a broker sold 100,000 shares in late 2011 and had been "sitting on the bid" (waiting for the seller to move) yet unable to get access to shares. Barker's reports indicated that there were no shares for sale in a transaction of that size. Barker suggests a plausible explanation whereby the broker may have loaned client shares to a short seller and the client/investor submitted a request to withdraw their shares. The broker was unable to force a recall of the loan due to restricted floating supply. As the "daisy chain" begins to domino, there will not be enough shares to cover all the open positions if they add up to more shares than are in circulation. (See the Appendix "Manipulative Market Activities identified by the Federal Reserve Bank of New York" for a definition of a "daisy chain" in fails.)

The parties contacting Barker are not deterred by the fact that Barker is publicly conducting this investigation and has contacted IIROC. This is further indication of the seriousness of the problem and the inability of financial regulation – reformed or not – to deter parties that are determined to perpetrate fraud in the open market for stock trading. IIROC required Barker to provide evidence eliminating every reasonable possibility for a legitimate explanation for FTDs and NSS before taking any action. After the follow-up letter naming specific parties, IIROC requested additional details on individual brokers. Barker complied and did not hear again from IIROC on the matter. Shortly after submitting the results of their research, the brokers named in Barker's letter did not have any subsequent trades "out of place" (i.e., no evidence of NSS) in BML for a period of time. Barker interprets this sudden change in activity to suggest that regulators are sharing information either directly with brokers or with parties (such as CDS) who are providing it to the brokers. There is, however, little to suggest that punitive actions are being taken against the broker-dealers identified with FTDs and NSS.

Conduct an event analysis
Summary: In the 2010 report, I recommended that Barker do an event study – where the information on corporate events (made public through press releases) is added to the database with stock prices and trade volume to determine if the observed changes are statistically significant. Such a study generally compares the stock price behavior (relative to some norm) for a range of dates before the event to the behavior during and after the event. An event analysis could tell if the abrupt changes in price and volume can be attributed to actual corporate events. If not, this adds weight to the suspicion of market manipulation. An analysis like this is especially useful when the overall market is experiencing volatility as is the case for junior mining stocks in Canada (PWC 2011). By pursuing the logic of event analysis, even without pursuing a technical analysis (i.e., based on methodology established in academic financial journals), Barker is able to more closely identify specific parties and specific dates – information that regulators often require before they will initiate further review.

Barker continues to make significant progress on maintaining the data for event analyses. The settlement data from the Canadian Depository for Securities, Ltd. (CDS) is consistently reported on T+4 (four business days after trade date). Despite this inexact alignment with T+3 settlements, the reports are valuable for estimating the magnitude of the problem and identifying time frames and parties. In addition, using revisions suggested in the 2010 Report, Barker created broker activity reports, both monthly and cumulative. These can be prepared to include a carryover balance from previous months or focused on specific dates for event analyses.

With the aligned data (cumulative since November 2010), Barker developed evidence that positive Company news forces more NSS. Two examples are included in *Appendix: Barker's Event Analysis*. These positive corporate events induced buying activity that pushed the price up. But those buy orders were countered with excessive selling of phantom shares (fails to deliver at settlement) which served to suppress the price. Using the refined methodology Barker has been able to identify the brokers. Approximately 3 million shares (net) were sold but not delivered around the Company's announcement of positive news in March 2011.

Document failures to receive
Summary: Information on investors' failure to receive shares at settlement would be of significant interest. The dollar value of shares purchased but not received is tantamount to a loan from the investor to the broker for the period from settlement to receipt. Some key facts that can be brought out are: was there a difference in the share price between when the money was debited from the investor's account to when shares were delivered to the investor? What is the broker's credit rating compared to the risk of other investments? Subsequent events surrounding the failure of MF Global and Peregrine in the US provide clear evidence that customer money is not always segregated as required by industry rules. A financial failure (e.g., bankruptcy) of

the broker-dealer between settlement date and the date when shares are received by the investor could cause serious harm. There was some evidence that investors failed to receive shares on the settlement date at the time of the 2010 Report.

In March 2011, shortly after the 2010 Report was completed, an insider shareholder intended to sell shares (for personal financial reasons). When the shares were deposited into a brokerage account, Barker's report methodology clearly captured data showing the shares were quickly lent out. The investor found another source for their financial needs and subsequently withdrew the shares from the brokerage. Barker's report methodology revealed the same broker purchasing a like number of shares on the open market before returning a certificate to the investor. This raises serious questions about why the broker didn't simply recall the loan – an option that reduces costs and financial risk to the lending broker. The broker involved sold 4,400,000 shares in March and delivered only 1,400,000 for settlement. This appears to be a clear-cut example of a broker-dealer "creat[ing] supply and perpetuat[ing] selling" in BML (Cirangle 2012, p. 18).

In another example, one broker failed to receive 426,000 shares of BML in May 2011 (purchased more shares than they received in settlement). The obvious question is: "why didn't that broker demand a buy-in?" (where the settling depository purchases shares on the open market, delivers them to the buyer and charges the cost back to the seller who failed to deliver). According to new research released by Public Safety Canada (Hicks et. al. 2011), brokers "may not want to report rule violations that would undermine confidence" in the securities industry, emphasizing the detrimental impact on investors. As described earlier, there is also a "tit for tat" attitude toward not reporting violations on trading partners in exchange for favorable treatment in the future (including not having their own violations reported). A failure to receive of this magnitude – in a stock that normally trades only tens of thousands of shares per day – can lead to a "daisy chain of cascading fails" (Fleming and Garbade 2005). Furthermore, as was revealed in the Overstock case, brokerage firms go so far as to have "policies to accommodate manipulative trading styles such as 'killing' required buy-ins, and providing clients with information that would enable them to 'sell into' buy-ins, resulting in matched trades" and maintaining fails indefinitely (Cirangle 2012, p9). Barker's reports reveal multitudes of matched trades in BML.

Despite such aggressive market manipulation in shares of BML, the routine reports provided to publicly traced companies are not showing any shares "out of the ordinary" – that is, Barker is not receiving reports from CDS, brokers' NOBO lists or the transfer agent for BML showing more shares in accounts than have been issued. This is the crux of the problem for companies with shares subject to market manipulation in a self-regulatory industry. The Company will not be able to see the real evidence unless and until they have access to the brokers' records on investor accounts. When NSS occurs, some individual investors' accounts are likely to be allocated the "fail to receive" (the other side of a "fail to deliver" or "naked short sale"). The brokers must be maintaining retail customer records for more shares than are in the brokers' CDS accounts.

The recently revealed emails in the Overstock.com case demonstrate this (Cirangle 2012). Only through their own "digging" can Barker identify who, when and how many shares are FTD/NSS. They have successfully tracked this in their reports. It is important to note, as we did in the 2010 Report, that this is the minimum extent of the problem – the number of shares

FTD/NSS is likely higher than in the Barker reports due to the nature of market manipulation, i.e., the determination on the part of the perpetrators to hide their activities. Using their reports, Barker has been able to estimate that 15% to 25% of customer shares at one broker-dealer [TD Waterhouse] are phantoms. The reports also show that another broker-dealer [Canaccord] has created about 2.2 million phantom shares since November 2010.

On the face of it, any of these facts may seem like a single incident of fraudulent market activity. Taken as a whole – which we do in the next section with the statistical analysis – these events paint a picture of widespread manipulation.

Updated statistical analysis

The 2010 Report included a statistical analysis of stock price volatility measured by the daily trading range as a percentage of the opening price using data from 2006 through mid-2010. That analysis revealed a volatility spike from March 2, 2007 through June 21, 2007. Further, volatility continued to increase, peaking in 2008. Despite a reduction in volatility in subsequent years, another spike arose in 2011 with volatility rising to a level higher than the previous peak (Table 1). This pattern is similar to what Fleming and Garbade (2005) saw in U.S. Treasury bond markets – an initial decline in manipulative market behavior when the problem is brought to light (after their 2002 article) and then a rebound to levels above previous peaks when no regulatory or enforcement repercussions are implemented.

Table 1 Intra-Day Stock Price Volatility

Dates	Trading Range Variance
2006	0.0060
2007	0.0104
2008	0.0257
2009	0.0192
2010	0.0130
2011	0.0281

Standard event analysis proceeds from here to compare the behavior of BML stock prices to a measure of the "market."[2] One way to do this is to compare BML to Global X S&P TSX Venture 30 Canada (NYSEArca:TSXV). TSXV is a fund designed to mimic the returns on securities of the TSX Venture Exchange, which is Canada's junior listings market for emerging companies. The comparison allows us to quantify deviations from the market that are specific to BML stock (i.e., non-systemic changes). BML's intra-day volatility is compared to that of TSXV for 2011 in Figure 1. The variance for TSXV in the period was 0.0004; for BML it is 0.0168 – about 45 times greater. A t-test indicates statistically significant differences at greater than the 99.99% level.

Figure 1 Intra-day Stock Price Volatility BML versus TSXV, 2011

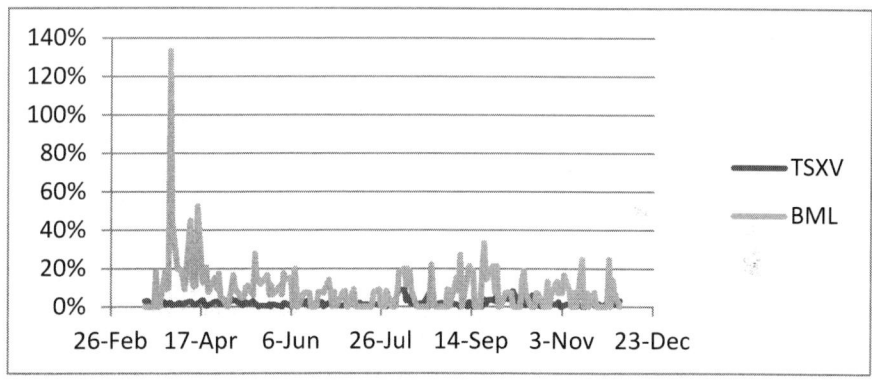

Sources: BML stock prices provided by Barker Minerals, Ltd. TSXV prices from www.finance.yahoo.com. Excluding the two weeks before and after the March 2011 stop-trading date does not make a material difference in these results. See the Event Analysis appendix in this report for specific analysis of March 2011.

Despite this intra-day volatility, the closing price of BML is remarkably stable – with a variance that is only 0.5% of the

---

[2] For good instructions on avoiding many common pitfalls in stock-price event analysis, see Rose Ackerman's chapter in Coffee, Lowenstein and Ackerman (1988). Ackerman provides a straight-forward discussion of how to structure a technical stock-price event study.

average closing price compared to nearly 38% for TSXV over the same period. This is supportive of the type of intra-day manipulation that greatly concerns Barker management: Massive trading volumes with erratic high and low bid/ask prices and a routine return to an artificially low closing price.

Our interpretation of the data is further supported by information provided to Barker by Buyins.net. Unsolicited, Barker received "RegSHO Compliance Alerts" which are summarized below. Buyins.net calculates a "Friction Factor" of zero (0) for normal price changes compared to trading activity. A negative "Friction Factor" indicates that excessive "selling caused the price to drop, which is evidence of manipulative activity." On October 6, 2011, the "Friction Factor" for BML was an extraordinary -142,100!

Table 2 Summary of data from Buyins.net

Date	Buyins.net "Friction Factor"	Short % trade volume
09/21/2011	0.0	84.62
10/06/2011	-142,110.53	21.62
10/11/2011	30,000.00	100.00
10/20/2011	-135,714.29	74.36

Barker's reports indicate three brokers primarily identified with naked short selling around the October 2011 dates.

Table 3 FTDs around Buyins.net data

Broker	Date	Sold but not delivered
Questrade	October 4, 2011	1,800
Questrade	October 5, 2011	6,000
Questrade	October 6, 2011	29,700
HSBC	October 11, 2011	30,000
HSBC	October 12, 2011	14,000
Jitney	October 14, 2011	10,000
Jitney	October 19, 2011	2,000

All of which is to further demonstrate clear evidence of price manipulation activity in BML shares taking place in public capital markets in the US and Canada. Broker-dealers are able to manipulate the appearance of a supply and demand for shares by consciously opting not to settle sales in shares of BML.

Barker minerals' strategy

According to research released by Public Safety Canada (Hicks et. al. 2011), in the securities industry "wrong-doing can be difficult to identify and the interpretation of motivations and behavior is not as clear as in other fields. ... The securities sector is an area of low visibility that requires proactive enforcement and prevention." Barker's tracking and reporting efforts provide the information that makes early intervention possible.

Barker's CEO, Louis Doyle, received Board approval to document and formalize the data tracking methodology as a potential commercial activity. The methodology will be called "Pro Long Strategy" (PLS) in reference to its ability to provide support to long-term shareholders and to counter naked short selling. PLS has been refined to the point where they know before they get reports from the transfer agent/registrar what the results will be. In essence, the transfer agent reports provide a cross-check to Barker's own analysis. Even when trading volume spikes (to millions of shares from tens of thousands) Barker's PLS reports make it possible to connect specific trades with settlement failures. The work done on refining reports during periods of normal trading volume gave them the confidence to continue to rely on the results when the volume increased.

Beyond implementing the Pro Long Strategy for tracking all trading and settlement records, Barker's multi-point strategy to counter manipulative behavior in stock markets includes:

- Filing regulatory complaints presenting data on abnormal events;
- Minimizing advance notice (in press releases) on financing activities while remaining conscientious about conforming to timely disclosure rules;
- Encouraging individual shareholder registration;
- Maintaining a historical event timeline which includes all corporate events and news releases alongside market trading and settlement activity.

Summary

Barker's strategy of making public statements about this investigation has begun to put some pressure on manipulators despite the lack of regulatory support. In mid-2011, Barker began receiving calls from brokers who "wanted to get out" of their naked short positions by buying legitimate shares from Barker (on the pretext of providing a cash infusion). These brokers are unable to get legitimate shares in the open market – where fails are rolled over and manipulators "sell into the buy-in" (Cirangle 2012). The only way out is for them to induce Barker to issue additional shares in exchange for cash. The frequency of these contacts from brokers provides some indication that Barker's strategy of public disclosure and pressure on regulators is beginning to have an impact.

Barker remains very selective about accepting financial partners and with good reason. The case of Eagletech is a cautionary tale in this regard. Eagletech Communications, Inc. is a Florida-based company that was destroyed by stock market manipulation under circumstances similar to that faced by Barker Minerals – a relatively small, junior company with valuable assets it had yet to bring to market. The U.S. Securities and Exchange Commission successfully prosecuted 17 individuals over the case of Eagletech.

Four individuals were convicted of criminal securities manipulation.

Conclusions

Through the efforts of Barker management, the evidence of manipulative activity is becoming increasingly obvious. Barker management has devoted hard work and effort not just to developing and maintaining this tracking methodology but also to keeping their business plan moving forward. This point bears emphasis: Barker executives have developed PLS while attending to the Company's business purpose – not an easy task. Eagletech is just one example of just how bad this can get. Many entrepreneurs have lost their battle in the open markets after relying on broker-dealer financing. Fortunately, Barker has access to other forms of financing including potential bulk sampling financing.

At this point, the NSS activity Barker is finding is not officially recognized by the Canadian government – hence, there is little or no regulatory pressure on brokers to settle the outstanding trades. Barker is not finding discrepancies in share registrations (at the transfer agent) or the position listing reports (at the depository). There are obviously anomalous patterns indicative of the market manipulation activities identified by the Federal Reserve Bank of New York (albeit unwittingly). The trading patterns of certain brokers (in confidential documents shown to me and submitted to IIROC) bear witness to the specifics. For example, one broker bought 1.93 million shares and sold 1.86 million shares in the same month – or about 16 times the broker's annual average monthly holdings in BML. This represents an "unusual amount of market activity" signaling an attempt to manipulate the market supply of the security (FRBNY 2007). This is not unlike Goldman Sachs "expressed ... intentions to create supply and perpetuate selling" in Overstock shares (Cirangle

2012, p5). It is clear "that concentrated short selling in a small number of small to mid-cap companies could be expected to have downward price effects" (Cirangle 2012, p6). Because shares are not borrowed to cover the settlement failures, the seller has no negative cost associated with the decision to sell. "In other words, the naked share sales [are] not a genuine expression of negative sentiment" (Cirangle, 2012, p8). Once the trader knows that the broker agrees to fail to deliver his sell orders, the trader has full knowledge that all fails will persist past any reporting period, so they are free to naked short sell million of shares for years on end. In private conversations with Barker executives, CDS managers admitted that there are fails on their records which have been open for eight years.

An "asset grab" like that experienced by Eagletech is a common outcome for unsuspecting entrepreneurs. "Naked short selling" and fails to deliver take place regardless of the real economic value of any legitimate "short sale strategy." Once the broker-dealers are in deep enough that they are unable to cover either the shorts or the fails at any price, the obvious long-run outcome is the takeover of assets by the broker-dealers – unless they are stopped.

Possible next steps

Barker can show evidence of where/when the fails occur and can trace the fails back to the trades at specific broker-dealers. The regulatory authorities in Canada have seen this evidence and have failed to take definitive action. So far, Barker has developed and refined the PLS methodology, plus sent formal complaints to regulators and made presentations to securities analysts explaining the problem by using their PLS reports. There is evidence that the reports shown to regulators were shared with CDS and the specific brokers engaged in the manipulative activities – but without sanction. Barker's concern here is that by letting the brokers know exactly where they are tracing the activity, the brokers might be able to find ways to hide it. Presentations to securities analysts have also not been effective. In the case of Overstock.com Inc. versus Gradient Analytics, Inc. and Rocker Partners (Marin County California Superior Court, August 2005) analysts were involved in the fraud (see OSTK 2005 and OSTK 2009). This could well be the problem in Canada, too, as these analysts are partnered with fund managers who operate internationally.

Although Barker has considered making the PLS methodology available to assist and encourage other companies to complain to regulators, broker-dealer financing sometimes comes with the placement of "inside" management – Board members put in place by broker-dealers to assist with the asset grab. Giving PLS to any such "puppet" managers could help them devise new strategies for hiding the activity even further.

Therefore, I recommend, at this point, that Barker establish the magnitude of the economic damage done to the Company and investors and begin to pursue civil litigation. The standard valuation for a publicly traded company, using the current market price, ignores the impact that the excessive ("phantom") shares have on the market efficient price mechanism. A valuation based on the value of the underlying assets could present a more appropriate starting point for estimating damages.

I also recommend that Barker consult lawyers about bringing action against CDS and/or specific broker-dealers identified through PLS reports. Ultimately, CDS is responsible for the value of the missing shares. As a result of novation – the process required for centralized clearing and settlement – all rights "to receive funds or securities must be asserted against CDS Clearing" (CDS, 2010). Filing a lawsuit against the CDS could bring the political process to bear on getting rules/regulations and enforcement tightened. It could also generate a significant amount of publicity, urging shareholders to remove their shares from the pool of unregistered shares available for backing fraudulent trades. A successful lawsuit against the broker-dealers identified in the PLS reports would provide Barker with access to internal records, including communications with analysts and traders and the internal records of investor accounts that are not backed by corresponding shares on deposit at CDS.

References

Anonymous (2010), "UBS loses first Lehman note arbitration case in US", *Structured Products*, vol. 6, no. 4, pp. 4.

Associated Press (2012). "Loss of customer cash at Peregrine, *Washington Post*, July 11, 2012

Barker Minerals Ltd. Website
http://www.barkerminerals.com/s/Background.asp

Canadian Depository for Securities Limited (CDS, 2010). "Note 15 Commitments and Contractual obligations," *Annual Report 2010*, Toronto.

Cauchi, Marietta (2009). "UBS fined for unauthorized trades," *Wall Street Journal Europe*, Brussels, Wall Street & Technology.

Coffee, John C. Jr., Louis Lowenstein, Susan Rose-Ackerman, eds. (1988). *Knights, Raiders and Targets: The Impact of Hostile Takeovers*. Oxford University Press, New York.

Entertainment Close – Up (2011). "Financial Industry Regulatory Authority Fines UBS Securities for Regulation SHO Violations and Supervisory Failures."

Fleming, Michael J. and Kenneth D. Garbade (2002). "When the Back Office Moved to the Front Burner: Settlement Fails in the Treasury Market after 9/11," *FRBNY Economic Policy Review*, November 2002, p35-57.

Fleming, Michael J. and Kenneth D. Garbade (2005). "Explaining Settlement Fails", *Current Issues in Economics and Finance*, 11(9), September 2005, Federal Reserve Bank of New York. Available online at www.newyorkfed.org/research/current_issues.

Global Investor (2011). "FINRA fines UBS $12m for short sale violations", 2011, *Global Investor*.

Hume, Lynn (2011). "FINRA Fines UBS $300,000", *The Bond Buyer*, [Online], 120 (33618), pp. 2.

Hicks, D., Kiedrowski, J., Gabor, T., Levi, M., and Melchers, R. (2011) *A Study of the Vulnerability of the Canadian Securities Sector to Organized Crime*. Ottawa, ON: Public Safety Canada.

Cirangle, Ellen A. (2012). *Overstock.com, Inc., et. al. v. Morgan Stanley & Co., et. al. Case CGC-07-460147*. Superior Court of the State of California, County of San Francisco, filed February 2, 2007.

Price Waterhouse (PWC, 2011). *Junior Mine 2011: Volatility, the new "business as usual"*, Online [www.pwc.com/ca/juniormine].

OSTK (2005). "John O'Quinn and His Legal Team File Lawsuit Against Gradient Analytics, Inc. and Rocker Partners LLP on Behalf of Overstock.com, Inc." Overstock.com Press Release (August 11, 2005). Online [http://investors.overstock.com, Investor Relations]

OSTK (2009) "Rocker Pays $5 Million to Overstock.com to Settle Lawsuit" Overstock.com Press Release (December 8, 2009). Online [http://investors.overstock.com, Investor Relations]

Reuters *Hedgeworld* (2011)."UBS Fined $12 Million in U.S. for Improper Short Sales", 2011, (Philadelphia, Pa.).

SEC v. Labella, Serubo, et. al. (2005). Case Civ. 05-852, United States District Court for the District of New Jersey.

Technology & Business Journal (2011). "Financial Industry Regulatory Authority FINRA; FINRA Fines UBS Securities $12 Million for Regulation SHO Violations and Supervisory Failures", pp. 402.

Technology Business Journal (2011). "FINRA Fines UBS Securities $12 Million for Regulation SHO Violations and Supervisory Failures", pp. 402.

Treasury Market Practices Group (TMPG, 2007). *Treasury Market Best Practices* published May 11, 2007, Federal Reserve Bank of New York www.newyorkfed.org/tmpg.

Trimbath, Susanne (2010a). Report for Barker Minerals: Review of Data and Documents, October 14, 2010 [corrected December 3, 2010].

Umair (2011). "UBS Securities faces $8M fine over short-sale lapses", *SNL Bank & Thrift Daily*.

APPENDIX 3: Manipulative Market Practices Derived from TMPG (2007)

Hold the Box: to hold settlement of an executed trade for a period of time [beyond T+3 or other industry standard settlement periods].

Inter-dealer voice brokers: [market participants] with electronic trading screens without having a record of the transaction published on the screen at the time of the transaction. Pricing practices that do not have an objective of resulting in a transaction also reduce efficient market price discovery.

Restrict the floating supply: [limit the number of shares delivered for settlement in the market] in order to generate price movements in that security or related markets.

Slamming the wire: the practice of holding back deliveries until immediately before the close of the securities wire with the intention of causing settlement fails in the market.

Strategic fails: the practice of selling short a security [in the repo market at or near zero percent] with little expectation of being able to obtain the security to make timely delivery.

Signals of trading activities that [manipulate] supply circulating in markets:

- an appreciable or unusual amount of market turnover in a particular security;
- changes in a market participant's normal securities lending or borrowing patterns in a security in which a market participant has a large position;
- elevated delivery or receive fails in a particular security and/or the presence of particular trades that persistently fail to settle;

- large concentration of holdings in the floating supply of a particular security (floating supply, at its largest, reflects the amount of the security originally issued [less closely held shares];
- placing a substantial percentage of floating supply in ... collateral with select counterparties that typically do not recirculate collateral;
- refraining from trading when holding a large position.

APPENDIX 4: Barker's Event Analysis

The analysis of each event is demonstrated in three graphs, along with a description of the event. The first graph presents an overlay of the price information on BML and TSXV, a fund that approximates the market for stock prices of companies similar to Barker (without volume data). The next two graphs show the price (high-low-close in a standard "candlestick" format) and volume data for BML and TSXV around the event.

In each example, the share price rose dramatically in minutes/seconds and then dropped on high sales volume which Barker can connect to FTDs. As the price per share rises on good news, the value of any short position would rise, resulting in margin calls or increased scrutiny by broker-dealer compliance staff or regulators. Barker views this as something similar to what might happen in a "short squeeze" – except that in this case many of the buy orders are fulfilled with phantom shares resulting in suppressed closing prices.

Example 1

On March 30, 2011 Barker Minerals requested a halt on the trading of their stock before the release of material news regarding the high grade silver mineralization on their Black Bear Project. At the time of the halt, the stock was trading at $0.075. After trading resumed the stock rose to $0.175 in thirty five minutes (a gain of 133%). Then it declined steadily to close the day at $0.105 (a gain of only 40%). The following day the opening price was at $0.10 and in twenty eight minutes the price rose to $0.14 (a gain of 40%) after which it declined almost in a steady manner to close at $0.11 for the day (a gain of only 10%). The March 2011 Broker Activity reports indicate sales of 4.3 million shares failed delivery from six brokers (and an additional 468,000 shares failed delivery from six other brokers). In March 2011, TD Waterhouse had 12 million shares in their CDS account, sold 5.4 million shares in open market trades yet failed to deliver 1.3 million shares. As explained in this report (see also Trimbath 2010), this is only possible if there are no "free" shares in the CDS account – i.e., all the shares are either out on loan or in customer-restricted accounts (e.g., tax-free retirement savings). Alternatively, as suggested in the text of this report, TD Waterhouse intentionally failed to deliver shares at settlement.

Table 4 Fails to Deliver, March 2011

Broker	FTDs
TD	1,347,149
BMO Nesbitt	1,063,000
Anonymous	1,056,500
RBC	343,480
Qtrade S.	251,572
CIBC W.M.	216,500
Leede	163,000
Global Securities	163,000
Dundee	50,000
National Bank Direct	42,000
HSBC	35,000
Pacific International	15,000

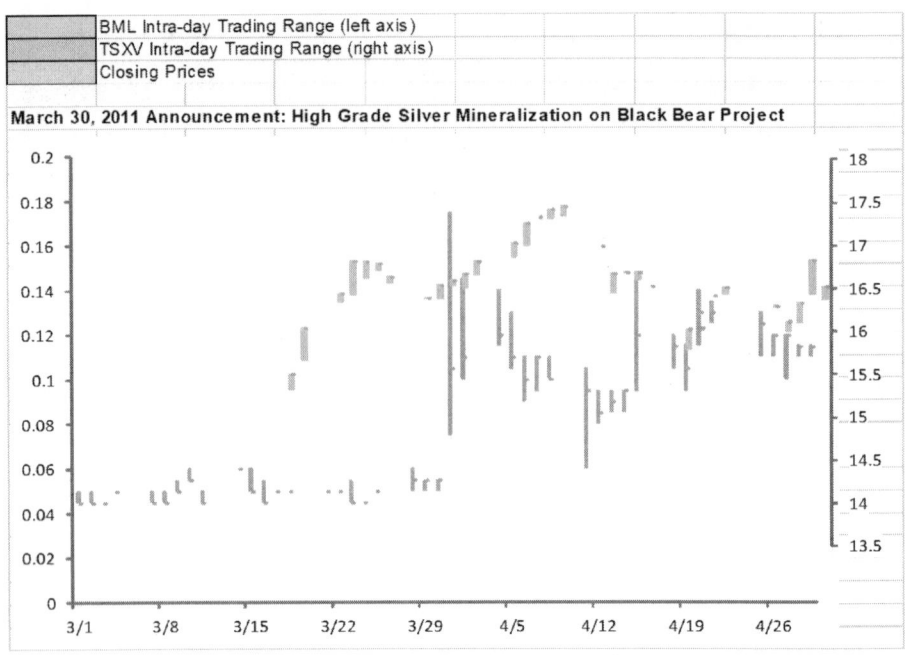

338 NAKED, SHORT AND GREEDY

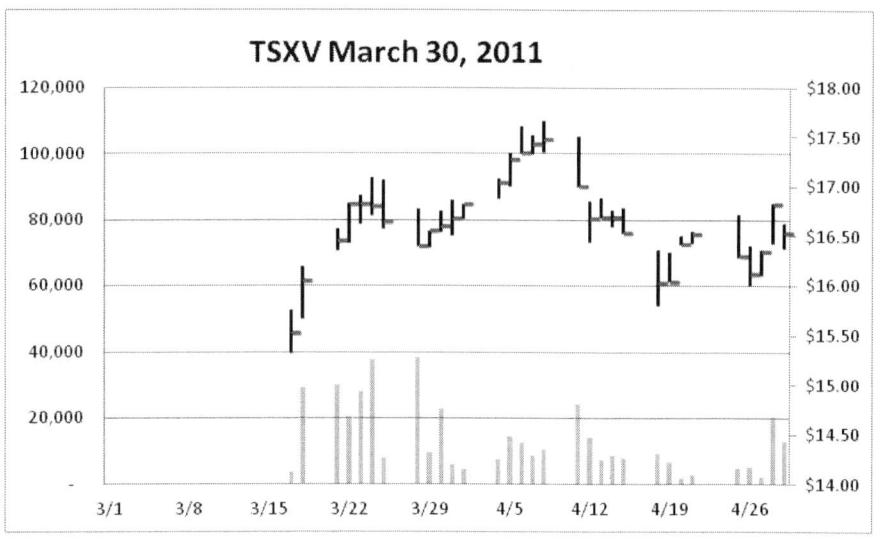

TSXV was initiated on March 17, 2011.

Example 2

On February 24, 2012, Barker Minerals requested a halt on the trading of their stock before the release of material news regarding a new gold discovery on their Frank Creek Project. At the time of the halt, the stock was trading at $0.05. After trading resumed the stock rose to $0.075 with the first trade. Sixty three seconds later the stock traded at $0.095 (a gain of 90%) after which it declined steadily to close the day at $0.065 (a gain of only 30%). The February 2012 Broker Activity reports indicate sales of 391,000 shares failed delivery from eight brokers.

Table 5 Fails to Deliver, February 2012

Broker	FTDs
CIBC W.M.	135,015
Scotia Capital	115,350
Questrade	46,000
BBS	40,000
Qtrade S.	35,000
Blackmont / Macquarie	12,000
Canaccord	7,000

Union 1,125

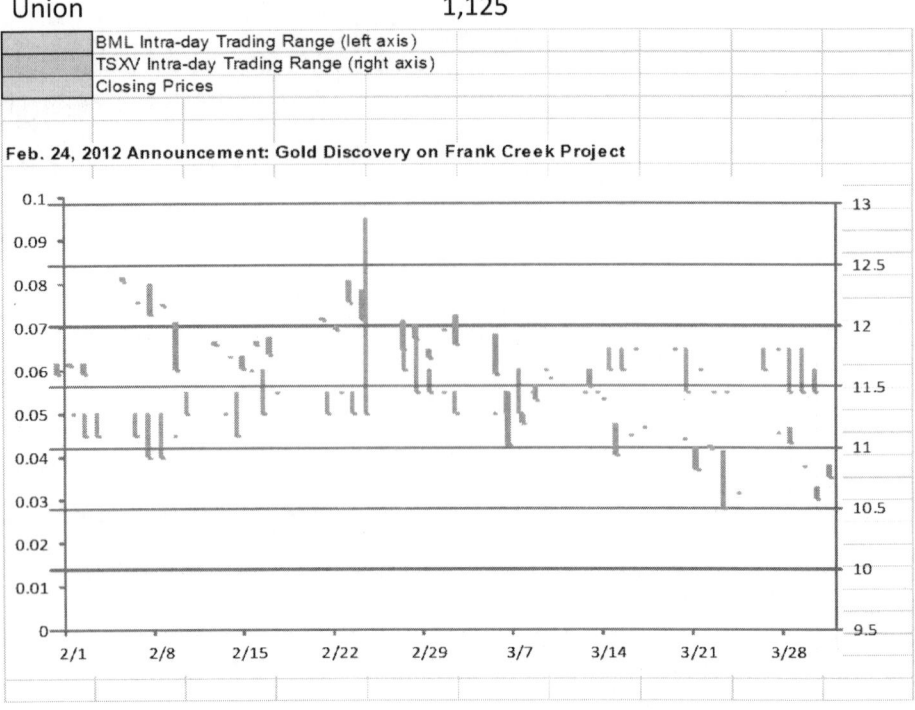

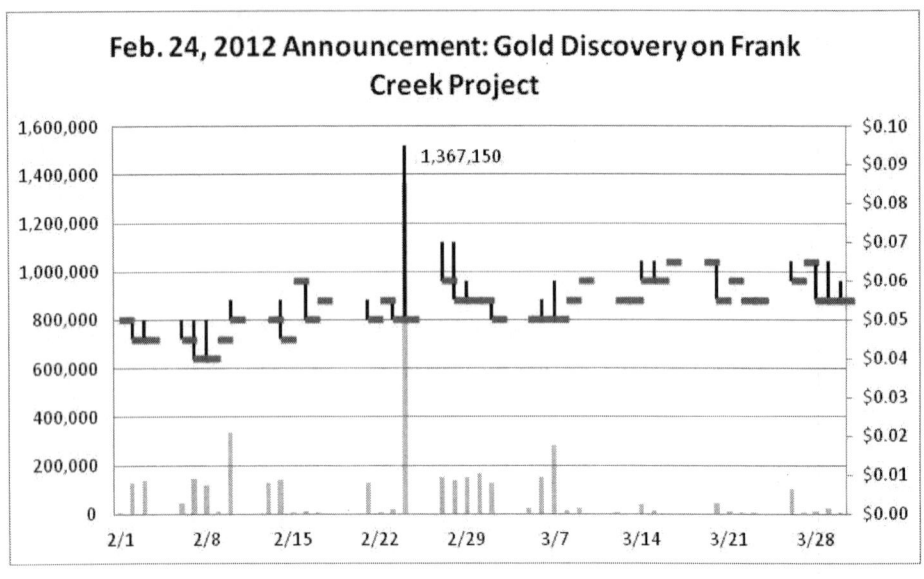

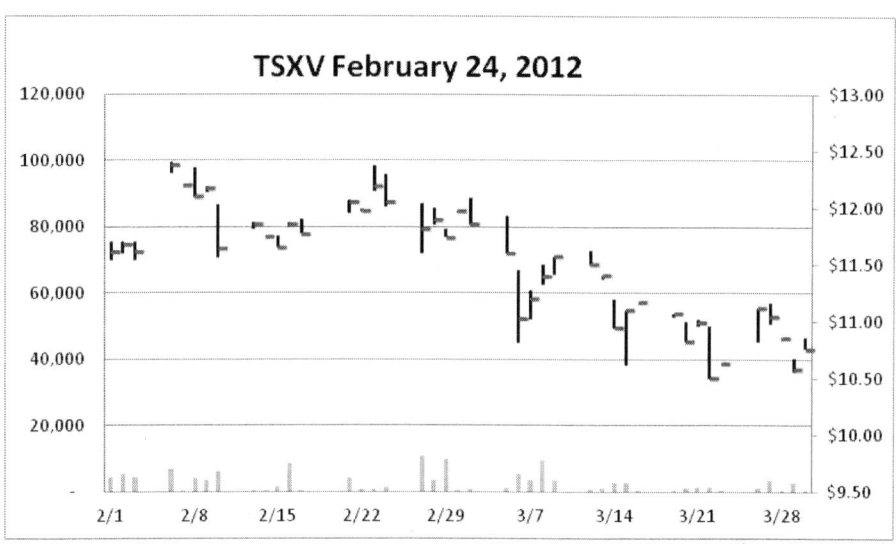

Index

Abelow, Bradley 162, 181
Alsin, Arne................................
..........174, 176, 178, 187, 257
Altenbach, Jim........... 174, 185
Angel, James J.............. 64, 134
Banking Committee................
.... 139, 155, 199, 200
Barker Minerals.................. 261
Bear Stearns ....
..119, 205, 209, 235, 262, 271
Bee, Samantha 206
Bennett, Senator (R-Utah)......
.... 139, 151, 198, 199
Benson, Todd..................... 132
Big Short, The........................ 228
Bolwell, Liz 228
Boni, Leslie... 47, 159, 163, 296
Brigagliano, James 134
Burnham, Drexel.......... 31, 231
Burrell, Bud..... iii, 42, 168, 228
Business Roundtable ....
.... 76, 151, 155, 156
Byrne, Patrick...48, 137, 139, 142, 144, 174, 176, 185-186, 191, 198, 202, 257, 274
Canadian Depository for Securitiesix, 152, 292, 293, 309, 312, 321, 332
Cardinale, Senator Gerald 162
Casavant, Urban 215
Casino Capitalism............. 249

Cede & Co 10, 152, 213, 284
Centralized clearing and settlement1, 15, 19, 27-29, 64, 109, 124, 171, 228, 280, 331
Chartered Financial Analysts Society of Los Angeles.. 185
Chepucavage, Peter J. 134
Chicago Board Options Exchange 121
Christian, Wes..........iii, 33, 37, 39, 45, 49, 124, 126, 131, 171, 182, 235, 242, 274
Citigroup 126
Clark, Don 126
CMKM Diamonds...ix, xi, 208
    certificate pull.................... 212
    document review 218
    phantom shares.................. 220
    UnShareholders.................. 217
Continuous net settlement. 22
Copeland, Kristina Leigh 229, 289
Corzine, Governor Jon...... 162
Cramer, Jim 120, 207
Credit default swaps. 233, 249
Credit rating agencies...... 249, 303, 321
Depository Trust and Clearing Corporation....... 2, 112, 184, 246, 287, 292

Depository Trust Company iii, 2, 11, 20, 62, 152, 181, 183, 239, 292, 348
DiStaso, Professor Marcia.. 39
Dodd-Frank Act .... ix, 7, 261
Donaldson, William 199
Dow Jones Industrial Average 23
Doyle, Louis........274, 277, 327
Drummond, Bob 73, 85, 136, 287
Drysdale Securities............. 62
Eagletech Communications 125, 131, 263, 282, 328
Economic efficiency...... 69- 71
Essary, Gayle 131
Failures to deliver................... 1, 11, 57, 60-62, 163, 178, 264-267, 270, 311, 313, 318
   data........................240
   effect on share price 206
   Europe................................236
   increase 242
   levels 83, 110
   multiplyingshares in circulation 128
   NASAA Forum....................134
   Ponzi scheme comparison.202
   proposed regulation...........111
   Wall Street Journal article .198
Fannie Mae 119, 237
FBI 170
Federal Reserve Bank............ iii, iv, 22, 23, 56, 64, 287, 296, 319, 329, 332, 333
   FTD reporting....................260

Fiduciary duty 27, 184, 221, 283, 284, 348
Financial Industry Regulatory Authority 10, 40, 318, 332, 333
Financial intermediaries......... .... 113, 284
Financial Services Committee 155
Finnerty, John 134
FOIA requests.......... 32, 64, 86
Freddie Mac 119, 237
Fridson, Marty.................... 157
Fuld, Richard 206
Funkhouser, Cameron K.. 134
Galper, Josh........................ 188
General Motors Acceptance Corporation (GMAC) ... 238
Goldman Sachs..........162, 172, 181, 204, 238, 262, 329
Government Accountability Office........... x, 130, 263, 292
Government bonds 18, 20, 56, 283
Great American Bubble Machine 204
Great Financial Crisis of 2008 .... 195, 204
Hagberg, Carl .... iii, 26-9, 46, 192, 266, 284
Harmer, Senator John (CA) 139,199, 282
Harrington, Cynthia . 185, 228
Hedge Funds..................... 139

Hodges, Al 223
Horowitz, Andrew 206
House Committee on Government Oversight and Reform 206
Huntsman, Governor Jon 140
Imperfect knowledge between parties 69
Initial public offering 8, 162, 293
Insana, Ron 132
Institutional investor 10
Investment Industry Regulatory Organization of Canada .... x, 276, 317
Jamieson, Dan 169, 232
Jett, Wayne............................ .... 72, 174-177, 185, 187
Jewell, Gary 33
Jobs and Growth Tax Relief Reconciliation Act .... x, 60, 114, 115
JP Morgan 209, 238, 248
JPMorgan Chase 172, 262
Kirkpatrick, Steve 215, 216
Kirzner, Israel 121
KPMG USAID Capital Markets Project 67
Kuhl, Robert 274, 277
Labella, Tonino 127, 314
Lambiase, Ralph................ 136
Lessons Not Learned 7, 13, 283, 286, 289
Long shares 223

Madoff, Bernie 117
Manufacturers Hanover Trust Company 20, 26
Matsumoto, Gary 167, 205
McKinnon, Thomson 62
Milken Institute .... iii, 31-33, 184, 197, 287, 289
Milken, Mike 31-34
Mitchell, Mark 195
Mohr, Sandra .... iii, 228, 289
Montrone, Tom iii, 27, 187, 190, 288
Morris, Nancy M. 67, 111
Mortgage bonds 233
Mortgage-backed bonds .. 240, 281
Naked Short and Greedy Event 174
Naked short selling 2, 12, 25, 46-49, 61, 66, 73, 79, 109, 119, 122, 131, 133, 144, 148, 150, 157, 159, 166, 170, 174, 180, 186, 195, 197, 228, 245, 253, 263-265, 270, 290, 299, 316, 326
  media stories....................... 166
  Overstock.com.................... 193
  small businesses targeted . 257
  small businesses, effect on 139
Nanopierce Amicus 75, 79
National Association of Securities Dealers .... x, xi, 134, 173, 174

National Securities Clearing Corporation .... xi, 2, 11, 21, 112, 182, 288

New Horizons Holdings .... xi, 208, 215, 216

New Jersey Senate Judiciary Committee 162, 181

New York Stock Exchange . 1, 10, 134, 163, 202, 295

Nichols, Dr. Lawrence 197

North American Securities Administrators Association .... xi, 133, 163, 285

O'Brien, Bob 143

O'Quinn, John 34, 37, 49, 127, 131, 133, 333

Olde Monmouth, transfer agent 189

Overstock.com...xi, 46, 48, 139, 143, 146, 167, 175, 185, 186, 257, 311, 323, 331, 333
   phantom shares 191

Over-voting 1, 27, 50-52, 73, 76, 137, 154, 156, 160, 164, 250
   Bloomberg Magazine report 191

Pacific Clearing Corporation 46, 183, 239

Pacific Depository Trust Company 67, 292

Pacific Securities Clearing Corporation 67, 292

Pajamahideen.....48, 61, 139, 143, 166, 184, 279

Patch, Dave 32, 63, 109, 169

Paulson, Henry Jr. 162

Phantom shareholders...... 236

Phantom shares 119, 220
   economics of......................... 16
   role of brokers 205

Phantom votes 247

Porter, Scott....................... 189

Post-trade processingiii, 11, 39, 41, 204, 229

Proxy voting 10

Ramtahal, Anand 74, 134

Registrar & Transfer Company 27

Regulation SHO..................... 11, 61, 155, 158, 175, 263, 265, 267, 292, 295, 332
   amendments......................... 72
   compliance 66
   economic incentives 68, 71
   Threshold List 63

Regulatory crisis......... 1, 5, 278

Rickert, Ben 228

Riley, Ray ....iii, 20, 23, 29, 33, 35, 266

Roundtable on the Savings and Loan Crisis.............. 197

Salomon Smith Barney 126, 128

Sanity Check, The.............. 143

Sarbanes-Oxley Act... 158, 167

Securities .... See Shares

Securities and Exchange Commission ....

1, 8, 67, 134, 160, 173, 174, 288, 292, 295, 328
  proposed Naked Short Selling Anti-Fraud Rule............. 269
Securities Industry Association..52, 65, 154, 295
Securities Lending Conference............. 169, 188
Securities Transfer Association ....
  iii, 20, 25, 50, 76, 154, 155, 156, 163, 187, 288, 289
  white paper............................ 51
Self-Regulatory Organization 10
Serubo, John126, 127, 314, 315
Settlement failure12, 138, 139, 233, 235, 291, 303
Settlement failures 15
Shapiro, Robert 134, 159
Shares
  authorized................................ 8
  buy-in 11
  clearing and settlement....... 11
  float... 9
  issued.. 9
  outstanding.......................... 8, 9
  phantom........................... 16, 54
  registered 9
  settlement.............................. 10
Shelby, Senator (R-Alabama) 199
Short sale................................ 12
  circuit breaker 120
  flipping.................................. 128
  price test............................... 120
  share price, effect on.......... 207

Stewart, Jon 206, 207
Stock lending 13, 77
Stock Shock 228, 289
Street name............................ 9
Tax treatment
  bond trades 56
  costs to taxpayers and investors......................... 57
  stock trades 59
Terminology........................... 8
The Securities Lending Conference 169
Thompson, Larry80, 83, 84, 131, 182
Transparency
  DTCC...................................... 81
  SEC.. 85
Trezza, Joe 179
Troster, Chris 189
Trump, Donald J................. 283
UnShareholders208, 223, 224, 262, 285
US Senate Banking Committee....................... 139
US Senate Judiciary Committee....................... 142
Valley Forge Securities 127, 314
Wall Street Conspiracy 125, 139, 199, 229, 289, 315
Weidner, David 206
Young, Rod 125, 130, 131, 263, 282

Endnotes

[1] For the elements that define a crisis in the context of the constitution, see
[2] See, for example, *Euromoney* March 2005 p.32 "The curious incident of the shares that didn't exist" and April 2005 p.40 "SEC seeks to curb naked ambition."
[3] See *Federal Register*, Vol. 69, No. 234, December 7, 2004, Rules and Regulations, 70852-70862.
[4] See SEC Release No. 34-52976; File No. SR-NSCC-2005-15; December 19, 2005.
[5] A good resource covering the early years of DTC and the subsequent creation of DTCC is *The Depository Trust Company* (2008, Paperback), by former DTC Chairman William T. Dentzer, Jr. from YBK Publishers, Inc., New York.
[6] There are some exceptions and these rules continue to change. The primary problem with fines for failing to deliver securities is that, where the rules provide for a fine, the request has to initiate with the party that failed to receive. One broker may be reluctant to request the fine this time so that the failing broker won't press for a fine against them the next time. A similar problem exists with most buy-in rules, as well.
[7] The seller may incur additional costs if the share price rises against the short bet. In that case, the short seller is subject to a "margin call" where they have to keep the cash on deposit within a certain "margin" of the original price when the shares were sold short. This is to ensure that the short seller will have sufficient means to purchase shares to cover the short sale (i.e., repay the stock loan).
[8] A 1988 mandate from the Department of Labor, known as the Avon Letter, established fiduciary duty that requires public pension funds to vote any shares in the best interest of the beneficiaries of the pension plan. The California pension funds revised their processes accordingly.
[9] NSCC no longer includes "due to" and "due from" values in their annual financial statements, plus the value covered by the stock borrow program. Instead, there is one number of "open positions." The stock borrow program was ended in 2014 due to lack of use. See Note 11 below.
[10] At that time, we were unaware that settlement failures, resulting in unlimited duration open positions at NSCC, were also contributing to the problems. The magnitude of the contribution of settlement fails would explode after 2001.

[11] NSCC proposed ending the stock borrow program at the end of 2013, due to lack of use (SR-NSCC-2013-13). The SEC received no comments on the proposed rule change and approved it on January 31, 2014.

[12] Trade settlement took place five business days after the trade date (T+5) when I started in the industry in the 1980s. It was shortened to T+3 in October 2014. The industry moved to T+2 for many financial instruments in September 2017.

[13] The Federal Reserve Board's Survey of Consumer Finances found 52% of households owned stocks in 2016 (most recent); 54% in Gallup's 2017 Economy and Personal Finance Survey (down from 62% before the financial crisis). The Gallup survey has a slightly higher percentage because the question asked households to consider money in 401(k) and IRA retirement funds.

[14] The share of pension fund money invested in the stock market varies slightly by source with most results coming in around 50%. For example, a Global Pension Asset Study by Towers Watson (a pension fund consultant) reported in 2011 that 44% of the average US pension fund is invested in the stock market. A Wells Fargo Securities report published on MarketWatch.com reported that defined benefit pension funds allocated 55% of their investment to stocks in 2018.

[15] Recall that "naked short selling" is terminology often used to marginalize critics of short selling and fails to deliver; we keep it in places where the meaning is clear or to be consistent with the actual terminology used in a particular context.

[16] The complete story of the CMKM withdrawal from DTC is available in Chapter 18.

[17] Some non-technical explanations for this and other financial and economic elements are available in the Primer in Chapter 1.

[18] In a 2019 example, Overstock.com declared "a blockchain-based dividend that critics said was concocted by ex-chief Patrick Byrne to stymie short sellers." See, for example: https://nypost.com/2019/09/18/overstock-says-it-will-loosen-restrictions-on-bizarre-crypto-dividend/ [Accessed September 28, 2019]

[19] A biographical sketch from www.carlhaberg.com: "[Carl] holds a BA [Bachelor of Arts degree] from New York University and a MS [Master of Science degree] from the Columbia University Graduate School of Business. He is a member of the American Arbitration Association, the Society of Corporate Secretaries and Governance Professionals (a former New York Chapter President and National Treasurer), the Shareholder

Services Association, the NASDAQ Board of Arbitration, the National Association of Stock Plan Professionals…"

[20] The impact of abusive short-selling and fails to deliver will be made especially clear in the story of Eagletech, Inc., in Chapter 9.

[21] Tom Montrone is a 1971 graduate of the United States Military Academy and received an MBA with honors from Iona College. He served on the board of directors and is a past-president of the Securities Transfer Association (STA). At the end of 2008, Tom purchased the remaining shares of R&T after being a minority shareholder. He sold R&T to Computershare Limited before retiring in 2014.

[22] The question of "fiduciary duty" is complicated and evolving from the perspective of the law. Even more complicated is whether the organization where an investor places their buy and sell orders is a fiduciary: investment advisors are but brokers are not. I won't go into it further here, but the interested reader will find a straight-forward, easy to follow explanation, along with tips on where to look for disclosures and what they mean, at http://www.highpassasset.com/blog/58-is-my-financial-advisor-a-fiduciary-or-a-stockbroker.html, by Ethan Braid, March 2013. [Accessed July 31, 2019]

[23] On June 4, 2003 the Securities and Exchange Commission made it impossible for an issuer to refuse to have its shares held at DTC. See SEC Release No. 34-47978; File No. SR-DTC-2003-02. See more in Part VII, Chapter 18.

[24] Many companies would contact me after struggling along on their own for years. Most of them would expect me and my team of experts to work without compensation. The exception would be Barker Minerals, which is covered in Chapter 21.

[25] We would never get information from NSCC on exactly who were the offending banks and brokers that were not delivering shares at settlement.

[26] My dissertation was published in 2002 as *Mergers and Efficiency: Changes Across Time*, Kluwer Academic Press (Springer), Boston.

[27] See "Without a Trace: The Importance of Information in Markets," by Susanne Trimbath, *LSTA Loan Market Chronicle*, The Loan Syndications and Trading Association, NY (2004).

[28] See "High Yield Financing and Efficiency-Enhancing Takeovers", by Susanne Trimbath, *Policy Briefs* (22), Milken Institute: Santa Monica, CA (2000).

[29] Initially, Dave used his General Electric work email to engage in e-conversations. Later, as he became increasingly active, he switched to a

personal email address. Although mostly a private person, Dave appeared on CNBC and in at least one documentary discussing "naked short selling" and fails to deliver.

[30] Wes was going to write a book of his own to tell the story of the criminal involvement, but to my knowledge it has not been published.

[31] Several of Mike's articles, including "Democratization of Capital" (*California Lawyer* magazine, July 2000), are available without charge at www.mikemilken.com.

[32] John O'Quinn died tragically in a car accident while driving to the airport on October 29, 2009. I never actually met Mr. O'Quinn.

[33] G. Themistocleous, C. Karavolias, S Kontou, N Gantaifis, et al. (2003) 'The accuracy of medical information on the Internet.' *Journal of Bone and Joint Surgery* (85, British volume), London, p. 228.

[34] "Iffy-pedia: up to six in ten articles on Wikipedia contain factual errors, by Amy Oliver for The Mail on Sunday, Published 06:21 EDT, 18 April 2012, Updated: 19:46 EDT, 18 April 2012. Although I caution students in the college classrooms where I teach about relying on Wikipedia and internet searches for academic research, it is a good place to start when you do not know anything about a subject. However, it is only a starting point. Full disclosure: I make a monetary donation to support Wikipedia most years.

[35] http://www.finra.org/industry/series7

[36] More on this in Chapter 7.

[37] Many of the businesses that printed certificates also printed currency for foreign governments. The US government has a Bureau of Engraving under the Department of Treasury that prints all of its money.

[38] For a more complete discussion of the scholarly research on these and other issues of financial market regulation, see Trimbath (2015).

[39] The case of Eagletech Communications, Inc. in Chapter 9 is a prime example.

[40] "Psst, Wanna Borrow Some Shares?" by Theresa W. Carey *Barron's* (Online and Print), This Week's Magazine, 17 July 2010.

[41] A graph showing the fails in US Treasury bond trades was removed because it is outdated. The value of fails in the Treasury market varies widely throughout the year. As of 12/17/2008, the fails were $428 billion. 10/10/2018 they were $180 billion. 6/19/2019 $292 billion. These figures represent only the fails involving the Primary Dealers, of which there were only 17 as of October 1, 2008, down from 22 in 2007. As of July 5, 2019, there were 25 Primary Dealers. A list of the Primary Dealers, as

well as current and historical date on fails in a variety of bond markets, is available at

https://www.newyorkfed.org/markets/primarydealers.html [Accessed July 5, 2019]. A link to my complete research report on Settlement Failures in US Bond Markets is included here, as it was sent to the IRS and the State Treasurers. An updated version was published in an academic journal (Trimbath, 2011).

[42] This is parallel to the dividend problem addressed by Section 6045(d) of the Jobs and Growth Tax Relief Reconciliation Act of 2003 (JGTRRA).

[43] For example, on September 22, 2008 corporate bonds paid 450 basis points over Treasuries. Financial companies, under distress at this time, would have significantly higher costs of capital.

[44] Section 6045(d) reflected the changes to information reporting for payments in lieu of dividends effected by the Jobs and Growth Tax Relief Reconciliation Act of 2003 (JGTRRA). Implementation was delayed to 2004 at the request of broker-dealers who commented that they needed additional time to implement system changes.

[45] Conversely, broker-dealers may not be reporting these payments as "in lieu." In that case, the investor does not suffer a monetary loss. Instead the loss accrues to the federal government (i.e., taxpayers). If "payments in lieu" are reported as bona fide dividend payments, the IRS will collect less revenue (income tax payments) than they would have had the payments been properly reported as "in lieu."

[46] The tax rate on qualified dividends is 5% or 15% (depending on the individual's income tax rate). If the individual has a regular income tax rate of 25% or higher, then the qualified dividend tax rate is 15%. If the individual's income tax rate is less than 25%, then qualified dividends are taxed at the 5% rate.

[47] The mean dividend yield for the S&P 1500 was 0.9% in 2003. See Jeffrey R. Brown, Nellie Liang and Scott J. Weisbenner, Executive Financial Incentives and Payout Policy: Firm Responses to the 2003 Dividend Tax Cut (December 2004). Available from the Social Science Research Network: http://ssrn.com/abstract=631182. Their calculation of the average dividend yield includes firms that do not pay dividends, making the calculation relevant even if there are non-dividend paying companies among those whose shares were not delivered to NSCC. The question of whether the failure to receive occurred on a dividend record date is less relevant because the value of shares that investors fail to receive has never been zero. In fact, most academic research on the

subject shows that the activity leading to payments in lieu of dividends actually increases around record dates.

[48] "[A]mong S&P 1500 non-dividend-paying firms, the fraction that initiated dividends jumped from only one in a hundred firms in 2001and 2002 to nearly one in ten firms in 2003." Ibid.

[49] A significant percentage of households reporting dividend income are either retired or earn less than $50,000 per year. Speaking in support of JGTRRA, James W. Struckert, Chairman of the SIA Regional Firms Committee, said "According to the most recent IRS data, 34.1 million tax returns (or 26.4 percent of total tax returns, representing 71 million people) reported some dividend income in 2000. Of all taxpayers that claimed some dividend income in 2000, nearly half (45.8 percent) earned less than $50,000 in adjusted gross income (including dividends). ... Importantly, almost half of all savings from the dividend exclusion would go to taxpayers 65 and older, thereby giving retirees an additional reliable, long-term source of income to supplement their social security earnings and other retirement savings. The average annual tax savings for the 9.8 million seniors receiving dividends would be $936." Testimony before the Subcommittee on Economic Policy of the Senate Committee on Banking, Housing, and Urban Affairs, May 22, 2003. Furthermore, interest paid on municipal bonds in the US is exempt from federal taxes. When bond trades fail the investor gets a payment in lieu of interest. Unlike dividends, these payments are not differentiated by the broker. As a result, the US government is missing out on $1.54 billion per year in tax revenue.

[50] Calculations for 2006 are available in the appendix to Settlement Failures in Bond Markets, available from the Social Science Research Network at http://ssrn.com/abstract=1016873. An updated paper, including calculations using data available through mid-2008, is available as Trimbath (2011).

[51] For a complete primer from the SEC, see "Key Points About Regulation SHO" at https://www.sec.gov/investor/pubs/regsho.htm.

[52] *American Banker*, Nov 16, 1984 v149 p21(1)

[53] *The Wall Street Journal*, Sept 8, 1989 pC1(W) pC1(E) col 3 (20 col in).

[54] NYSE Threshold List went from 73 stocks on 1/7/2005 to 96 stocks on 9/18/2008. Each stock exchange kept its own list of stocks where the fails to deliver met the threshold. The total number of stocks on the Threshold List as of May 2006, about 1 year after compliance reporting started, was 298 for all exchanges.

[55] See NASAA Public Forum in Chapter 10.

[56] Comments by David E. Patch Jr., November 6, 2003, RE: Release Nos. 34-48709; File No. S7-23-03.

[57] See, for example, "Short-Selling Crackdown Extends to New York, London" by Michael Tsang, September 18, 2008, Bloomberg.com.

[58] NSCC Rules and Procedures, version March 2007, page 43. Read more on this in the final chapter.

[59] The SEC making it unlawful to lie would remind me of my August 2007 meeting with the FBI where they asked me if stealing was illegal. See Chapter 12.

[60] The letter can be seen at https://www.sec.gov/comments/s7-08-09/s70809-1716.pdf.

[61] Many of the academics who wrote adoringly about short sellers and even settlement failures (as an investment strategy) were supported by financing from banks and brokers. For example, one academic proponent of short selling was Professor Owen A. Lamont of the Yale School of Management, which raised $300 million in a campaign headed by a Goldman Sachs Group retiree. At the time of the fundraising campaign, and as Lamont was publishing papers on the benefits of short selling, about 10% of the regulatory events disclosed by Goldman Sachs were for violations of rules governing short sales. A good, non-technical treatment on this point can be viewed in *Inside Job*, a 2011 documentary directed by Charles Ferguson, produced by Audrey Marrs and Charles Ferguson, released by Sony Pictures Classics.

[62] Pet Quarters, Inc. (Case No. 4-04-CV-001528 JLH, United States District Court, Eastern District Of Arkansas, Western Division) and Nanopierce Technologies, Inc. (Case No. CV04-01079, Dept. No. 4, Second Judicial District Court, County Of Washoe, State Of Nevada).

[63] According to the documentary, in 2010 another company victimized by phantom share multiplication received no recognition for the invention of a cancer treatment, which was bought by a company in Sweden in 2010. The reader interested in Viragen should view the documentary for a more complete discussion of the story of Viragen.

[64] Securities and Exchange Commission v. Tonino Labella, et al., Civil Action No. 05-CIV-852 (WGB) (D.N.J.). On December 18, 2006, the SEC barred the lead defendant, Tonino Labella, from association with any broker or dealer.

[65] See United States v. Labella, No. 05-CR-87 (D.N.J.). In this case, Labella and others pled guilty to conspiracy to commit securities fraud and wire fraud.

[66] The story is told by the company founder, Rodney Young, in the film documentary *The Wall Street Conspiracy* (WSC, 2012). The documentary also includes the story of how the company went public, including an interview with one of the brokers admitting their intention was always to destroy the company with abusive trading strategies designed to take over Eagletech's assets, including patents to telecommunication inventions.

[67] Just before the episode finally aired, Gayle handed out leaflets to DTCC employees and visitors entering the building it occupied in New York City. Mr. Essary passed away in August 2006.

[68] See http://www.nasaa.org/about-us/

[69] The quotes in this section were taken from a transcript of the audio of a live webcast of the NASAA Listens Forum. The transcript was posted to a website that is no longer active (www.ncans.com).

[70] A copy of an NYSE Audit of the voting function at its member firms is included in Chapter 8 in the attachment to my comments on Reg SHO.

[71] One-share/One-vote: "The restriction on NYSE, AMEX, and NASDAQ [listed] companies forbidding them from taking any actions which would significantly dilute or restrict the voting rights of current shareholders." http://www.investorwords.com/3417/one_share_one_vote_rule.html#ixzz5l0i26a3H

[72] The results of this committee's work is the letter sent from the SIA to the NYSE that we discussed in Chapter 8. See attachment to Trimbath's comments on Reg SHO.

[73] Documented events. Bankers name withheld at the request of Mr. Byrne. After sending me copies of the email correspondence, he subsequently used similar quotes in some of his slideshow presentations on the topic.

[74] "Byrne's War: Overstock.com's Patrick Byrne is On a Self-Imposed Mission to Save Main Street from Wall Street" by Colin Kelly, Jr. April 18, 2006. *Connect Magazine* (connect-utah.com).

[75] Harmer was state senator from 1966-1974 and briefly served as Lieutenant Governor under Ronald Reagan (1974-1975).

[76] A summary of Reg SHO and related rules and amendments, along with Trimbath's comment letters to the SEC, are included in Chapter 8.

[77] Eugene Melnyk is a Canadian businessman who was the founder, chairman and CEO of Biovail Corporation, a Canadian drug company. Gradient Analytics, Inc. is a financial forensics research firm serving institutional investors. Biovail filed a lawsuit against Gradient in 2006

alleging that Gradient colluded with hedge funds to manipulate the stock price, similar to a suit filed by Overstock a few years earlier. Gradient counter-sued Biovail; the two settled their cases in 2010.

[78] A good place to find out about making a direct purchase of shares from companies like Exxon, Coca-Cola and Walmart is: https://www-us.computershare.com/Investor/#DirectStock/Index. Many have starting options as low as a few hundred dollars and allow shareholders to either reinvest dividends or take receive them as cash payments.

[79] Available at https://www.law.cornell.edu/ucc/8; Accessed July 10, 2019.

[80] *Wall Street Journal* "NJ Corzine Taps Ex-Goldman Colleague For State Treasurer" 13 Jan 2006 12:13

[81] For example, see Out Takes, *Investment Dealers' Digest*, Jan 18, 1999, Securities Data Publishing.

[82] "Proposal to make DTC stock lender causes participant angst." *Operations Management*, April 8, 2002 v8 i14 p2(1). Euromoney Institutional Investor PLC

[83] CFRN broadcasts live on the internet at www.cfrn.net.

[84] Available as a playlist on Gary Matsumoto's YouTube Channel at https://youtu.be/HjkbChSBc0A?list=PL7CFF70F2937191E8. [Accessed July 22, 2019.] This is the pre-broadcast version; the spelling of my first name was corrected when the program went live.

[85] Gary would tell me later that he hoped to become personal friends with Patrick Byrne after the special aired – perhaps presaging my exclusion from the final cut while there was time to show video of Patrick Byrne riding a Segway in the Overstock warehouse and driving his Jeep into the mountains around Utah. In an email Gary said that it was not his decision to cut me from the final program.

[86] "SEC seen shy on naked shorting", April 23, 2007. Investment News is available online at https://www.investmentnews.com [Accessed July 28, 2019]. Some articles are available to read after registration, without subscription. The most recent articles in Investment News from Mr. Jamieson are in late-2013. He is currently Editor at Large for Financial Advisor magazine https://www.linkedin.com/in/dajamieson [Accessed July 28, 2019].

[87] After reviewing my proposal for the event, Patrick Byrne provided a small stipend to cover any shortage between the cost of the event and revenue from registration fees. At the time, he declined any notation of sponsorship either personally or for his company.

[88] Wayne Jett disclosed that Classical Capital LLC, which managed $2.93 million in investments at the time of the event, had a small investment in Overstock.com (OSTK) and no investment in other companies that have made claims or filed lawsuits related to short-sale abuses.

[89] Mr. Altenbach is a partner at Florentez Investment Management in Los Angeles. He frequently contributes articles on financial topics for print and online media.

[90] At time of the event, Alsin and/or Alsin Capital Management disclosed investments in Overstock.com (OSTK). Alsin wrote several articles for RealMoney.com (a "premium service" from TheStreet which is owned by CNBC buffoon-commentator Jim Cramer) presenting evidence of abusive short selling in OSTK and other stocks.

[91] Electronic Trading Group, LLC v. Banc of America Securities LLC, et al. 06 CV 2859, USDC SD NY. I assisted the plaintiff's attorneys with the efficient markets arguments in this case.

[92] A significant amount of the material Patrick used for this and other public comments at the time can still be found online at DeepCapture.com.

[93] Recall Patrick Byrne's saga in trying to get delivery of shares (Chapter 10). He was able to get that information as a high-value client at the bank. Most investors are not able to find out.

[94] "The Stock Market is Patently Unfair," by Arne Alsin, April 25, 2006, updated December 22, 2006. Available online https://www.thestreet.com/story/10281714/1/the-stock-market-is-patently-unfair.html [Accessed July 26, 2019]. Arne made a copy of the original article available to the audience at the event.

[95] "DTCC Questions Facts in Naked Shorts Squabble" by Christopher Faille, Financial Correspondent, Thomson Reuters (HedgeWorld.com), March 16, 2006.

[96] Ms. Harrington was Principal at Cynthia Harrington & Associates in Los Angeles, with expertise in Behavioral Finance and Neuroeconomics. She is currently CEO at Candidate Success.

[97] Examples might be charging the transfer agents increased fees, denying payment for an agent's fee billing or unreasonably delaying processing.

[98] In September 2008, Vodia Group rebranded as Finadium, "an independent consultancy in capital markets with unique expertise in securities, finance, collateral, and derivatives."

[99] United States District Court, Southern District of New York, Olde Monmouth Stock Transfer Co., Inc. v. Depository Trust & Clearing Corporation and Depository Trust Company, 07 CV 0990 (CSH).

[100] The application service provider will not be named because they are still in business under the same company name, claiming to "obtain, aggregate, track and analyze shareholder trading information" under a patent pending system.

[101] See Barth, Trimbath and Yago (eds. 2004) for a summary of the event.

[102] "Blame the 'Stock Vault'? Clearinghouse Faulted on Short-Selling Abuse; Finding the Naked Truth," by John R. Emshwiller and Kara Scannell, *Wall Street Journal*, July 5, 2007.

[103] "Some lawmakers also shorted stocks, congressional records show" by Robert O'Harrow Jr. and Dan Keating May 5 2010, Politics section, *Washington Post* https://www.washingtonpost.com/politics/some-lawmakers-also-shorted-stocks-congressional-records-show/2012/01/28/gIQANRMXYQ_story.html?noredirect=on&utm_term=.655d5f70f302. Their story was based on financial disclosure documents assembled by the Center for Responsible Politics. A similar story, using data from the same source, appeared in the *New York Times* on May 4, 2010.

[104] "Naked Short Sales Hint Fraud in Bringing Down Lehman" by Gary Matsumoto - Mar 19, 2009, Bloomberg.com.

[105] NSCC Financial Statements as of and for the Years Ended December 31, 2016 and 2015, p. 28.

[106] The Money Honey Bee segment: It takes a financial wizard like Samantha Bee to understand the lucrative business of short selling." (4:34), March 16, 2009, The Daily Show with Jon Stewart. Produced by Stuart Miller, Edited by Einar Westerlund. Available on the original URL from the WayBack Machine (archived March 13, 2016) www.cc.com/video-clips/7pous8/the-daily-show-with-jon-stewart-the-money-honey-bee [Accessed July 24, 2019]. Also available via Bing.com at https://binged.it/2YmQqxs [Accessed July 24, 2019]

[107] James J. Cramer is co-founder and major shareholder in TheStreet.com, which also received a subpoena.

[108] After CMKM Diamonds Inc. stopped trading, the acronym "CMKX" came into wide use. It is typical for financial sources to either add the letter "X" to a three-letter stock symbol or to substitute "X" for the fourth letter to denote a stock that is no longer trading and for which there are no formal price quotes available.

[109] Source: Slideshow distributed as CMKM/NHHI Shareholder Meeting #38, January 30, 2015. Meeting dates, call in numbers, etc. were posted to http://cmkxunofficial.proboards.com. Mr. Kirkpatrick declined our

request for a statement; any information contained herein that is attributed to Mr. Kirkpatrick comes only from public sources.

[110] $6,399,876,138 as of December 31, 2007.

[111] If you skipped ahead to get here and these concepts are not clear to you, please go back to the Primer in Part I.

[112] One notable exception will be the Canadian firm Barker Minerals; see Chapter 21.

[113] In the 1970s and 1980s, an "Uncola" ad campaign for the American soft drink 7 Up was designed to highlight differences between 7 Up and other soft drinks on the market with cola flavoring. Likewise, the UnShareholder designation is meant to distinguish investors who had neither shares nor entitlements from the bona fide shareholders of public companies.

[114] See NASDAQ Uniform Practice Code, Section 11530, "Delivery of Securities Called for Redemption or Which Are Deemed Worthless" for the correct procedure, which requires that the broker return the original price paid by the buyer if the shares are deemed worthless after the original trade date.

[115] See Securities and Exchange Commission Release No. 34-49930; File No. SR-DTC-2003-09.

[116] For example, *The Big Short*, based on a book by Michael Lewis, would come out in 2015; *Inside Job*, narrated by Matt Damon, came out in 2010. In an ironic twist, Matt Damon would appear a year later as the TV front man for Ameritrade, one of the worst offenders in fails to deliver. See Chapter 18 for data on Ameritrade provided by shareholders and investors.

[117] I am grateful to Regina Maasich for editing the raw transcript into a readable form.

[118] "Delivery failures plague Treasury market," by Dan Jamieson, *Investment News*, Oct 19, 2008.

[119] The settlement failures in US Treasury bonds among the 19 primary dealers would be at least $5 trillion for 8 weeks after this interview.

[120] "Connect to the future," by Karl van Gestel, Global Investor, suppl. *Custody Compendium*, London (Sep 2002): p5-6.

[121] I was able to meet with the report's author the following year in London (December 16, 2009, Oxford and Cambridge Club). James Economides, co-founder of Amaces (an advisory firm) was quoted in "Comparing Settlement Data", Richard Greensted, *Global Investor* (London), March 2006 (03), Page 1. He said that as much as 19.1% of trades in the UK failed to settle (based on a study of institutional

investors). After analyzing more than 1.5 million trades over two years, Economides suspected that custodians were using the process to boost their earnings. In the article, he is quoted as saying, "You might expect that, over time, there would be a relationship and correlation between failing purchases and sales and the total number of purchases and sales. … But there are a number of custodians where this is absolutely not the case. The ratio of sales to purchases is around 1:1.1 and failed sales to failed purchases is 1:8 and, in some instances, up to 1:15."

[122] Industry reports indicate that about 40% of shareholders vote in corporate elections. With that figure in mind, the actual votes turned in are closer to about 217% of the shares outstanding.

[123] In 2008, when the music stopped, we would find out just how many senior managers at international financial institutions did not understand finance, especially credit default swaps. Many CEOs would offer the excuse that they didn't understand the associated risks when they authorized the activity.

[124] The "Reg SHO Threshold List" contains the names of firms where more than a threshold level of FTDs were reported by NSCC. See Chapter 8 for a complete discussion of the SECs attempts to regulate naked short selling. The set of rules are generally referred to as "Reg SHO".

[125] Available at https://www.gao.gov/products/GAO-09-318R [Accessed July 31, 2009]

[126] Available at https://www.gao.gov/products/GAO-09-483 [Accessed July 31, 2009]

[127] The GAO received: the 2007 working paper version of "Trade Settlement Failures in U.S. Bond Markets" (published as Trimbath 2011), including an unpublished appendix on fails in US equity markets; the STA Article (see Chapter 6); and copies of comments to the SEC on proposals for Reg SHO and related rule changes (see Chapter 8).

[128] See Chapter 18 in Part VII.

[129] See "Will NSS torpedo the Trump bull market by Richard Levick, 26 September 2018, Forbes.com.

[130] For complete details, see the company's March 5, 2019 press release linked from https://barkermineralsltd.yolasite.com/

[131] I found one author that used the term "regulatory crisis" in this broader sense, specifically in the context of banking regulations. Pablo Triana wrote "It is fitting that financial mandarins should feel obliged to show contrition and atonement. For the 2007 crisis was, at its core, a regulatory crisis. Either because of enforcing of conceptually flawed

rules (the reliance on VaR and credit metrics) or neglectful policing of rules (giving a free pass to the abuse of the trading book), bank regulators made it possible for the big banks to toxify their balance sheets with bad leverage." p 209 (digital) in *The Number That Killed Us: A Story of Modern Banking, Flawed Mathematics, and a Big Financial Crisis* (2011), Wiley & Sons, Incorporated.

[132] For the long-term view on financial crises, see Reinhart and Rogoff (2009).

[133] While the Fed is finding it difficult to reduce its balance sheet, 60% of the US money supply sits as excess reserves earning interest for the banks. The process available to the Fed to reduce their balance sheet would ultimately raise interest rates. That means the banks would earn even more money on excess reserves.

[134] "A registered clearing agency may summarily suspend and close the accounts of a participant who ..., (ii) is in default of any delivery of funds or securities to the clearing agency ..." Securities and Exchange Act of 1934, Section 17A.a.5.(C).

[135] Short interest on the NASDAQ was up again in early July 2019.

[136] On 3 July 2019, ECSDA published the latest draft of the *Settlement Discipline Penalties Framework*, including recommended penalties for settlement failures both within and across central securities depositories. It also recommended that each of its 40 national and international central securities depositories across 36 countries report the value of fail transactions to its respective regulatory authority.

[137] "Frequency and cost of settlement failures to rise – report" by Andrew Neil, *Global Investor* (London, May 17, 2017)

[138] The future of free enterprise was discussed at the start of the World Economic Forum's annual meeting in January 2012. In an opening panel Sharan Burrow, general secretary of the International Trade Union Confederation said, "There's too much power, it's time to reset. If you've got a group that is too big to fail, what it means is that you are the biggest bullies on the planet. The financial sector has lost its moral compass." Other panelists included Carlyle Group LP (CG) co-founder David Rubenstein and Bank of America Corp. Chief Executive Officer Brian Moynihan.

[139] See note 23 above.